Sylvia Kennedy was born in London and graduated
from Bristol University. She has lived in France,
Sweden and New York, pursuing various careers as
chef, disc jockey, EFL teacher, information officer for
the British Tourist Authority, publishers' reader and
freelance writer; she now lives in London. *See
Ouarzazate and Die* is her first book.

SEE OUARZAZATE AND DIE
Travels Through Morocco

Sylvia Kennedy

LITTLE, BROWN AND COMPANY
Boston   New York   Toronto   London

First U.S. edition

ISBN 0–316–48923–9

10 9 8 7 6 5 4 3 2 1

Printed in Great Britain

This book is dedicated to the memory of
Miguel Perestrello
21 June 1962–12 October 1992
'I love you, my little tiger.'

CONTENTS

◆

◆ ACKNOWLEDGMENTS ◆

It is almost impossible to single out and thank individual Moroccans amongst the many I met. However, I am immensely grateful to the staff of the Hotel Panorama (Meknès), Les Mimosas (Safi) and the Hotel Majestic (Rabat) for their assistance on every level and on numerous occasions. I would also like to pay tribute to the Grand Hotel de France (Tunis), whose staff made a point of ensuring my safety and, putting personal feelings aside, welcomed me generously at a sensitive time in Arab-Western relations.

On the home front, I wish to thank everyone at Streatham Surgery, in particular Dr Peter Ashby and Dr Andrew Saunders, for their enduring interest and concern, the medical kits they compiled and the pre- and post-trip care they lavished on all of us.

Mary Loring of Scribners proved to be the proverbial tower of strength and encouragement from beginning to end, tempering a keen critical intelligence with affectionate pats on the back.

Tony Oaklands not only lived under the shadow of this book for over a year, but also drove over two thousand kilometres to make it possible, tended children in my absences and read and re-read the manuscript. His generosity and long-suffering good nature were all the more remarkable given his attachment to comfort, lush golf courses and roast pork dinners – all of which were singularly lacking in the Maghreb. Finally, I would like to thank my travelling companions, Michelle Dermody, Miyuki Hirayama and Sheila Hodgson, and my three irrepressible sons, Alexis, Caspian and Blaise, for being there, for tolerating so much and for making it all so hugely enjoyable

◆ INTRODUCTION ◆

It is the evening of 15 August 1990 and six of us are standing around a mountain of luggage in Casablanca Arrivals Hall, trying to track down a rental car large enough to take a double buggy draped in straw hats with red ribbon ties, packets of disposable nappies and what, at our last count, added up to eleven pieces of baggage – not including handbags. Miyuki, whom I first met in 1985 when she came to London to study English, has been waiting for us at the airport since midday and has contacted twenty-nine Marrakeshi hotels in the Green Guide she procured from her new-found allies at the tourist information window. All to no avail. Over thirty hours of flying from Tokyo have taken their toll on her. Miyuki's oddly flat, blue cotton hat is welded to her head with sweat and she is so exhausted she seems shrill and positively merry, rather than the reserved, studiously polite Japanese chemist of former summers. Her broken English and lack of French notwithstanding, Miyuki continues to feed dirhams into the pay-phone, as if determined to concentrate on one task rather than panic at finding herself in such an alien environment. From time to time, she casts sidelong glances at the milling crowds, our heap of suitcases and the unfamiliar Arabic signs and posters, shaking her head in wonder, before returning to her mechanical friend and calls to Marrakesh.

Michelle, the babies' nanny and co-conspirator, has never met Miyuki before, but realises that they will be sharing a room for ten days and eyes her up rather dubiously. Organised and energetic, Michelle has packed and colour-coded her own and the babies' bags with low cunning and imagination and she is currently sitting braced against a marble column. cups of orange juice at her feet. calmly reading them *The Ugly Duckling*. Like so many Australian travellers. Michelle takes her trips seriously. She has been digesting guides. studying maps and reading potted histories of the Maghreb for months now. passing on a diluted. almost shorthand image of Morocco to the babies in the process. As far as I can make out. Blaise and Caspian have selectively edited her information and are expecting numerous dust storms. poultry. snakes and visits from Allah. They also apparently know that jackals have 'dirty teeth' coated in rabies. and that they must wear their sunblock and hats at all times.

The Moroccan Tourist Board in London warned us firmly against taking the babies inland for prolonged stretches over the summer months. since temperatures can soar to thirty-seven degrees centigrade from the end of July onwards and cholera outbreaks are common. As a result. much of this leg of my meander around Morocco has been designed to take advantage of the Atlantic coast's breezes and lower temperatures. with the odd stop at the imperial cities thrown in – epidemics permitting.

The itinerary seems daunting tonight as we wait for Tony – who will be doing all the driving and taking most of the photographs – to finish his inspection of the available motor pool. The minutes tick by and then suddenly he is there. grinning and tossing car keys. reaching down for the largest bags.

Standing outside on the large semi-circular drive which sweeps across the airport entrance. we share an unvoiced moment of tense excitement. as we survey the unfathomable stretch of blackness ahead. Michelle and I hold the babies' hands and exchange smiles. satisfied that weeks of planning have finally brought us here. to Morocco. to search for sultans and sorcerers. the kif trade and the Koran. Miyuki looks thoughtful. ready for whatever the next few days will bring. And Tony breaks the spell. slamming down the bonnet with a loud thump. urging us to take the first step into Morocco and its adventures as he whoops: 'Marrakesh. here we come.'

PART ONE
(August–September 1990)

TRAVELS EN FAMILLE

Cast
Blaise & Caspian: my two- and three-year-old sons.
Michelle: exuberant, jovial Australian nanny.
Miyuki: bemused, gentle Japanese chemist.
Tony: AKA 'Moustache', the macho man with a
heart of gold.

◆ *Chapter One* ◆

At the age of fifteen, I remember kneeling on the floor in front of an outspread map of the world and compiling a list of places I intended to see before I died. Needless to say, the choice was dictated more by the resonance of the syllables than any more meaningful criteria, but Marrakesh made the grade, along with Samarkand, Petra and the Mississippi. Marrakesh seemed to promise a blend of intrigue, heat and exoticism beyond comprehension, a stew of veiled women, shady men in fedoras creeping down narrow bazaar alleys, pyramids of spices and raucous foreign tongues. During the 1960s and '70s the tougher, more street-wise rock stars and their retinues also felt drawn to take the legendary Marrakesh Express for simpler, more hedonistic reasons: the abundance of drugs, prostitutes of both sexes and all ages, the cheapness of daily life, the raw beauty of the mountainous setting and the contrast it provided to their normal environments. Jimi Hendrix and the Rolling Stones, Alain Delon, Yves St Laurent and Nastassia Kinski – to name but a few – have all come to Marrakesh. Some to dabble in the colourful poverty, others to settle on a semi-permanent basis and, at least in St Laurent's case, to contribute as well as exploit.

I had decided to stop off in Marrakesh in order to attend the moussem at Setti Fatma, an annual occasion which lures Berber tribesmen, who otherwise rarely leave their villages days away in the High Atlas, down into the Ourika Valley for two or three days of festivities. Moussems are a curious phenomenon since, strictly speaking, Islam frowns on cults of personality and yet, the length and breadth of the country, you see whitewashed domed buildings, known as koubbas marking the resting places of venerated local saints. Individuals and groups come to pray for intercession, or for guidance, to ask for fertility or safe-keeping on a journey, or simply to share in the 'baraka' or luck which making this type of pilgrimage is supposed to bring. I have always found the koubba a heartbreakingly solemn and emotional sight. The austere lines and unadorned exteriors somehow speak of a life dedicated to the glory of God rather than the accumulation of material goods, an impression which is reinforced by the fact that they often spring out of the landscape at a remote spot or dominate an otherwise completely barren area. Externally, nothing twinkles, shimmers or distracts from the statement of respect which is the building. Unlike so many Catholic shrines in Europe, there are no attempts at flower arranging, photographs of dead relatives and babies' booties to be seen. The message seems to be – here was a man or woman of God. Remember and learn from their example.

Marrakesh was hot. Very hot. The dry, immobile air burnt the back of the throat and even strong sunglasses failed to cut out the glare as we spilled out at Djemaa el Fna – the Place of the Dead – and staggered on to the nearest café terrace to get our bearings. The first thing that caught our eye was the ring of snow-topped mountains which encircle the city. Reaching Marrakesh is reaching the threshold of the desert and hence Africa. Europe and Andalusia have not left their mark on this part of Morocco, which looks south in spite of the colonial administrative legacy found outside the Almoravide walls, and Marrakesh has not been fundamentally altered by its contacts with the French. The High Atlas and Marrakesh's place within its peaks still define its function – gateway to north and south and gathering place of the peoples. Twilight was falling and the scene which sprawled to right and left testified to the city's incredible energy and sense of purpose. The air was thick with dust and noise, as men dragged packages on carts towards the CTM terminal to our right; donkeys ambled by, their cargoes swaying perilously from mangy right to equally mangy left flank. A woman darted past in a smart black nylon caftan with large orange tea roses and mules, her arms outstretched to catch a toddler; the men in the next-door newspaper kiosk under the green canvas awning yelled out greetings; and a stream of moped riders, blue petits taxis and local buses roared out in spurts to cut across the view, belching filth from their exhausts. On the edge of the square the thirty or forty nut and orange juice stallholders were starting to light their kerosene lamps, and groups of tables and crates were being assembled further in, as men chopped hunks of lamb into even cubes, diced oval slabs of liver, stirred beans in oil and tomato and added extra spoonfuls of water to the ready-assembled pigeon and chicken tagines. Suddenly my eye was caught by a pathetic sight – two grey barbary apes on thick metal chains, being half-dragged, half-whipped along. They disappeared into a sea of backs and legs gathered around a preacher, who punctuated his words by waving a small green Koran in his right hand and spitting into the dust, avoiding the blanket which held numerous sun-bleached pamphlets. His audience came and went, drifting on to the next circle. Tarot card readers squatted on their heels, ready to grab a passing ankle and pull you to the ground with hennaed fingers, whipping out their large greasy packs as you regained your balance.

In the days that followed, I was constantly and short-sightedly being nobbled by these older Berber ladies and, as they came to know my face, the price fell from thirty to five dirhams. In the end, I never succumbed, not because I have disrespect for the craft or the cards, rather out of a growing aversion to being touched and a resulting disinclination to have anything to do with the shoulder-tappers, arm-holders, calf-squeezers and their ilk. I find it difficult to ignore or accept the physical familiarity shown towards European women – a disrespect which is totally understandable, given Islam's strictures and the fact that so many tourists stroll around in lycra bicycling shorts and cropped tops, tossing their hair back nonchalantly in response to what they conceive of as admiring looks. This is a mistaken view. Moroccan men both lust after and condemn, in equal measure, the glimpses of thighs, breasts and even arms afforded them, and since they have internalised the division between the virgin and the whore, in the end it is contempt and not admiration which wins out. The bazaarist's hand on the shoulder is not a sign of friendship, but evidence of his giving in to temptation and scoring a quick 'grope'. After all, no Moroccan woman is going to allow a casual acquaintance, let alone a shopkeeper, to fondle her arm or, most common and repulsive of all, to shake her hand in greeting while suggestively poking his index finger in and out of her palm. On the other hand, of course, there is little point in making a stand on such an essentially petty issue, either. I found that pointedly and silently removing the offending digits worked well and the occasional recidivist normally responded to a curt 'Would you like a stranger to touch your mother and sister in this way?' Needless to say, he would not...

By 7:00 p.m. the sky was darkening rapidly and Djemaa el Fna was no longer an open space, for people were pushing in from all the side roads to participate in what is Morocco's largest and most compelling open-air theatre. I edged round the crowds, passing a depressing group of men, women and children holding up second-hand clothes, grey trousers, a short woollen overcoat, trainers and T-shirts, as the call to prayer, distorted and probably a recording, but magnificent for all that, was taken up by the town's mosques. There is no God but God...

In the distance the sharp outlines of the mountain peaks could still just be distinguished from the deep grey of the sky. while the elegant twelfth-century Almohad Koutoubia minaret. Morocco's most distinctive landmark. loomed over the swelling tide of men and beasts.

Unlike Fez and Meknès. Marrakesh is relatively flat and thus ideally suited to the horse-drawn carriage trade so beloved of natives and visitors alike. The main rank is round the corner from the post office and drivers were preparing for the busiest time of day. Tourists from the new town who had spent the afternoon shopping in the medina realised their buffet suppers were about to be served and decided to treat themselves to a ride home. daunted by the way Marrakesh changes as the sun disappears to reveal alleys. smells and corners which have hitherto remained invisible. Smiling and embarrassed. yet barely restraining the impulse to wave at passers-by. they trotted off. canopies down. harnesses jingling. for the ten-dirham ride which would cost them at least seventy. The warm earthy smell of dung steamed in the heat on already over-heated roads and steam rose from beneath iron-shod hoofs as the caleches thrust into the throng. In theory one should be able to negotiate a price in advance: in practice the glut of tourists makes it a seller's market and here. as in Sousse. another North African tourist town. negotiations are virtually pointless. the drivers insolent if you argue the toss. Only the horses and their plaited manes and tails and gleaming brass hardware conjure up visions of bygone days.

Somewhere in the distance I heard the faint but mesmerising sound of drumming. but this was overlaid by an eruption of hysterical laughter close by. as a cobra attempted to sidle away from its handler. basket. umbrella and audience and break for the border. The snake charmer grabbed it (all the snakes have been rendered harmless by being forced to drink water. prior to which they discharge their venom) and pretended to bite off its head, before unceremoniously thrusting the poor creature back into its cardboard box and returning his attention to its obedient friend and co-worker, who was patiently half-raised, waiting for the piping notes and the movement (snakes are deaf) to start again. A group of children dressed in maroon, clashing hand-cymbals in their palms and swinging their heads so the tassles on their skull caps turn through three hundred and sixty degrees, pounced. One threw his arm around my waist – he must have been all of five – whispering 'Give me a sweet, a biro, a dirham.' I refused and felt his fingers trying to undo the clasp of my wrist-watch, the safety-chain of my bangle. Should I react? Cry out? Smack him? I didn't know. Whenever tourists and touts come into conflict, the police seem to take the side of the Moroccan, to accuse the visitor of being at fault, of starting the argument. Perhaps this is a tactic. After all, unofficial guides pay the police a percentage of their daily takings anyway, in order to remain unharassed and on the streets, so there is little percentage in squeezing them. The tourist, however, is easily intimidated, at an obvious disadvantage and will quite happily hand over a fiver, rather than lose time in bureaucratic wrangling and the unpleasantness of a run-in with Morocco's infamously brutal and self-governing lawmen. In the circumstances I disentangled myself, did nothing and was rewarded with a chant of 'bloody Inglish, bloody Inglish' for the few yards it took me to dodge this worldly-wise little pickpocket.

Later, sitting in my room, watching the babies sleep, doubtlessly dreaming of the yards of snake which had been draped around their necks as they squealed in the double buggy, I became angry. Angry for the first and not the last time at a society which corrupts the very young, at myself for my initial reaction: it's the Third World and the kid has to eat, so why not steal? Somehow, this is no argument, not on moral grounds, but I simply believe five-year-olds should be protected from the corrupting drives of economic necessity and allowed to ignore where the meals they eat, the clothes they wear, come from. The magic element which makes childhood a time of wonder and intuition, fantasy and empathy is each child's birthright and should not be determined by wealth and hence class. Upper middle-class Moroccans – and never make the mistake of ignoring their existence and talking of Morocco as if it were populated only by quaintly dressed peasants, asses and hustlers – would no more condone their wives begging for alms, their infants suckling a breast by restaurant doorways, or their toddlers working as pickpockets than you or I.

This train of thought leads nowhere fast but merely sparks off counter-arguments and doubts about travelling in, understanding or clearly seeing any foreign land. As such it was promptly suppressed in favour of attempting to nap in the suffocating heat of the Hotel Ali – which I shall not grace with a description and have now added to the select list of places where I would gleefully consign my worst enemies.

Somehow or other the night slipped by and predictably enough it was another charnel-house by 9:00 a.m., with temperatures in the low nineties as I slipped out of the Ali straight into the arms of two lurking teenagers looking for clients. Abdul, a wiry, generous-mouthed and nervous young man of eighteen wearing a greasy yellow paisley shirt, seemed to have no physical deformities and a fair grasp of English and was totally lacking in glints in the eye or pushy enthusiasm. In short, he appeared destined to another day of empty traps and this decided me. I'd take him to Setti Fatma. Abdul accepted my offer of forty dirhams (£2.80) for the day instantly and cheered up – only to look at me with incredulity with I told him where we were going.

'It is no good, this moussem,' he said. 'It's too far away. I will show you El Badi, the Saadian tombs and the medina. All the tourists like the Saadian tombs so we will go now before it's too crowded. You'll love it.'

PART ONE

I interrupted him. 'Listen Abdul. I don't want to go into town. I've come here to see the moussem, but if you aren't interested then I'll just have to find someone else who is.'

'No, no, it's all right.' Abdul wavered then conceded. 'I'll take you there and I'll show you the seven waterfalls. I am Berber and these are my people, you know. My father is Berber, my mother is Berber. Welcome to my country.'

And with this emotional outburst he held out his hand proudly. I shook it, stifling a giggle. Poor Abdul wasn't to know that I have developed a strong distrust of anyone who starts off a conversation with those seemingly innocuous words of description 'I am Berber'. In my experience this is a sure sign that some form of rip-off is on the cards, along the lines of 'I am Berber. This is an antique Berber dagger which has been in my family for hundreds of years and I will give it to you for only seven hundred dirhams because I like you and I know you will respect our traditions!' The dagger is invariably made of tin, the sheath bends out of shape as you pull the tip and the blade leaves an oily, green sheen on the fingers. Alternatively, we find the 'Trust me. I know a good hotel (where the touts get over forty per cent commission). I am Berber and now you are my family, my sister.'

Having accumulated over a dozen 'brothers' during my last stay in Morocco, all of whom severed our 'kinship' ties when I told them I would not marry them for a passport, bring over a colour TV (with remote control) on my next trip or sponsor a visa application, Abdul almost scored an own goal. Yet there was something highly appealing about him, an inborn kindness and softness which was only occasionally blitzed by a bolt of greed over the days that followed. As we set off for Setti Fatma, I felt glad of his company, moved by his attempts to describe the entirely nondescript landscape which unrolled on the other side of the massive Bab er Rob – the gate which traditionally displayed severed criminals' heads in Marrakesh.

◆

The Ourika Valley. which locals referred to as 'Marrakesh's paradise', is a lush. cool and calm oasis south of the city. Almond trees, oleanders, peaches, apples and tomatoes dot the warmly-red mountainsides, and patches of grass cling to the slopes. The river is fast-flowing and it is easy to visualise how the many ruined buildings on the valley floor came to be swept away by the winter floods. No Berbers live down in the valley and as we passed yet another large home. its flank walls missing, foot-bridge ripped up and roof askew. Abdul told me that this was formerly a Saudi family's house and lasted barely two seasons before it was dashed to pieces. Apparently the Berber tribesmen had warned the businessman who built the house that he needed to go far. far higher up to get out of the way of the flash floods which literally tear chunks of rock face out of the mountains between November and March. or send down avalanches of polished giant boulders which flatten anything they encounter – from the constantly rebuilt bridges to the roads themselves. As the battered wreck of a formerly vast terraced garden and two-storey house testified. he dismissed their advice.

Somewhere along the way. after I had been badgering him for a coffee stop. Abdul finally decided that we could leap out of the car. He had been turning down café after café. promising me 'a special place, a better place', and this turned out to be a terraced dump on a main road, the 'beautiful view' that of a cliff-face. Pretty young girls wearing what appeared to be white nylon nighties with embroidered hems and plastic slip-ons hid their faces behind spreadeagled hands as we climbed a filthy ladder to reach a small flat concrete area boasting five iron tables and swarms of flies. Lo and behold. the reason for this macabre rest-stop soon became clear when Hassan. Abdul's oldest and dearest friend. plonked himself nonchalantly at our table and asked for a lift to Setti Fatma. Stifling a surge of irritation. I agreed to drive him the few remaining kilometres and sipped the lukewarm, thick brew that passed for coffee in its sugar-coated small glass. Abdul was happy. He had a client, the client had a car, arriving by car would add to his status, and being able to assist Hassan, in particular, obviously pleased him immensely, in terms of one-upmanship.

Looking at Hassan, I could empathise with Abdul's poseur-need-to-impress instinct, since Hassan was obviously doing well and made no bones about letting everyone know as much. I loathed him on sight and the more he spoke – of his shop, the camel-skin bags, pouffes and slippers he sells, the superb, shocking price he will offer me, his good, his best friend, of the French girl he dates – blonde, of course – and the house he has in the park – the more the loathing grew. Hassan was the only Moroccan I met who owned a lighter and though this may be quite insignificant on one level, it is a curious deviation from the norm. Every other Moroccan male I knew spent his time bumming lights from passers-by or, in worst cases, trying to pocket my cheap pink Bic! This idiosyncrasy, combined with his Levi's 501s and the thick gold chain he wore around his neck, made me wary of Hassan.

As we finally approached Setti Fatma, I looked around in vain for any sign of the gathering of the clans. Dozens of pick-ups crammed with people squashed between the wire-sides; impossibly large local buses, grands taxis, private cars, carts and traps jammed the narrow valley road which passed through a tiny village. There was no point in driving on, and soon we had joined the vast throng walking up the path parallel to the river bed, which was edged with tents and alive with paddling children and women scrubbing clothes, washing their hair or dunking small babies. The tide of visitors grew in numbers as the road narrowed and our walk turned into a bare crawl. Rock and mineral sellers, bearing trays of semi-precious stones, with ill-spelt name stickers, emerged from nowhere and thrust their boxes in front of me: asses knocked me flying as they chopped a way through with ne'er a word of apology, and improvised drink-stalls, bottles set up under trickling streams, proliferated.

Abdul and Hassan informed me that the best vantage point from which to look down upon the moussem was up by the waterfalls, and so we started what turned out to be the most physically wearing and frightening climb of my life.

At first the ascent was more a lurching stroll than a climb, following a broadly curving four-in-one gradient path past a café where a group of Berber musicians playing drums and gimbris stamped their feet, while a group of middle-aged women swayed and clapped in a loose circle around them, their soles slapping and pattering in time to the beat, heads thrown back and throats and tongues giving voice to the distinctive semi-wailing of the North African nomad. Crowds of teenagers clutching Fanta bottles lounged in the shade of the walnut trees, for the sun was shrivellingly hot by now, gossiping and barely glancing at the entertainers. I felt a shiver of pleasure at the sound and made as if to stop, only to be told that there were five other levels to the next café and the journey would be rewarding. So, ever onward.

Adjusting my shoulder-straps and hitching up my cotton skirt, I followed the boys along what soon turned into a monstrous rock face, whose steep, smooth sides yielded no visible hand or footholds. The crumbling ochre ledges over-looked deep ravines and the scrubby bushes and odd pieces of root provided no levers or support. As the path faded and then disappeared some thirty minutes into the climb, I began to panic and, throwing caution and elegance to the wind, scrambled rather than walked, shinnying up the rocks by digging my fingers into the unstable soil, crashing over narrow, swaying bridges made of a single tree trunk suspended over a positively Miltonian chasm, through overhangs and under thorn-like thickets. Soon, my knees were bleeding, I had what appeared to be vertigo and I was panting, quite out of breath. The idea of balancing and hopping across another series of boulders and minute stepping stones terrified me, since the fast current tugged at my ankles with an insistence bordering on savagery and I was sure that it could only be a matter of seconds now before I finally lost my foothold and fell in.

Seen from the safety of a helicopter or, better still, a car window, the rugged and massive peaks might have inspired a sense of grandeur. Instead I was submerged beneath a tide of primitive fear. In short, I sensed I'd rather jump than fall, as fall I surely must, and ended up digging broken nails into both Abdul and Hassan's hands for security, and being half-dragged to the top. Collapsing at the nearest café table, I looked up at the reason for having undertaken this nightmare journey – the waterfall – and all the misery of the last two hours was instantly forgotten.

This was the real McCoy, the waterfall of innumerable adventure tales and unbridled imagination: tons of crashing spume and spray exploding down a dank cliff to roar into the deep pool below, churning up the water over, over and yet over again. High up on a ledge, I could just make out the seventh, and top, cascade, and a group of young boys peering into the icy sheet which seemed to be falling vertically with horrifying force towards us. Quite a large group of people had assembled on our level – Berber women, their babies strapped to their backs with large sheets of cotton wrapped, cocoon-like, around their bottoms and backs, adolescents with ghetto-blasters playing Rick Astley cassettes, families carrying yellow melons and flat loaves of unleavened bread, even a group of women dancers who stood waist-deep in the pool under the walnut trees, mock belly-waggling and singing traditional songs with much clapping and twisting. Abdul pointed out a long sloping cliff-face which cut through the trees and reminisced about the time he had slept the night up here and abruptly woken to discover a troupe of barbary apes drinking and smashing walnuts mere yards from his sleeping-bag. Not to be outdone, Hassan launched into a story about his two-week trek to Lake Ifni with porters and asses and the panther spore they came across three days out of base camp.

The air of festivity soon dispelled my exhaustion. Even the frequent bursts of fat raindrops which added an extra sheen of slipperiness to the already glossy boulders, boulders down which we would soon be descending, seemed attractive and refreshing in my euphoric state of mind. Of course, city girls are prone to these ridiculous poetic excesses and as soon as I surveyed the near-vertical short climb and distinctly vertiginous thin paths which lay ahead, panic reasserted itself and I promptly refused to budge, wildly promising Abdul and Hassan that I would be ready soon, that I merely needed a few minutes to prepare myself.

Abdul was quite happy to comply but Hassan saw through the pathetic bleatings and said the magic words which shifted me: 'I will hold your hand and I won't let go.' And off we crawled. I suddenly remembered that a Cambridge team led by Dr. Graham Drucker was due to arrive that same day to hunt for traces of the Barbary leopard, believed to be alive and well in the high peaks...

An hour later, having followed a long bramble-snarled trail in the blinding heat, criss-crossing the Atlas slopes according to some plan I could not understand, I watched my Russell and Bromley sandals slowly unglue in the river we were wading down as we came to a clearing which held the sanctuary of Setti Fatma herself. Non-Muslims are, of course, barred from entering the old white shrine, which holds three tombs and is small, perhaps twenty-four by twenty feet. Just outside I noticed a flat, circular area, worn bare of grass, with a short tree stump in the middle, presumably to tether sacrificial animals brought here by the tribes, since thin dull grey entrails and fat black ones, covered in a sheen of dust, lay coiled at its base. A large container stood outside the entranceway to the koubba and a solemn farmer was dishing out tins full of freezing mountain water. I thought about cholera. I considered dysentery. I mused on typhoid. And I drank three tins' worth. Abdul assured me that anyone who drinks here on the saint's day will have good health all year to come and poured a container-full over his own head to make sure every top organ was included in the promise, not just those from the mouth down. Beggars and Koranic chanters clustered around the path which sloped away from the koubba, down into the valley and, looking below, I finally saw the moussem in all its glory – a blue tent-city spreading out to right and left.

As we joined the throng of families returning from paying their respects at the shrine, the jigsaw-like scene I had glimpsed from above dissolved into dozens of scattered activities. Huge sheets of grey plastic lay spread out beneath the trees on the fringes of the clearing, weighed down with the ever-present boulders, and people squatted there, dunking Berber bread into bowls of mutton and bean soup or drinking mint tea and chewing on lamb kebabs. Children and dogs darted in and out; men selling white and pink plastic necklaces, the type that snap together, strolled around the outskirts of the crowd, their wares draped over their arms, discarded fragments of bones crunching underfoot. Young women breast-fed their infants in large, gossiping groups, beggars cruised, younger children lounged in the trees or listened to the numerous musicians dotted between the food stalls. A couple of well-muscled teenagers were busily chopping logs with axes, the shards flying in the air, occasionally eliciting a click or hiss of disapproval from unlucky passers-by who examined themselves for blood as they walked on. The atmosphere was relaxed, slow and familial.

Given the fact that most Berbers only come down from their

villages every three months or so, this moussem was clearly a social occasion and not, like so many urban ones, an organised cultural event. There were no folklore exhibitions nor earnest discussion groups, no flag ceremonies nor military and administrative representatives, no talk of state and people, nationhood and Islam – just hundreds, if not thousands, of farmers, their wives and children sunning themselves, laughing and putting away vast quantities of lamb. No one wanted to sell me anything, or talk to me, and this status of 'honorary invisibility' was as welcome as it was unexpected. I removed my poor sandals, tucked my bag under my head, quickly surveyed the nearest stretch of plastic for bones and grease and promptly fell asleep under a smutty cloud of charcoal fumes, surrounded by empty Schweppes bottles and Merit cigarette packets, vaguely listening to distant chanting.

Abdul woke me late in the afternoon looking concerned and started raving about hats. As I looked up at him blearily I became aware of two things: the crowd had grown and with it the noise level and I had a headache which was tearing my skull in half. It was obviously time to leave and track down the Anadin. Raising myself gingerly I tried to work out where we'd parked the car. The answer was forty-five minutes' wading downstream against the tide. By the time we finally staggered out of the riverbed and onto tarmac, my shoes were long since gone with the stream, there was a peculiar mouldy green sheen between every toe and under each nail and I was having difficulty focussing on my surroundings. Everything seemed to be swimming and shaking as I peered at it, bulging out and collapsing in on itself over and over again. I half fell, half threw myself into the car. People were still pouring into the village and the one road which led in and, of course, out was blocked since it could only accommodate good drivers going in opposite directions at the same time, namely drivers capable of passing one another and leaving two inches between vehicles without leaping out to inspect paintwork or expecting the convoy of vehicles to stop for their manoeuvres. Such men and women are rare and in the end it took us three hours to jostle and bump our way back to Marrakesh. Once back at the Ali I somehow made it to bed and floated in and out of consciousness for the next fifteen hours, icy towels on my forehead, retching whenever I could bear to raise my neck. In short, the victim of sunstroke and my own stupidity. At one point in the night I remember half-waking and pinching my cheeks and stomach, any fleshy part of my boiling body, over and over again to try and halt the tumble back into semi-consciousness since my dreams relived the climb and each time they started up again I convinced myself that the ending would surely change and I would fall to my death. A dozen aspirin tablets and four litres of Sidi Harazam later I could finally both stand up and remain awake. It was time to buy a straw hat.

It will not surprise the reader to learn that, along with everything else under the sun, straw hats can also be bought on the Djemaa el Fna and that I decamped from the Hotel Ali as soon as I was able to lift a suitcase and drag it to the Companie Transports Marocaine. The CTM Marrakesh is something of a legend amongst travellers, because not only does the hotel occupy probably the most central position in town, on the square, but it also costs six pounds a night for a double room and boasts a large roof terrace where orange juice, fresh baguettes, butter, date jam and an enormous flat cup of strong good coffee can be bought for fifteen dirhams every morning.

The hotel has seen better days and is neither well upkept nor smart. Mounting the broad staircase to the right of the ground-floor reception with its desk and saggy sofa, I reached a rectangular courtyard, with rooms leading off all round and multi-coloured glass screens, huge banana and hibiscus plants in pots and a grass-matted roof. Water was being sluiced across the red terracotta tiles and the matting cast long shadows on the arches which surrounded the central area of the open courtyard. The doors, window shutters and slim columns which linked the broad arches were all painted light blue, while the walls, parapets and ceilings were white. I stood stock still, admiring the selection of underwear and shirts hanging from the ornamental trees and resolved to add my own to the collection as soon as 8:00 p.m. arrived and the promised hot water started to pump through what was surely highly dubious plumbing. Two elderly maids were slinging garbage into the centre of the courtyard, emptying bins by throwing the contents underarm to join the existing mini-mountain and it seemed discourteous to interrupt both the rhythmic bowling of apple cores, plastic bottles and old newspapers and their harmonious humming.

The younger of the two, Fatima, stepped over her bucket and wiped her hands on her cover-all, smiled, passed me a key to room fifteen. Room fifteen had a broken lock, a knee-high pile of shredded strips of leather by the doorway and an evil array of used tampons, crusty torn pink knickers and the odd bra on the floor … What the hell could have been going on here? I dragged my bag out and asked Fatima who was staying there. "A tour group," she answered. "The Spanish are pigs." I smiled weakly and tried again.

Number sixteen looked more promising – a large room with a curtain on a pole in one corner, behind which stood a giant shower tray and accoutrements, an orange-streaked European toilet with a very short metal chain, a broken mirror which sliced off my chin and a deep porcelain basin with no plug. The bathroom, for such it was, was partly whitewashed and partly tiled but, more to the point, it had no telltale splodges on the ground testifying to recently crushed cockroaches and pieces of

PART ONE

Le Matin were even tucked behind the wastepipe for use as toilet paper. The main bedroom, although illuminated by miserly forty-watt bulbs, had impeccably clean sheets on a saggy bed, the shutters closed, and the net curtains, a weird blue, complemented the café chair and its thick blue and white nylon webbing. It was blessedly cool and I felt excited by the prospect of staying in such a lush, dark place and gave aloof Fatima a peck on the cheek. She left the room, glancing at me with a look halfway between repressed amusement and incredulity. After all, her eyes said, this is just another chore, another room; what's the big deal?

The CTM company, which owns a large network of buses, hotels and cafés, is surprisingly efficient and reliable and was to prove a mainstay throughout the trip on every level, from providing crisp cheese omelettes to air-conditioned coaches and Jackie Chan videos.

All this time, unbeknown to me, Abdul had been standing outside patiently stalking me, his street 'spies' having reported the change of location. Just as he gave up and wandered away to check out other prospects – Abdul prefers the Germans, saying the French bring cameras; the Germans bring their wallets – I emerged opposite orange juice stall Number Ten and asked for two large glasses. The young boy switched on the electric liquidiser and handed over the first. It was watered down and had the sour tinge of blood oranges. I drank it anyway and set off towards the main entrance to the medina, rue Souk Semarine.

Tourism is virtually a year-round, rather than a seasonal, source of income in the city, for only during July and August, when temperatures regularly hit fifty degrees centigrade and the Marrakeshis leave for the coast, does the struggle between the tourist and his assailant become a slightly more equal one. Marrakesh has been an important trading centre for centuries, dominating the High Atlas strategically, politically and economically. Caravans from the south, Berbers from the remote

20

mountain villages and traders from central Morocco have long congregated here to barter goods, auction slaves, sell gold and ivory and buy the basic necessities for their survival in the souks of the sprawling medina.

The goods may have changed, but the city remains a trader's paradise and all too frequently a shopper's nightmare. The local tourist office wages a constant war against false guides, carpet sellers who work in cahoots with official guides, hoteliers who totally ignore the standardised classifications and prices for rooms, antique dealers who bury their goods for a number of weeks to simulate the patina of age and chancers who try any and every scam known to human ingenuity to part you from your dirhams. If you're in the right frame of mind, the streets of Marrakesh present a heady, colourful obstacle course, nothing more; if, however, you are in any way physically or emotionally depleted, the steady stream of persistent, often rude if not downright menacing hustlers can reduce you to tears of frustration, and create a siege mentality unequalled outside Fez-el-Bali.

Intent on finding a royal blue cotton gandora to sleep in and protect me against mosquitoes, I scanned bolts of embroidered cloth, silks and cottons which were piled on all sides. Treadle sewing machines whirred inside the shops, whose outsides displayed so-called air-conditioned trousers (Ali Baba pantaloons in pretty white and pastel shades with minute flowers and leaves in the pattern), children's gandoras in light blue, grey, light green and a particularly repellent ochre brown, striped adult djellabas in wool and cotton and the most lurid bri-nylon kaftans you can imagine – bright orange with yellow and black, olive green with gold embroidery and thick gold edgings, black and red with tassels in polyester. The range of colours was infinite and startling, but I wondered why women here wear so much synthetic material in the heat. Moroccan cotton is excellent, and from Tangier to Fez the souks are awash with copies of

Western fashion, from Levi's to Chanel-logo T-shirts, made of pure cotton.

After a fruitless half hour of popping on garments I did not wish to buy, I decided to aim for the kissaria, the heart of the medina closest to the mosque, where jewellery and clothes for important gatherings such as circumcisions and weddings are sold. Perhaps I'd find the blue there. Unfortunately, the blood oranges seemed to have addled my brain since, however I walked through the narrow, twisting alleys, past hole-in-the-wall workshops, grocers, communal ovens and inverted carcasses, I constantly came back to the one place in Marrakesh medina which is only of limited interest in my books – the metal-workers' quarter; in particular one corner of the metal-workers' quarter where a middle-aged man in glasses was recycling and cannibalising bicycles.

After three attempts, all aborted by cul de sacs or dead-ends, I finally asked a passer-by for the directions to the Koutoubia and was led past the wrought-iron stylists and into a narrow road full of tables and chairs, wardrobes and chests of drawers. The joinery was crude but young boys were painting the furniture to traditional designs, covering the unplaned edges and the ragged legs with a variety of rich base coats in turquoise, maroon, dark blue, and applying the patterns over the top with the thinnest of brushes. Working upright in small whitewashed booths, on whose walls they wiped the brushes, they were bent over in concentration, tiny pots of gold leaf and acrylics in every hue perched on ledges behind them. The outlines which they followed had already been pencilled in on the base coat and yet even a small, say three feet in diameter table, with simple, unturned legs, took a boy ten days to complete. I had a go on an offcut, but the brush-hairs separated as I tried to follow the curved line; according to Mohammed, my tutor, I had 'a weak wrist'. I hope it's a criticism he uses discriminatingly and sparingly.

As we moved on, the hammering and blow-torching of the wretched metal-workers was replaced by the syncopated humming and banging of the Marrakesh medina. The dyers' souk had been having a blitz on carmine red and royal blue, for the pavements were awash in streams of the same and thick skeins of wool assaulted my eyes as they hung drying over long wooden poles. A lone water seller had joined forces with a man carrying a peregrine falcon and the former was clashing his bronze cups and ringing his bell for snap-happy tourists: two for the price of one. Dodging down a side alley full of busy cobblers, children playing football and women carrying cloth-covered trays to the communal oven, I emerged by a large Berber pharmacy. The cross-eyed boy running the small shop was adjusting the screen of dead bodies around the entrance with a hooked pole: dried hedgehog, jackal and fox pelts, eagle feathers still on the wing, porcupine quills and a dry, immensely long snakeskin from the Sahara. Just inside the doorway on a flat table lay heaps of henna, antimony, Berber shampoo, clay pots of cochineal and dozens of herbs, while the walls of the shop contained jars of minerals, including the perfumed soft stones which are rubbed on the wrists and give off a warm, rose and jasmine-like scent. Looking closer I saw eggs, what looked like bird hearts and foetuses (of unknown origin) and a disgusting collection of severed chameleons' heads. A small wicker cage by the pelts held four or five old chameleons, one dragging a hind leg, and a jam jar with crude holes punched through the lid was home to a sprig of mint and a dozen fingernail-sized babies.

It was some years ago that I first spotted chameleons and understood their function in Berber medicine – crush with three herbs to prevent hair loss, crush with five herbs for headaches, throw, alive of course, on cooking fire to bring good luck. Intrigued, I bought four in London and managed to keep my charges alive longer than London Zoo's self-confessed best efforts. I developed a fondness for the creatures which still brings a sheen to my eyes when I see their graves in my South London garden. At home, the chameleons lived free in, aptly enough, the chameleons' room – so called to remind everyone that the slow-moving, often camouflaged creatures were loose and liable to be trodden upon. On hot days they basked in a chicken wire box, ten feet by ten, high on a white garden wall, lounging on sycamore branches and zipping out their tongues, fat and pink, to catch flies and bees or the odd spider, earwig or caterpillar I found for them, their eyes constantly moving round three hundred and sixty degrees. At night each one had to be held with its mouth beneath a dripping tap until it caught its fill of water drops. If you moved them too abruptly, the water shot out like a geyser and the whole long-winded arm-aching business had to start again. Since garden insects are not plentiful enough to feed a chameleon in England, unlike in Morocco where most families keep one caged in the kitchen to catch passing flies, I had to supplement their diet with boxes of live crickets and young locusts. This was a gamble, since nonchalantly throwing two hundred crickets into your best furnished room twice a week necessitates true faith in the chameleon's hunting ability and speed – otherwise, good-bye carpet, sofa and curtains. Incidentally, they never failed in the race against time – and the cricket's jaws.

Three years of typing with a chameleon on your shoulder, or down your blouse, watching the news with a string of chameleons suspended by hooked toes from the curtains by your head and getting to the point where they no longer puffed out suspiciously when you extended your hand, all left their mark – a tide of rage whenever I see them now, only half-dead, strung upside-down to dry in the sun, turning on a piece of string, their eyes bulging, blindly searching for food even in extremis. I know all too well, however, the futility of arguing the case for animal rights in a poor country where there is little enough respect for human rights, and progress (i.e. aspirin) in all its forms is associated with repression and corruption, while ancient beliefs (porcupine pelts) conjure up notions of a past golden age and are revered accordingly.

I declined a jackal pelt for two hundred and fifty dirhams to protect me against the evil eye and was making to move on, when a hand tapped me on the shoulder. Its owner, one Jamal, looked reminiscent of a young Cliff Richard in shades, and had apparently overheard and been offended by the pharmacist's sales spiel. He drew me aside and told me that he wanted to show me something which really did overcome the evil eye.

Curious, if slightly dubious, I trotted along until we reached an expensive antique shop, boasting a large and impressive collection of Arab and Berber musical instruments, whose doors he unlocked. Once inside Jamal revealed himself to be a Koranic scholar whose soul, as he put it, 'was at rest and not in the world', while he was preparing for his mission in life, to preach the faith in countries which had deviated from the true path. He would not specify where this might be, but over the hour that followed I gained the impression that Jamal was aiming to go to Iran, since his enigmatic comments on the great Satan being other than we thought seemed to indicate the Peacock Throne. His quiet voice and the intense glare he had perfected were threatening, and as he launched into a version of the origins of the hand of Fatima, held to be a symbol of protection throughout the Muslim world, I felt battered and pressurised. Apparently, Fatima was the mother of Christ, not the daughter of Mohammed, and when the women in her village discovered that she was pregnant they questioned her closely as to the identity of the father. Fatima constantly maintained she was still a virgin, which strained their credulity to the point where they eventually decided to stone her to discover the truth. By this time, Fatima had borne her child and when the crowd of jeering women arrived at her hut, she clutched the infant Jesus to her breast and held out her hand to ward them off. The evil-thinking villagers were stopped in their tracks, Jamal informed me that he had worked all this out from his own researches, an achievement which astounded me, but perhaps not for the reasons he might have imagined.

Now that he was launched on his theme of mock-the-jackal, he began to line up a selection of Koranic diplomas in front of me, apparently another extra-sure form of protection. When a Koranic scholar has finally learnt to recite the whole of the holy book, he is presented with one of these exquisite wooden boards as a reward. The boards are quite small, ten by twelve inches seems to be the average size, and are slightly convex. On the back, you find the Arabic alphabet, but it is the outer face which demands examination. Thrust outwards, it is adorned with intricate patterns and representations of the mihrab (prayer niche), mosque lights and decorations, along with verses from the Koran. The dyes which are used all come from the natural world: mint creates the green tints, saffron the yellow, blue comes from indigo and red from cochineal, and these subtle shades combine well with the thick, light wood. Jamal handled each piece lovingly and asked me, rhetorically I presume, whether these can truly be compared with an animal corpse. Apropos of nothing, he suddenly added that he converted two Germans to Islam last year and, as if on impulse, added that he would gladly now read the Koran aloud to me, since I have 'baraka', i.e. luck, or, more specifically I suspect, a pendant made in Kuwait with Allah written on it in silver.

This wretched pendant, which I have worn day and night for six years and which I no longer even feel next to my skin, became the bane of my life in the weeks that followed. Men swore at me for owning it, warned me that the impure of heart would lose it, admonished me to wear it with respect and so on. Infuriatingly enough, everyone I met united in telling me what I already knew. Allah is the name of God. I got to the point where I hid it under T-shirts and reversed the chain for good measure for fear of ramming it down the next 'translator's' neck. I have taken the precaution of never buying any object with a written inscription without first having the message translated and, like most mildly superstitious magical-thinkers, I am particularly careful about what I place next to my skin, to absorb my spirit, as it were. The common Moslem belief that they have a monopoly on respect for the spiritual world is one of Islam's least attractive traits and frequently angers me, as did Jamal's final shots at conversion, trick questions such as 'Is it better to be materially or spiritually well off?' His anxious, concerned expression forced a polite, banal answer out of me, rather than the sharp retort I would have made to any door-bashing evangelist in London who also posed questions I answered at catechism classes at the age of six.

I suddenly felt ill at ease and made my excuses, saying that I wanted to see the Medersa Ben Youssef and the koubba before they shut. I scuttled gratefully back into the streets to be borne away by the tide of asses, shoppers and porters. My last glimpse of Jamal was of a rigid-backed white-clad figure sitting cross-legged at a low table, surrounded by Koranic diplomas. I could have sworn he was smiling at the carved tablets, smiling at the prospect of the martyrdom I couldn't understand but which he referred to so naturally, so casually. I felt unexpected tears come to my eyes, the hairs rise up on my neck, for in that split second I believed he might well get his wish.

It is probably a good thing that the Medersa Ben Youseff offers another vision of the Moslem faith. A home for theological students until 1960, when it became too small to cater for the city's growing needs, this medersa a triumph of decorative art and a haven of peace. Entering the heart of the medersa, which formerly housed up to seven hundred theological students for the six years it took them to memorise the Koran along with the teachings and commentaries on the scriptures, it is almost a shock to walk straight into what looks like an off-white marble bath, decorated with griffins, eagles, leaves and flowers. Apparently this solid, cheerful object was brought over to Morocco by the expansionist Almoravides, a confederation of desert tribes who rebelled against the authoritarian rule and high taxation imposed by the caliphs of Baghdad. Led by a succession of tribal emirs, of whom Youssef ben Tachfin, the founder of Marrakesh, was perhaps the most renowned, the Almoravides fought to re-establish Islamic orthodoxy and gain territory for the faith on the battlefield. By the beginning of the twelfth century, their empire stretched from the Balearic Islands to the border of Senegal, from the Atlantic coast to Algiers. Eventually this souvenir of the Andalusian campaign was ensconced here in the sixteenth century by the Saadians, who wanted to make Marrakesh not only their political capital, but also the intellectual capital of the country.

Wandering through the quiet and deserted tiled courtyard, with its ablutions basin and lines of stumpy yet powerful Kufic script reminding me of the glory of God and duty of man, the simplicity of the building and the utter sense of repose it instils in the visitor once again confirmed the joy to be found in meditation and faith. The small wooden rooms upstairs are monastic in their lack of adornment, yet even here it is easy to spot human pride at work since at regular intervals you come across strips of ornately painted ceiling marking the entrance to larger cells with heavily carved windows and wider lofts – the homes of the imams. The stucco-work shines in the sunlight and the visitor almost cocks an ear, hoping to hear the echoes of the millions of chanted verses which have murmured through these cells and the elegant prayer hall below. I leaned on a thick wooden railing overlooking the courtyard and felt content, drinking in the plasterwork and tiling, sinking back into the ages-old certainties.

In contrast, the recently excavated Koubba el Baroudiyn, which stands nearby some three yards below street level, is a total non-event. Like so many architectural 'discoveries' of yore, its beauty lies in the reconstructive and imaginative eye of the beholder. Guide-book writers are particularly prone to seeing a smudged tile, or a broken piece of plaster and building a whole theory of contrasts, boldness and light-play, with historical antecedents and parallels around it. The koubba's most interesting feature must be the fact that it shows how frequently Marrakesh was destroyed and then rebuilt on top of its own rubbish – nothing more.

The medersa had whetted my appetite for simplicity and I decided to find my travelling companion and old friend Miyuki to interest her in photo-opportunities. Like so many Japanese tourists, Miyuki owns a fiendishly sophisticated small black camera bulging with gadgets, lenses which click and shriek, auto-everything, manual override for the impossible shot. It also takes strikingly good pictures and in three days Miyuki had already exposed around twelve reels of Fuji film. Only the crippling heat, sheer exhaustion precipitated by the strange diet of kebabs, bread and water and sharing a room with the babies had driven her back into the CTM to sleep that morning.

Miyuki was sitting outside the hotel with none other than Abdul as I pushed through the traffic and reached the pavement, unscathed. Abdul was still wearing the same paisley shirt and looked miserable. Apparently he had lost a tooth the previous night and the dentist, one of thousands, nay millions who practise in Morocco, had told him it was "one of those things". In addition, he disliked the clients he had lined up for the morrow and was further depressed to discover that Tony was away playing golf, so he was left with me – and I don't shop. To cheer him up, Miyuki promised to buy a gandora. Abdul appeared unimpressed and resignedly asked us what we wanted to see throwing in the fact that we had been drinking from juice stalls Nos. 10 and 4 and only No. 12 doesn't dilute the orange.

The Saadian tombs were mooted once again, but we bartered a visit to el Badi, the ruined Saadian palace, first, in exchange for a glance at the tombs. Abdul could not comprehend this choice of destination and told us that real tourists didn't go there, but my avoidance tactics were scuppered when Miyuki, who had been following the conversation with her ears and co-ordinating her understanding of the argument via a guide-book, perked up and said the guide-book assured her the tombs were very beautiful. The guide-book won, as it did throughout our trip, and Miyuki shoved thirty rolls of film into her bag, giggled and toddled off with Abdul, accepting with equanimity the 'sayonaras' which marked her progress through the streets.

The sixteenth-century el Badi palace is superb, shimmering rich warm orange walls surrounding a courtyard with pool and four sunken gardens. An Italian girl was kneeling by the pool washing her hair, but apart from the sacred storks casually flapping in their nests on the turrets, the palace was empty. The guardian emerged and told us that this was the first time in eighteen years the storks had not flown away to cooler climes in the summer, because the weather had been so mild. It was forty degrees centigrade! I looked at him blankly and smiled while I pondered a stork's definition of heat. Clambering over a wide but rickety bridge, it was possible to see the judgment chamber where Koranic sentences of beheading, amputation and imprisonment were handed down by Ahmed el Mansour. The prisoners, both male and female, were sent to underground cells nearby where they quickly went blind due to lack of light. Shallow niches mark the spot where the guards habitually placed their lamps in the passages. Food was thrown in through gaps between doors. The fabled marble columns have not withstood time as well as these dank pits, ironically enough, since Moulay Ishmael, in his merciless quest for building materials for admittedly wonderful Meknès, came to the el Badi in 1696 and helped himself to the Italian marble, the cedar doors, the mosaics and the gold, which was smelted here to embellish ceilings and walls. He left the el Badi as we now find it – a vast glowing emptiness which only comes alive in July when the local tourist office mounts a fantasia-cum-folkore extravaganza with Berber dancers, dervishes, riders and singers performing above the covered-over pool.

Just as we were leaving, the long-absent guardian of stork-migration materialised and asked for a forty dirham tip (two days' wages). I gave him twenty dirhams for no good reason apart from a great liking for the building, and lunged at Miyuki to prevent her following suit as I realised that he was recounting a classic lie: 'We guardians receive no wages but rely on tips.' The mood was shattered.

Abdul, being an unofficial guide, was barred from entering sites of historical interest, accompanying a client in a taxi or even from walking down the road with one, for fear of being spotted by the tourist police. He had, therefore, been sitting in the street and sidled out to enquire how we had got on. My enthusiastic adjective-barrage held his interest for a minute, but he was more outraged by the guardian's ploy to secure money than interested in talk of honey-coloured walls and clear reflections on water. Perhaps he would file this tactic away for leaner times. As we marched through the Marrakesh mellah en route to the tombs, Abdul pointed out the Jewish inhabitants: in practice this meant every obese woman with a sweaty moon face and swollen ankles and every beak-nosed man. I was outraged by this racism, but Abdul wouldn't hear of it and insisted that these truly were the remaining Jews of the area. Nevertheless, as we penetrated the mess of tall houses, with their rectangular balconies and their upper floors almost touching, there was indeed something stereotypical about the men at the sewing machines or hemming and stitching by hand, needles held between their teeth or hanging over their lips, ready to be threaded, as they flipped over large flapping sheets of polyester. There was a sense of a disappearing community in the air, underscored by our discovery of a synagogue perched above a short staircase with its sad brown door and simple bronze star. There are no functioning synagogues left in Marrakesh, since they have all been converted into schools and colleges and the post Six-Day-War exodus appears to have finally ripped the heart out of the community.

In contrast, the guide-toting and camera-clicking tourist community was alive, well and assembled en masse outside the Saadian tombs, final resting place for descendants of the prophet (the Shorfa), and the Saadian, Merenid and Alaouite princes. The indisputable beauty of the open-air graves, the richly decorated mausoleums and dark, solemn prayer hall was ruined by the tramp of feet. Nikon flashes and syncopated spiels issuing from the numerous guides, who hustled out one group as soon as humanly possible, the quicker to marshal together the next dirham-dispensers. Pushed aside to make room for tripods, I peered over half a dozen heads inside, avoiding spluttering hose-pipes watering the grass and wide-angled lenses outside. Like so many unique, inspiring settings, it had been debased by over-exposure and failed to move me.

The same cannot be said of our next stop, Yves St Laurent's strange Jardin Majorelle, a botanical garden in the New Town which was originally created by French artist Louis Majorelle and has now been revamped with gallons of royal blue paint. The jardinières, both square and round, the pavilions and the peripheral infrastructure (three-foot-high bins, walls, trims and steps) scream out 'designer blue' but, astonishingly enough, it seems to suit this tiny, dainty garden with its bamboo arches overhanging paths broken by goldfish pools, lily ponds and pavilions. Miyuki became very excited at the sight of Malaysian bamboo, bursting into a speech about obviously much-mourned Japanese cuisine, pandas and koi carp, frantically snapping the giant cacti which surrounded us and made up the majority of the exhibits. The garden, she remarked, was the opposite of bonsai and its discipline. And of course she was right, for here everything was just too big, from the oak-tree high cacti to the enormous drooping light-coloured blooms popping in the heat. The goldfish were huge, as were the messy bananas, palms, rubber plants and dragonara. We felt dwarfed and repelled by the size of it all, the military rigidity of the cacti out of place in a city which spreads and crawls with life, rather than marches to a beat. And yet the graffiti etched into the stands of bamboo bore testimony to courtship amongst the almost forced lushness, and a cockerel and its entourage occasionally broke down the sense of order as they wandered across our path and refused to give way. When the shock of the overbearing first impression passed, however, the calm and the bright colours wove their spell, although this garden must surely be one of the great irrelevancies of Marrakesh – a crazed colonial statement rather than a meaningful or provocative one.

In our quest for the ultimate small garden, Miyuki and I decided to see the much vaunted terraces of the nearby Mamounia Hotel. The Mamounia is Morocco's most famous hotel and has played host to the world's rich, powerful and infamous. It is so remote from mainstream Moroccan life that it could be on another planet – 'planet international'. The colossally affluent interior with its ancient kilims, black marble, shopping arcades, tasteful glassed-in displays of jewellery, slot machines and man-high flower arrangements guarded by doormen in traditional costume, was enough to send us, more humble visitors, into full retreat, self-consciously wiping our shoes as we walked out – not in. We just managed a peek at the Bougainvillaea-clad wall by the pool and the fabulous, red-painted cedar ceilings of the main reception before shame overcame confidence. This was one garden which would have to wait for another day and smarter garb.

Marrakesh, which seems to disappear each time you pop inside another historical testimony to an era, another set of priorities, reasserts itself on the streets and on the air. Sitting there that final hot night, listening to the rhythm of the city, eating tagine (a stew of meat or fruit with vegetables and spices) and salad, watching yet another group of grey apes, their teeth removed with pliers by their smiling owners, making their way across the square, to mingle with the throng, I felt depleted, longed for a haven – and immediately thought of the High Atlas, and more specifically of the ruined mosque of Tin Mal, the only mosque in Morocco that non-Moslems are allowed to enter.

The High Atlas, which rises south of the Marrakesh plain, the Berber homeland, is crossed by three main passes, the Tiz-n-Test (2092m) to Taroudant, the Tiz-n-Tichka (2260m) to Ouarzazate and Tiz-n-Babaou to Agadir. Only the Tiz-n-Babaou is guaranteed to be open all year round and provides the dullest and least spectacular route across what are unimaginably stunning peaks. I am not a great admirer of European mountain ranges, with their ski resorts and cable cars, but the High Atlas is a world apart, rather than a developed national attraction, a world of farmers and shepherds who eke out a living in the age-old fashion, driving their herds to seek pasture, cultivating their land. Leaving Marrakesh for Taroudant, we drove down a long straight road lined with gum trees and prickly-pear cacti whose fruit is sold by the bucket by little boys who dart out into the traffic and make windmill-motions with their arms. I had never tried a prickly pear and, not wanting to buy thirty, in case it proved foul,

I hopped out by a large bush and pulled one off. The minute sharp hairs which are clustered in the wart-like dimples that cover the fruit instantly embedded themselves in my fingers. Panicking, I passed the fruit to Miyuki, and tried to pull the prickles out with my teeth. As a result, the roof of my mouth, my tongue and gums all received a lavish coating of needles. Miyuki, who had no idea what she was being given, had also discovered the reason why the fruit was so named and was squealing 'Oh, oh,' and rummaging for tweezers – having passed the fruit on. Of course, the more vigorously you attempt to pull the vicious barbs out, the more likely it is you will drop them onto neighbouring knees and shirts and embed them in arms. Within a matter of minutes, the car was a sea of grimacing faces, everyone intently examining their digits. Profanities thickened the air and it was made clear to me that I was not only brainless but potentially dangerous. Surely, it was argued, the name might have given me a clue? I was too busy gingerly trying to dislodge the feathered stings from inside my lower lip to reply but my first impression of the Atlas valleys and peaks in August was somewhat marred by self-inflicted wounds.

A far cry from pottering along the tarmac road which leads into the fertile Ourika valley, with its streams, birds and lushness, crossing the Atlas mountain passes is a treacherous, often worrying business. The further we climbed the less pleasurable the drive became, and even the beige, red and ochre landscape with the Berbers' flat-roofed mud and pise (adobe) houses wedged into sheer rockfaces, overlooking suicide-inspiring ravines, could not distract from the front-end loaders, graders and tractors which were shovelling mounds of slurry, slate and shale, or shifting basalt and granite slabs to clear the road. The Tiz-n-Test winds steeply and is cursed with S-bends, innumerable blind corners on the trot and unprotected sides. Common accident sites have been marked off with heaps of boulders or thin plywood bars, whose feet are themselves gradually slipping down the slope with the constant movement of the topsoil. Since the road zig-zags so relentlessly, every so often it is possible to look directly ahead across the next peak to see if anything wheeled is coming down. Buses make this trip several times a day and 'hoot' all the way, voicing wild notes of despair. It is not a comforting sight to glimpse a broad, swaying, local bus, crammed with passengers, trumpeting towards you at forty kilometres per hour, but the drivers are competent enough and if you park up tight to the cliffside and shut your eyes and pray, it's all over in a matter of seconds. People are not the main obstacle in the High Atlas for they are few and far between once you have left the cultivated foothills and the towns behind: the distant silhouette of a mule and rider framed against the skyline, the herder and his flock of black and white sheep going somewhere inaccessible, woodcutters loading sawn-up logs into trucks and heading ever-upwards. Goats present more of a problem as dozens at a time pick their way across the road, the odd stragglers dashing to catch up with the main herd, or stand stock-still and bleating in front of you, before scrambling up a seemingly unscramblable sheet of rock and setting off a mini-landslide in their wake.

The drive from Marrakesh to the village of Tahanaoute was almost biblically idyllic, as we passed donkeys with brown ceramic jugs hanging on each side. The donkeys drank at canals, where the jugs were filled to the brim by young children who waved at each passing car before turning back to their tasks. Women were much in evidence at their labours, stacking red-mud bricks, carrying on their heads woven baskets filled with straw, thumping washing in large wooden tubs or sweeping the dust from their low pink-and-orange houses, headscarves protecting their heads from the piercing heat. In fact, Islam enjoins the covering of the head for both men and women at all times so that Allah's scribes, the honest recorders, angels who register all our acts and thoughts and are believed to live in our brains, are protected symbolically. The younger, urban generation seems to be drifting away from this observance, but in the countryside it is rare to find girls with their heads uncovered.

As usual, and for reasons which I cannot fathom, wherever I find myself in rural Morocco, there is always a solitary man to be spotted squatting on his heels under a tree, eyes peering into the middle distance, gandora hitched up to the knees, often with a donkey tethered to a branch or grazing a nearby hedge. These immobile male figures appear in the middle of nowhere or lie, face down, in the fields, seemingly miles from anywhere. And yet women and their tasks are much in evidence: washing flapping on trees, struggling along, bundles of twigs tied to their backs in slings. Children armed with sticks drive herds of sheep or the odd cow, mongrel dogs snapping along at their heels, while, low in the valley, rickety shelters held up by poles have been constructed for byres. There is a rhythm which relaxes the senses, a purposefulness to all the quiet activity, a timelessness to the division of labour, so far removed from the mercantile free-for-all of Marrakesh. Here the children don't hustle kif (cannabis) and fight to accompany tourists; the men aren't glued to café tables waiting for an unsuspecting ingénue to drop out of a tour bus and the women live within secure, if harsh, traditional patterns and bonds, rather than in the twilight world of the semi-liberated Rabati girl with this generation's – if not the next's – half-articulated burden of guilt and insecurity. Transitional generations are martyrs for their successors and although no one wishes to freeze Morocco in a rural backwater because it 'looks pretty', the flight to the city has nothing to recommend it in this land where unemployment stands at over sixty per cent and social security benefits are non-existent.

An hour and a half into the journey we ran smack into the weekly souk at Tahanaoute: a sea of 'Berber taxis' (asses) and carts laden with vegetables and fruit, all converging inside a square off the main road. Rural souks are much of a muchness and not worth attending just because they are there, out of some misguided sense of quaintness or photographic need. Like all markets – street, covered, galleried or hyper – they exist to sell, and the hustlers descend like flies the minute you fail to drive past. Ibrahim, a self-styled Tuareg, managed to grab my arm, thrust a poor, thick tin bracelet around it and in the space of a minute, had invited me to come and watch his wife weaving, meet his children and eat couscous. Having lost the veneer of smiling patience all travellers carry about them during their first few days in the Maghreb, without having achieved the insolence of the French, who treat their former colony as a vassal state which is still morally if not legally theirs, I was not to be pushed so hard. I thrust on by, leaving him to a befuddled, smiling Miyuki who did not understand a word he was saying, but nodded her head good-naturedly somewhere above the tent-like gandora Abdul had sneakily forced her to buy in Marrakesh while my back was turned.

An old man named Mohammed had been watching this little attack and counter-thrust and ambled over to ask me what I was looking for here. Glue, I told him. Glue to stick together a pair of flip-flops. Holding my arm to guide me to the nearest shoe-mender, Mohammed moved briskly through the men guarding rusty screws, army knives, screwdrivers, colanders and broken wristwatches, past the bright mountains of peppers and over to a young boy, who passionlessly surveyed the plastic sandal, grinned and made to whack a half-inch nail through the hanging strap. I yelped. He jumped. The glue-pot came out and a liberal swish of paste was applied, all for the princely sum of one dirham.

Mohammed was proud of himself, for having secured the visitors and paraded us around the market so everyone could see. I resolved to give him some money, since his lack of hidden goods – he had come unprepared for strangers – left him nothing to sell. Instead, he showed me his eight hundred dirham she-ass and the baby, which he hoped to sell for five hundred dirhams. He also warned me conspiratorially never, but never, to run over a cow, since they were prohibitively expensive. I assured him that I would do my best and commiserated with his lack of takers for the spindly-legged but endearing, velvet-coated baby ass. Before he could articulate the gleam that flashed through his pupils, I hastily added that Customs would seize it on sight, but that I wanted to contribute to its welfare and his profit margin. Notes changed hands, farewells were made and, retrieving the flip-flop from the top of a tent where it had been left to dry, I strolled back to the car – only to discover Miyuki idly turning over the seven plastic and glass necklaces with metal tongues, two bracelets, two kohl container pendants and the wooden dagger Ibrahim had sold her. She looked glassy-eyed and a touch mad – this was all proving far removed from Tokyo and the famous guide-book was useless up in the hills. I duly admired the heap of goodies and felt a trifle too smug for my own good, since a mere fifteen kilometres further on, at the village of Asni, I found myself buying two equally useless round enamelled boxes, from a young man named Hassan.

The third son of a Berber farmer who scratches a living from the soil where the mountains meet the plains, Hassan cannot find full-time work in Marrakesh or on the land. He left school at the age of fourteen and has no self-assertiveness to his manner and thus no inborn talent for the only work open to him in Asni – selling knickknacks to anyone who stops for petrol or a drink at one of the ramshackle cafés. Hassan lives below the official poverty line, namely one hundred and fifty dirhams a week minimum wage and, like all but two of his six brothers and sisters, appears to be waiting for something to happen. In the meantime, he lounges in the village along with the majority of his peers, chatting at the entrance to the main and only square, watching the cars and the road, sleeping away the afternoons and smoking kif in the evenings in order to tranquillise himself the better to pass out. A friend of his eldest brother's has given Hassan half a dozen enamelled boxes and a dozen tin bracelets, which he keeps in a brown drawstring cloth bag on a sale or return basis, and this is how he survives. At harvest time, he picks up the odd day's work and he is always available for casual labour, standing in at the café for an hour or so, running errands. There is no alternative to this stagnant form of time-wasting and Hassan keeps dreaming that he will meet a rich Christian woman who will marry him and take him away, show him sexual perversions of every kind and shower him with electrical goods and Western clothes. Unlike the smooth-tongued medina salesman of Tangier, who comes into contact with Europeans on an hourly basis twelve months a year and has a heap of letters and cards from Spanish, British and Italian girls to prove it (and why, pray, do so many of them bear a Sheffield postmark?), Hassan's chances of talking his way into a new passport are nil. And yet, like innumerable Moroccan youths, getting out, sponsorship, a ticket to the West is an obsession.

I have been approached on countless occasions, in parks, at cafés and on street corners by boys who tell me they want to practise their English and, once encouraged to talk, immediately launch into the 'I want to leave this country, there is nothing here for me' confessional mode. Most end up handing over a sad square of paper with name, address and date of birth printed carefully on it. The whole business is reminiscent of marooned sailors launching messages in bottles, hoping against hope and experience that one day they might reach a friendly shore. It is difficult to persuade anyone in Hassan's situation that they might find London, for example, unfriendly and crowded, might find it difficult to get work or accommodation and that the fabulous wages we earn cannot be translated into local currency, since they are geared to London prices. The tanned effervescent twenty-year-old girl with money to burn and all the time in the world to sunbathe and knock back vodka, turns into a hardworking secretary who catches the 8.15 and watches her pennies so that she puts enough aside for the quarterly gas bill. Should Hassan ever manage to turn up on her doorstep, chances are she would be at best embarrassed, at worst horrified and dismissive. Whichever way one looks at his situation, it is bound by the small square which is Asni – a few donkeys tethered against a low wall, their saddles at their feet, a grocer leaning half-asleep on his counter while flies buzz over his bread, land on his yoghurt.

In one corner by a broken-down car an old man was sitting on a backless wooden stool, fiddling with a rubber patch and a tyre, while a group of giggling girls squatted near a box of kittens, prodding inside to get a spitting reaction. I felt terminally depressed and cut out, distanced myself from Hassan and his insistent but unconvincing sales-pitch, as he lit matches and held them against the orange-and-blue enamelled lids of two distorted pill boxes. The pool of trinkets in front of me grew, it was hot and humid, his voice droned on and on. I stood up abruptly and handed him forty dirhams for the boxes – one third of his asking price. He refused the money, but I could see that he was going to take it in the end and, as the car engine turned over, and doors slammed, he materialised and popped the boxes on the dashboard, snatched the notes almost apologetically and moved back, to wave and then return to his spot – ready for the next car.

The road to Tin Mal winds on up, getting steeper and more barren, through the pretty village of Ourigane whose prohibitively expensive Roseraie Hotel parking lot is always crammed with tourist coaches. On the other side of the road stands Le Sanglier qui Fume, immortalised by Paul Bowles and still famed for its cuisine. Madame, the owner, is said to be French by some, Hungarian by others, and presides over the bar in the main reception area eavesdropping on conversations and keeping her distance. Her strong features bear the ravages of disappointments, and yet she seems willing to live up to her 'legend in her own lifetime' status, snapping low-voiced commands at the numerous waiters who move between the outside diners and the bar, with its glass and cane coffee tables, hunting trophies and postcard stands.

The clientele is French and the eighty-dirhams and ninety-dirhams menus are classic routier meals featuring veal and tripe, fruit tartes and fromage blanc. Time seems to have stood still here, but when you wander outside, the signs of neglect and decline already visible in the owner's attitude are reflected in the crumbling outbuildings, long and dry grass, overgrown bushes and sheds full of litter and broken metal which house tiny brown lizards. The sanglier (boar) himself is penned below the terrace, and snuffles contentedly in a mess of mud and stones while a steady stream of water pours down on his grey, bristly snout. He is magnificently ugly and totally disinterested in human contact, preferring to sieve through the slurry at his feet. Somehow, even his presence could not lift the day and I suspected that this had something to do with this isolated terrain, home of long-established independent communities, all of whom make a living from passing foreign visitors, and not from the land. Their struggle to survive is more hopeless than that of their peers in town since traffic is lighter; hence their efforts to succeed are both more insistent and less warranted. Like the odd palm tree spotted in a riverbed edged with olives, gums and fruit trees, or the three camels tied outside the restaurant to be photographed by the visitors, they stand out because they are all artificial additions to the landscape.

When we finally reached it, Tin Mal was both 'right and fitting' and surely the most arresting religious site in the country. Perched high above a shallow stream full of fish and frogs, it looks down over the N'fis valley and the nearby Agadir N'gouf, a sturdy castle built by the local Gondaffi caid in 1907, after his rivals, the Glaoui and M'touggi, had ransacked the valley and burnt his kasbah of Talaat n Yacoub. A steep but shady path winds up the hillside to the settlement of Tin Mal and the mosque seems to recede and then loom up above with every turn. Suddenly it is just ahead – an enormous, awe-inspiring ruin, open to the cloudless sky: the one building spared by the Merenids (who raised the village and slaughtered every inhabitant in 1276) which reflects Ibn Tumert's vision of reform and rejuvenation, an obsession which drove him to compel the Berber tribes of the High Atlas valley to acknowledge him as Mahdi, bringing them in line with his new morality, his new puritanical message. In 1124 he started preaching his message of reform and by 1128 the Almoravides felt sufficiently threatened by his success to mount an attack on this remote and well-fortified alternative centre of religious power. They failed and yet it was left to Ibn Tumert's successor, the politically ambitious Abdel Moumen, to use the forces mustered behind the flag of Islam to establish the Almohad dynasty and move its administrative centre away from the peaks of the Atlas down to Marrakesh in 1148.

Standing on the threshold of the mosque, I sensed that strong mixture of ambition translated into architecture which makes the el Badi unforgettable. Had I been a twelfth-century Berber woman, I too would doubtless have worshipped at this place and felt that it was blessed for its purpose. A heap of rubble just inside the main courtyard testifies to the collapse of three arches in the last year, and salt erosion is visible in the remaining columns and arches. Only one cupola has been left reasonably intact. A new bridge is being built so that the materials needed to carry out repairs can be transported over the river; even so, the inaccessibility of the site and the frequent rockfalls which shut the Tiz-n-Test will make restoration difficult and seasonal. Wandering through the courtyard I tried to imagine the aisles and screens which separated the women from the men so they could slip in to worship via their own entry, the crowds at the ablutions fountain, an imam directing prayers or the khatib giving the weekly Friday sermon. I could almost see the serried ranks of Berber warriors, each with their new Arabic name, saddling up and preparing to spread the word of Allah.

◆ *Chapter Two* ◆

The day the temperature soared to forty-three degrees
centigrade by 11:00 a.m. was the day we left Marrakesh for
Essaouira, the Moroccans' favourite coastal resort. Stocking up on
a four-dirham block of ice at the Bab Doukkala I added banana,
grape and apple tartlets, four baguettes and half a dozen bottles
of Sidi Ali to the provisions, honked the Koutoubia in farewell
and sped out of old dusty Marrakesh.

A Moroccan saying describing the imperial cities speaks of the
gaiety of the Marrakeshi, the chic of the Fassi, the arrogance of
the Rabati and the hostility of the Meknessi. I can't tell if it's
accurate on every score at this juncture but Marrakesh is
certainly gay as long as you are passing through or part of the
indigenous local economy. Essaouira, our destination, enjoys an
enviable reputation as a relaxing holiday spot at home with
Moroccans, and as a centre of woodwork and quaint blue
painted houses abroad. I have never heard anyone say a deroga-
tory word about the town. Cat Stevens still spends his summers
here and Jimi Hendrix graced it with his presence during his
drug-induced blitz on Moroccan sensibilities before a particularly sordid murder at a nearby village made hippies personae
non gratae on this stretch of the Moroccan coast. To this day,
however, every hotel keeper in Essaouira quietly confides that
you have chosen to stay in the same hotel as Jimi Hendrix did
and waits for expressions of awe and sighs. I feel it is highly

unlikely that even Jimi Hendrix, whose eyesight was probably impaired by his 'highs', could have sunk to the level of some of the damp, dark, salt-damaged dives Essaouira offers the traveller. Buoyed up by the rapidly falling temperature as we climbed into the mountains above Marrakesh and the realisation that the phenomenon, the breeze, still exists on this planet, I forgot about Essaouira and the problem of accommodation and concentrated on the road and scenery – arid dusty plains, broken by the odd road-side stall.

Chichaoua was the first place that looked as if it might have Schweppes bitter lemon and a toilet. There was no sign of the carpets for which the town is famous, just a large café on a roundabout whose tables were smothered in clouds of flies. This was because all the garbage from the restaurant inside had been tipped over a low adjacent wall and left to rot. I resolved to look into urban garbage disposal at the next big town, a suggestion which was greeted with incredulity and roars of laughter. Only Miyuki smiled pleasantly and agreed, doubtless planning her angles and her apertures.

As soon as we sat down, the usual collection of souvenir sellers appeared, but this motley crew was composed of geriatrics, not teenagers, and they were bearing the strangest collection of goods imaginable. A fat, bald man presented me with a donkey hobbler and tried to persuade me that it was a dog collar by barking into my black coffee. He gave the game away somewhat by winking at his companions at the next table. Another produced a huge tin shackle with two heavy balls, four inches in diameter at each end, obviously an animal device. Using a mixture of mime and French he told me it was for arthritis. I tried it on to show him I'd lose my balance wearing such a contraption, whereupon, nothing daunted, he turned it on its side, and presto, it became a door-knocker. The watching crowd collapsed laughing, and even the merchant saw the joke and dropped the idea. The shoe-shine boys who are a feature of all café life had ascertained by now that there was no leather in view and had put their boxes away in favour of washing the car windows. When the drinks had been paid for and we returned to the car they swarmed around asking for money, trousers, kisses and sweets. These children were not young but on the borderline of teenagerhood and thus were no longer content with asking, or trading on their innocent looks and vulnerability.

Sensing another rumpus in the air I passed out the standard two dirhams for the unnecessary wash and opened the doors. A swarm of hands tried to grab our fruit tartlets, our road map, bags of rancid grapes, the babies' plastic sunglasses or an empty matchbox, shoving us, as well as each other, in the few seconds that elapsed between getting in and closing the doors. My last impression of Chichaoua was a shower of pebbles raining down on the bonnet and a thick dribble of phlegm descending down the newly washed windscreen as the car pulled away with a screech of tyres.

Two hours later we arrived in Essaouira and my worst fears were confirmed. There were no rooms. Driving along the long esplanade up to the elegant Hotel Des Isles and the town gates, the last two kilometres of sea wall were virtually hidden from view by windsurfers: the people, the sticker-encrusted vans, the gear. In short, Wind City was full of seekers after the ultimate wave. It was much cooler and very busy. Old men carrying striped, plastic shopping bags and women in white haiks mixed with the backpacking brigade, fishermen, craftsmen and the primarily Marrakeshi holidaymakers in the crowded streets. A policeman on duty outside Bab es Sebaa pointed out a young man in a crisp white djellabah, fawn trousers and Raybans who, he said, was from the tourist board and in charge of coordinating the supply of local rooms with demand. Ahmed introduced himself and confirmed our sad plight before becoming businesslike and telling us he had just the thing, a house by Bab Doukkala, the main gate at the opposite end of town.

The house had a small open courtyard with two bedrooms which between them boasted eight beds, two chairs and the usual collection of brushed nylon animal-motif blankets. A shower ran off the butane gas cylinder, as did a dodgy looking stove in the kitchenette, and a toilet completed the accommodation. We bargained down badly from a criminal eight hundred dirhams plus fifty dirhams commission to Ahmed, to a horrendous six hundred dirhams plus fifty dirhams commission to Ahmed, then shook hands and met the other residents, Luigi and family from Padua. Luigi was in his early fifties and the epitome of the 'seen it all, done it all, know it all' traveller. He was wearing a Tuareg costume – indigo blue cloth which leaves stains on the skin, hence the blue-men tag of tourist pamphlets – and a headdress which looked odd with his thin ponytail and Armani slacks. Having just returned from Rissani where the temperatures hit sixty degrees centigrade and he had slept in a tent on a flat roof under the stars, he was full of the joys of the desert, the nobility of the people, the bartering economy, the chunky jewellery of the women, their proud demeanour and how they all commune with nature and live a life of romance. He did a slow-shuffling Tuareg dance to demonstrate his point. I deferred judgment but admired the get-up, jewellery and dagger he had bought for twenty pounds. Luigi needed an audience who would be awed by the places he had seen, the miles he had travelled, his expertise, and once he had established the fact that we had not been to the Drâa Valley or Zagora he definitely felt in a position of strength and lectured us on Essaouira and its environs. I gently interrupted and told him that I had spent a summer here not long ago, but he ignored the message and started to rummage for photographs. It was definitely time to go for a walk, a coffee, in short, anything that would preserve us from forty packets of Konika film, all doubtlessly featuring Luigi.

Historical records tell us that the Phoenicians were the first to see the potential of Essaouira, the Little Ramparts, as an Atlantic base, and by the eleventh century it had developed into Morocco's chief port. This made it a target for Portuguese expansionist ambitions, and in 1506 it was captured by King Manuel. The Portuguese, whose cannons still rust on the Scala, held on to Essaouira and the outlying isles of Mogador for a mere thirty-five years after which the town lost its pre-eminent position when the Saadians moved the focus of trade to southerly Agadir. It was not until 1760 that Essaouira's fortunes revived when Sultan Sidi Mohammed expanded the medina and moved the Jews north from Agadir, removing Customs duties at the same time and thus turning Essaouira into an important port. Today Essaouira no longer exports animal pelts and ostrich feathers but fish. Tons and tons of sardines.

The most permanent souvenir of the European presence must be the well-organised grid-style street plan of the town with a main artery crossing from the Bab Doukkala down to the port, and smaller intersecting roads going off to right and left at almost perfect right-angles. The social heart of the town is the square, Place Moulay Hassan, a minute's walk from the sandy beach, lined with cheap hotels which change travellers cheques; kiosks which sell Mars bars and Kit Kats; restaurants, banks and patisseries. It is sufficiently sheltered from the stinging winds which are a feature of Essaouira, to provide a sunny, cobbled al fresco flop house for locals and visitors alike. In the summer months every available café table is taken, and a steady continual stream of people and café waiters walk to the north end, passing Mishmish, the square's dog, and the tiled but defunct fountain, to line up outside Chez Driss, a family-run patisserie where trays of steaming petit pains au chocolat, crisp brioches and hot crumbly croissants hit the counters every two or three minutes to be snapped up by the half dozen, butter oozing wildly into the brown paper sheets in which they are expertly wrapped. So much better than the hard dough of Marrakesh.

But Chez Driss is a morning extravaganza and as night was falling we wandered out into the great empty wasteland outside Bab Doukkala to join the hundreds of evening strollers who were pouring out of their flats and houses to shop, promenade and snack. The huge patch of dirt had come alive, a children's funfair ride was lit up in the far corner and strange fairground stalls with plates and TVs were attracting crowds of people, three or four deep. Presumably, the plates could be won since there was a spinning board with arrows on the back wall. Prickly pear sellers were out with their barrows as were the T-shirt and sock merchants who had spread their wares on large blankets by the side of the road. A line of grey plastic poodles rocking on aluminium rockers nodded in the breeze, their black eyes startled and their ugly ill-cast features totally moronic in the fading light. A barrage of flying fishheads was thrown into the street from the local grill café where a dozen diners were clustered around a small table watching an old dubbed John Wayne movie, mesmerised, their chins up in the air. The heads had sharp pointed teeth frozen in vicious snarls as they lay there in the pool of light. I shuddered.

Somewhere in the middle of this stony nothingness I could hear a man shouting 'Allah' and a young Berber in traditional garb, with long black curly hair, accompanied by three drummers, was dragging snakes from under a blanket and draping them over his shoulders pretending to hypnotise them and bite off their heads. The crowd cooed, recoiled, screamed. I felt the usual Western revulsion at animal shows, felt sorry for the patient snake and moved on past the unintelligible jester and dancers to have a go at the rifle range, shooting at an arched iron frame supporting nineteen pieces of chalk, and the kind of plastic figures which used to come free in cornflakes packets. The object of the exercise was to shoot the figures, not the chalk. I missed everything. Tony hit a plastic Indian and was severely reprimanded. We had obviously misunderstood the rules somewhere along the line.

The babies still interpreted the evening call to prayer as the voice of Wee Willie Winkie who has tracked them down (thank God, Moslems don't share our nursery rhymes and understand my offspring's frantic reactions and excitement). Tonight it seemed especially loud as we joined the men and women pouring under the dark urine-spattered arches of the Bab Doukkala into the Rue Mohammed Zerkhtouni. Music was tearing into the salty air, odd snatches of jarringly sharp singing issuing from every hole in the wall stall, adding to the chattering of the promenaders, the cries of encouragement from the plastic, shoe, leather and kaftan sellers. Small red-green apples, melons, wasp-covered boxes of black grapes and onions seemed to be the fresh produce of the day, for every fruit stall offered identical merchandise though in different quantities and arrangements. Doughnuts were being fried in large oil tubs on street corners, expertly popped onto string to be carried away. Hairdressers were clipping hair with sharp scissors and the usual revolting selection of baby-pink lamb carcasses swayed in the breeze.

Walking twenty to twenty-five abreast, the inhabitants of Essaouira caught each other's eyes, barely pausing long enough to exchange a smile before being whisked off and further on by the crowd. It was difficult to stop. It necessitated shoving out of the stream and then back into the main body of cigarette sellers, beggars, women gripping snivelling children and groups of swaggering young men. Since the road was so narrow, the sense of togetherness was overpowering and only frail old men in their striped djellabahs and white turbans, obviously intent on doing their shopping judging by the thin plastic bags they were clutching, had the nerve to stop the traffic or act as temporary road blocks when they spotted something interesting in the dozens of stalls lining the street. I began to enjoy the eyeing up and the fashion parade aspect of it all, and noticed that Tony's Batman T-shirt with its profile of the two protagonists (for which he was subsequently offered three hundred dirhams) was receiving many admiring glances. Bursts of song, clapping and laughter vied with snatches of greetings and conversation, and I could hear strains of music down a dark, arched alleyway where tagines were being set out on trestle tables. A disturbed young man was shoplifting without a care in the world, stuffing individual teabags and handfuls of raisins into the pockets of his woollen cloak. He was gently pushed away and a fist was raised in his face to emphasise that he would not be welcomed back. I saw him shuffling into the next grocer's shop to try again. Almost as if a gun had been fired, at around 9:30 p.m. the streets began to empty and soon there was no one to be seen. The day's crescendo had peaked. Essaouira, which boasts no Western night life of the kind to be found in Agadir, Marrakesh or Rabat, was effectively dead.

The morning came all too soon in the house, since a rooster, colour and lineage unknown, woke us all with his crowing. At first I was charmed, then irritated and finally murderous. It had been a bad night since we were so close to the mosque that the 4:15 a.m. call to prayer, with its refrain 'Why sleep if you can pray?' had me sitting bolt upright, muttering about the lack of choice. The courtyard was awash in dust, our clothes stiff with salt. The two café chairs were sticky with seaspray and the beach towel had flown up, out, and away. There was no point in breakfasting amongst all this damp and Essaouira was still shrouded in a heavy fog-like mist which made an already depressing dump of a house intolerable. Miyuki and I left together and strolled down to Place Moulay Hassan for a machine-made cup of mint tea, which was sweet, cool and lacked any mint flavour. A young man named Abdul, a dapper mechanic from Tetouan, joined us, complaining about the number of Marrakeshis in town, and the lack of hotel rooms. He was wearing an acrylic sweatshirt embellished with three pigs, and tight jeans, and had the confidence of the employed youth who will never know the agony and despair of hanging out.

Abdul was thrilled about Saddam Hussein's invasion of Kuwait, maintaining that Kuwait was an American colony and that it should distribute its wealth to help its Arab brothers rather than place it in a development bank for already rich Kuwaitis. According to Abdul, and every other Moroccan I spoke to, Saddam Hussein is the greatest Arab leader since Nasser, and Kuwait, formerly a part of Iraq anyway, has no right to sovereignty. The most virulent criticism was reserved for the Americans, who have defiled the sacred places of Islam with their presence and whose defeat is prophesied amongst much table-bashing and "you will see whose side God is on" rhetoric. I was uninspired by this view, one I heard the length and breadth of Morocco and Tunisia. I was in Tunis in March 1990 on the day when Saddam Hussein told his troop commanders that in case of attack they were to retaliate against Israel, at their own discretion. I will long remember the excitement in the café where I was sitting, as the newspaper vendor passed from table to table, the waving of the front page with its portraits of Hussein, the nods and smiles, the anticipation of Israeli defeat. The humiliations of the Six Day War and the continuing exist-ence of the State of Israel, coupled with indignation at the world's indifference to the plight of the Palestinians, has left the Arab community rightly sceptical about the West's impartiality and respect for international law. Where were the Americans and Europeans when Israel moved into the Golan Heights, into Lebanon, into the West Bank, and how is it that Israeli expansion is acceptable and any Iraqi expansion is a crime? Abdul was looking for an argument and, finding none, suddenly switched tack and complimented Miyuki on her culture – karate and Bruce Lee. Miyuki looked pained and bewildered but took an exquisite revenge by giving Abdul one of her infamous bright fruit balls – anything dried and Japanese is a kiss of death to the palate. Abdul spat it out immediately and looked at Miyuki in utter horror. 'You no like?' she enquired sweetly.

Essaouira is rightly renowned for its joinery and carving, a far cry from the tatty, shoddy, chipboard cupboards and chairs of the Marrakesh medina, and there is none of the pressurised selling of third-rate rubbish common to tourist towns in its workshops. Instead, a walk through the craftsmen's quarter reveals dozens of ateliers where the focus is on the work and not on the retailing. Children and youngsters seal wooden slabs of thuya, a local type of juniper, with squares of rag and polish finished pieces, while decapitated cans containing preservative are warmed over gas cylinders, alongside the pincers needed to remove them from the heat. The scraps of wood, offcuts and still untouched thuya roots lie at the doorways in tangled heaps. There is an air of calm and concentration as apprentices plane and cut, and the master craftsmen inlay pieces of mother-of-pearl, ebony, silver and lemonwood into cedar box lids. The quality of work varies from one workshop to another: sometimes an exquisite card box is marred by a badly placed hinge or a heavily ornamented chair is held together by screws visible to the naked eye, thumped in through the top joints. More often than not the cheaper items are slightly lopsided, the chessboard not quite square, the domino boxes almost rectangular, the bangles, book-ends and earrings rough to the touch. Yet when the work is good, it is excellent. A dining table six feet in diameter, French polished till it gleams, inlaid with lemonwood and mother-of-pearl, takes one craftsman and two apprentices a year to complete. A blanket box which is sold for two thousand dirhams and a chest of drawers which costs in the region of three thousand will take three months. Wealthy Moroccans drive directly to Essaouira to purchase their furniture, as do the better hotel chains and numerous businessmen. I toyed with the idea of buying a simple rectangle, cone or ball or a sculpture of a woman draped in a haik, her face masked with an ebony insert. Both were too heavy but testified to the Moroccans' mastery of the abstract form, the shape; in contrast, the sad odd cat, bird, or lizard reflect the age-old Islamic strictures against representing human or animal forms in art.

Another type of woodwork which is also thriving in Essaouira is the traditional boat-building business which dominates the skyline down at the port. Gaunt orange skeletons sit up on blocks, seagulls wheeling around the heads of the men working high up on the hull planks. These are fishing boats in the making, the fishing boats which make Essaouira Morocco's third largest exporter of sardines. Strolling down the quay I was startled by a man who stood, legs akimbo, holding a filthy brown burnous close around his chest. He looked like all the representations of Jesus Christ I have ever seen – the high cheekbones, spaniel eyes, thick brown hair, melancholy gaze and sweet smile. I was captivated and circled him to peep until he noticed my gawping face and asked if he could be of any assistance. Mohammed, for such was his name, was thirty-two and a fleet supervisor. I asked him questions, barely listening to the answers, watching his face with rapt attention. He must have thought I was slow-witted or dangerous, but generously agreed to take me round the yard.

Half a dozen boats, the annual turnover, were visible in various stages of production, and when finished they will cost around forty thousand pounds. The engine is another sixty-five thousand pounds or so, and when the price of the extras and internal fittings is added on, you have to budget around one hundred and fifty thousand pounds for a vessel, which is, however, ready to go to sea, complete with crew. There was a chaotic piecemeal look to the work in progress, rusty ladders thrown up against decks which stood twenty-five to thirty feet off the ground, main hulls in outline stage stretched out, dragon-necked, waiting for planking to give them a body, a more convincing mass. Two ships' cabins stood on the ground, their little doors swinging on hinges, looking pale in the light. These were made of eucalyptus rather than the mahogany used for the main structural parts of the hull or the softwood planks used for the cladding. The boats are about sixty feet long when finished, painted a cheery blue and white with ornamental cladding on the outside and between the deck and the top of the guardrail. At this stage in the proceedings, however, they all looked grey and orange in their undercoats. Mohammed told me that the foreman was a Frenchman and everything was built to a plan which he drew on the ground for the workers to follow. The Frenchman was autocratic and dismissive when I finally went to meet him, and categorically refused to allow me access to anything at all.

Apart from the rich smell of the sawn wood and the pleasing logic to all the stages of production, what most struck me was the industry of the place and the duplication of effort necessitated by old-fashioned tools. I sat and watched a man using a small axe to rebate a rectangular timber block to make a joint. He was not wearing protective goggles and took twenty five minutes to complete this task. Men squatted on the ground, eye-shields up on their foreheads, using oxy-acetylate blowtorches to weld the steel plates which would be bolted onto the bottom of the hull. A pair of children scrambled over the side of the hull using a large punch and hammer to countersink thousands of nails spaced six inches apart, an arduous, boring job, while others filled gaps between the planks with what looked like hemp, and then mastic over the top. I shouted up and asked how long it would take to dry. 'Three days,' came the answer. It's not surprising that this yard only produces four to six boats a year. Mohammed was called away by the supervisor and the two men stood there, shoulder to shoulder, surveying something being lowered on a winch. The noise was deafening, a clanging, banging, sawing cacophony, and yet it did have its own rhythm, and progress, insofar as I could see, was being made. The axeman was on his third timber block, the children were three feet lower down the hull, the torches had moved to another section. I sat on a barrel and watched for a while. Essaouira is a working port, after all, once you are away from the cafés and tourist information office. Looking round at the grill café umbrellas, the sign pointing to Chez Sam, Fish Restaurant, the screeching, dipping gulls diving for garbage, and the sardine fleet preparing for its 6 p.m. departure, the wood-carvers seemed like an afterthought, an indulgence by comparison. One hundred yards away from Chez Driss, the holidaymaker recedes, and the fisherman asserts his superior rights to the coastline and the town built to service it.

Mohammed told me that I should go to the next jetty and find his friend Nasser, captain of the Sidi Ali, and look at the working, finished product. As I moved on to the landing quay, a sardine boat was just coming in. A crowd of women and restaurant runners started clapping as it docked, before leaping aboard for first pickings. When the hullabaloo died down I spotted the Sidi Ali twenty yards further on. A dozen or so men were lounging on deck, drinking glasses of tea atop a pile of nets and ropes. It was a hot day but they were all wearing thick woollen jumpers, rolled-up jeans and boots. When I called out my business, Nasser's brother uncoiled himself and hauled me onto the gently swaying craft. Ali had just finished a year's schooling at the Marine School where he had earned his seagoing diploma. He was proud of working for his brother and not one of the rich owners who treat fishing as an investment, know nothing of the sea and pay bad wages for a sixteen-hour day. The Sidi Ali normally went out at 4:00 a.m. and returned at 6:00 p.m., but today the crew was preparing for three days to a week at sea. Hence Nasser's absence, for other captains had alerted them to heavy catches south of El Jadida and favourable weather conditions in the area. Unlike sardine boats, which can only fish their own waters, deep-sea vessels can go wherever they wish and the Sidi Ali frequently ventured up as far north as Larache and south to Agadir. As a result, this crew considered themselves more than a cut above the sardiners. I had to confess at this juncture, that I couldn't distinguish the two boats and was immediately dragged to see a small wooden boat attached to a rundown larger craft. Apparently the smaller boat hauled the latter's nets round in a circle before being winched up so that its contents could be thrown into the bilges. The Sidi Ali's catch, on the other hand, ends up being sorted, iced and then gutted on the quayside by numerous men squatting on their haunches who align the silvery blank-eyed fish in symmetrical rows on greaseproof paper, all facing right.

Looking at the young lads in their twenties and round the boat it was impossible to find the life they live enviable. The boat was cramped, wet and smelly, the accommodation rusty, and the dangers of the sea are very real. The crew's hands were cut and calloused from handling the catch, their skin grease-streaked, their nails broken, and their hair slightly matted. I couldn't imagine their ever feeling clean, although the mechanic had changed into a crisp, pink cotton shirt for his time off. The galley, which was a narrow space behind a flush iron door to the left of the stairs, held a small gas cooker and a huge old frying pan, a tray with glasses and two inches of still greasy water slopping gently from right to left on the floor. The beds were bunks covered in dark grey nylon blankets – no sheets or pillowcases here. Two crewmen lodged on the bridge another ten below deck near the pulsating engine, a green-grey monstrosity whose intricacies I could not even begin to understand. There was a peculiarly unpleasant smell on the air, a mixture of wool, fish, damp and gas. Nasser's brother was proud of the boat and invited me to come to sea with them for a few days to try her out, but I declined politely. Tentatively mounting a few iron steps into the cabin I was astonished to see the mass of sophisticated equipment on board, ship-to-shore radio, radar, built-in compass, a sonar and numerous little plastic covered boxes with dials whose Arabic names meant nothing to me. Everything here was spotless, down to the polished, beautifully smooth hardwood wheel. I stood on the bridge and fantasised.

Back on shore Miyuki was sitting beatifically on a wall tearing pointed heads from small grey bodies. I had forgotten how much the Japanese love fish and, watching her stubby fingers rummaging through stomachs and gills, I sensed a cultural divide yawning. She offered me a devilish looking flat thing and a slice of lemon, extolling the grill cafés by the sea wall, and we shared a bottle of Sidi Harazam while planning how to tackle the next obstacle – buying her a bus ticket to Casablanca. The local bus companies had all recently moved out past Bab Doukkala to a central station, a desolate spot reached after navigating through a series of wastelands via a rubble-strewn path. We set off. Hunched against the wind we passed a man sitting on an orange box, plastic bags, a lone black cow grazing between two red football stands. The ground was littered with broken bicycles, old mattresses and vegetable peelings. A group of young goats were ambushing and attacking each other down an alley. Essaouira, only a five-minute walk away, seemed a dream as the stones became larger, and making progress consisted of climbing boulders rather than walking. Other travellers, lugging suitcases and bags with large thick handles, emerged from side streets or stood near the grand taxi rank by the bus station forecourt. This was not a place to be after dark, when a broken neck would be the inevitable result rather than a possibility.

Inside the station we traipsed from one ticket office to another recounting our problem. We had to be in Casablanca by 1:00 p.m. the next day. A violent debate flared up between the kiosk men, half of whom thought, nay vowed, that she should take the 6:00 a.m. bus which arrived in Casa at some point between noon and 2:00 p.m. The rest were equally convinced that the 5:00 a.m. was the better bet since it arrived at midday. The 6:00 a.m. lobby, when pressed, said that the bus would get there earlier if full (since it could pass all passengers waiting en route), and at 2:00 p.m. if empty. 'How does it look at the moment?' I eventually asked.

'Oh, no tickets sold yet,' came the reply.

So the 5:00 a.m. it was. Unfortunately, two further facts emerged. The 5:00 a.m. left at 4:30 a.m. and we couldn't buy a ticket until the other driver, coming from Casablanca to Essaouira, arrived – since he had all the tickets. 'And what time will he get here?'

'Ah, between 6:00 and 8:00 p.m.'

Nothing, but nothing, had been achieved by all this verbal jousting. Miyuki and I decided to find the others and eat our first hot meal in Essaouira, away from the rooster, who was now crowing round the clock and deserved garotting, and our landlord who was sitting outside the front door manipulating a pocket calculator. The Riad Restaurant in the centre of the medina was financed three years ago when its owner, Mustapha, sold a Chinese vase to raise the original capital. He can't be doing badly since he told us that the premises had been hired by the British Embassy staff to celebrate a photo exhibition by Owen Logan, a sensitive, exciting photographer who concentrates on facial expressions and captures private moments with almost obscene clarity. The emigrating family, the bashful woman, the blind musician, the protective mother, all reproach and challenge from the page. Unsurprisingly, on looking through the catalogue Mustapha handed me, I found the usual input from Europe's main man in the Maghreb, Paul Bowles, namely three of his stories. It's always odd to come across pockets of Western cultural activity in Morocco, since the country is so demanding and insistent that one begins to feel cut off from the Western world with its preoccupations. This is abetted by the fact that the government-controlled media devote as little space to us as we do to North Africa. Occasionally you see a line about a strike, the pound, the poll tax demonstrations. For the most part, however, particularly in the smaller towns, Europe is no more. It is easy to see why the Riad was singled out by the Embassy. The food is good and the décor mock oriental with many concessions made to comfort. The diner has a choice between sitting at tables with freshly laundered linen and flower posies or going through to a backroom with its low plastic-covered round tables, pouffes and divans. Bric-a-brac theoretically adds ambience, but although few people will exclaim over individual ornamental rifles, brass trays and ceramic pots, it's the ensemble which counts.

Having spent ten minutes warning the babies about good manners, I committed the opening gaffe myself, glibly and shortsightedly stubbing out my cigarette in a bowl of argan oil, a local delicacy derived from the argan tree, which only grows between Essaouira and Agadir and is famed for the fact that goats climb to its top to eat the leaves. The waiter didn't blink an eye, but continued serving the couscous, vegetable tagines and grilled fish we had ordered, all of it perfectly cooked and hot, the vegetables steaming, their shapes preserved, their colours distinguishable. We ate as if we had never eaten before and gulped it down in minutes, taking the watching serenader, a gimbri player, by surprise, since he only woke up to the fact that the table had been cleared when Miyuki challenged Mustapha to an origami competition. His rabbit hopped, Miyuki's dove flapped, so a second round was clearly called for and both rose to the occasion, Mustapha producing a penis performing the sex act and Miyuki replying with a headless man removing and putting on his trousers. Most peculiar!

Miyuki left at four that morning, her suitcase sitting on its neat, retractable wheels, her straw hat pinned to her hair. She was the only passenger. It would be a long, long trip.

Essaouira was beginning to bore me by the fourth day. Abdul and his friends still sat at the café, their faces turned to the sun, shades clamped on noses, baying about Arab dignity and drinking white coffees. There is a limit to the number of strolls one can take to the bastion and along the ramparts, although the green Portuguese cannons, nine feet long and forged in the late eighteenth century, still impressed as they stared out over the sea, redundant but ever-ready. Made of the finest imported Mexican and Peruvian copper, they still bore their message of a Christian God, honour and fidelity and the expansionist dreams of man, though their mouths were silenced a century ago. Nothing will happen here now and no one will hoist them by the art-deco fish that form their handles, and call them into service again. Instead, swarthy kif sellers will continue to lounge against their barrels, hissing prices, and spaced out German blondes seeking a cause for tears or confrontation will kick bottle tops past them, or stand, cameras dangling and forgotten, looking for a pick-up, for conversation, for a plan of action.

The surfers are everywhere, their vans plastered with stickers – Hawaii OK, Horny, Sin City Africa, Our Bus, Out of Work – their androgynous bodies poured into tight-fitting gear. Many seem to come from Holland and Germany, while the number clad in Fosters T-shirts advertise a strong Australian presence. Short of entering the 'How long-This long-Which way-That way' circuit, I can only marvel at their singlemindedness, and the fact that they have managed to retain their wet suits in a country where foreign clothes are highly desirable. It is a minor miracle to get out of Morocco without losing the T-shirt off your back, though I doubt whether the Italian I saw wearing a Beast Erotica picture featuring a caged Mandy Smith lookalike in chains, obviously about to perform oral sex, would have had many takers! When the film *Perverse Pleasures* was being advertised on hoardings in Meknès, every poster had the woman's breasts defaced and the Alsatian's genitals removed. I feared the Italian was skating on thin ice and well on his way to a slashed chest.

By the time I could recognise most faces on the evening walkabout and even the pastries at Chez Driss no longer appealed to me, Essaouira's spell was obviously waning. A pretty holiday destination, with its blue and white painted houses, its odd local museum and its sandy, cool beach, Essaouira is a place for foreigners to fritter away time rather than to live. No Westerner could easily suffer the hardships of sailing and fishing, the occupations which constitute the life of the town. Here, one is a mere onlooker and the sun is insufficiently strong to push one into a coma of tanning on the beach. The days are long, very long, and the nights repetitive and predictable in their pattern. In a sense, Essaouira is still an exclusively local town, and outsiders, whether Moroccans or foreigners, simply hand over their money in exchange for a seat at one café table and then the next, remaining peripheral, albeit tolerated.

The newspapers were full of 20 August, which is the twenty-seventh anniversary of the Revolution of the King and the People, a national holiday, celebrated lackadaisically in the country itself but rammed down everyone's throats by the press for days before and after the holiday. In keeping with the king's policy of emphasising the common struggle which led to independence in 1956 and the saintly status of Mohammed V, the Father of the Nation (shades of the Shah, here), the newspapers had been reprinting ancient tales of French atrocities, urban guerrilla warfare and confrontations with the colonial administration for weeks. The government was actively seeking to tap into a reservoir of international pride, nostalgia and anti-French sentiment which reinforced loyalty to the current religious and secular leader, Hassan II. Myths and martyrs are crucial to this type of striving for legitimacy and loyalty and there was something disturbing about the way in which the old excerpts had been infiltrated into current news. On numerous occasions I found myself trying in vain to establish whether the bomb planted under a Casablanca bus, the High Atlas Valley killings and the mass protests I was reading about, had happened a matter of days or thirty-seven years ago. Of course, I should have realised that all riots these days go unreported!

The intense anti-European sentiment of yesteryear is kept alive in contemporary Morocco by this blitz of opening old wounds, and I am convinced that the widespread antipathy towards the French is the result of a centrally organised campaign of recrimination. After all, when the king felt threatened in the early 1970s following two assassination attempts carried out by the military, bread riots, and defections within the ruling elite, his first reaction after a massive clean-up of the visible opposition was to seize upon a common enemy, the Spanish. The Green March of 1975, when three hundred and fifty thousand citizens, Korans in hand, walked into the former Spanish Sahara, was less a popular upsurge of righteous nationalism than a clever smoke-screen. Reclaiming the Western Sahara obviously appealed to the strong Moroccan sense of nationhood and remains a popular issue, but as the years pass, the cost of fighting this desert war against the Algerian-backed POLISARIO (a federation of Saharan tribes who want to remain independent) becomes more evident: the price of dynastic ambition percolates down the economy and affects every family's spending power. Criticism is slowly beginning to rumble. The long promised referendum, which should, in theory, allow the inhabitants of the area to determine their own destiny, has been postponed innumerable times by the king, who wants the result to be indicative rather than binding. In the meantime, thanks to the lack of resolution, when times are tough the Algerians can be tossed across the ideological divide to join the French as the root of all evil in the land.

And where there is a 'baddy', logic dictates that a 'goody' must ride onto the scene to fight for the powers of light. Enter Mohammed V, whose honourable, selfless and admirable political career is in grave danger of being besmirched and cheapened by the regime. Mohammed V, the last Sultan and first King of twentieth-century Morocco, rallied most of the country – discounting the belligerently independent inhabitants of the Rif, the self-seeking Sufi sheiks and Thami el Glaoui of Marrakesh – against the colonial powers. His intelligent campaign for independence earned him two years of exile in Madagascar and, in 1955, a triumphant homecoming to take up the reins of power. In the six years which remained to him, the king embarked on a huge drive to create full employment via public works programmes, and attempted to modify traditional personal government by one man, by placing it within a multi-party constitutional framework. It seems both inevitable and criminal that the name of a man who had no truck with guile or corruption should be wheeled out regularly to cover up his son's shortcomings by acting as a focus for blind religious and secular devotion. Thus, just as in England we have the folk tale of 'the brave little boats of Dunkirk', which disguises a far more complex and sordid reality, so on 20 August, Morocco is treated to its own myth, 'the King, the Revolution and the People'. These days, the equation must surely be the King versus the People equals the Revolution.

PART ONE

Nevertheless, the pages of *Le Matin* proclaimed that the king had decided to reward former combatants and their families with travel concessions on the railways and domestic flights. He also decided that this category of citizens is entitled to free medical assistance, plots of ground and bursaries for the education of their children. No hard figures were supplied, however, and I could not help wondering how many people would claim all these gifts so many years on. It seemed too little, too late, and merely added to the artificial nature of the festivities themselves – fishing, drawing and football competitions, organised games and the eternal rallies and speeches immortalising the heroic struggle for independence and the role of Mohammed V in that struggle. I am convinced there can be nothing left to say that has not been repeated innumerable times over the last twenty-nine years since his death, so restrict myself to musing over the cult of the personality with all its attendant repression, insecurity and volatile political structure. After all, Morocco has an appalling record of human rights violations and any criticism of the king or the desert war is prohibited outright.

The first sign of the forthcoming public celebrations materialised outside Essaouira, at Tanmeld. A young man riding a donkey, waving the Moroccan flag at the end of a long stick, was singing to himself. (Why should I be surprised? After all, the newspapers promised us patriotic songs amongst all the other competitions.) He stopped to ask if we wanted to take a photograph. I felt so depressed by all the deprivation I had seen in the last few weeks, depressed by the lactating bitch lying in the dust sucking her own swollen teats, that I was certainly in no mood for this fellow's flag-waving rejoicing. He accepted my refusal cheerfully, shook his pole in farewell and rode on. Perhaps it is just a matter of acceptance and the Will of God after all. Perhaps I was being too materialistic and sentimental and everything really was fine. But the hordes of faces imploring embassy staff for exit visas, the beggars, the maimed and the degraded dispelled this doubt and I relapsed into fulminating against the men in their new Mercedes who cut us up on the road, and a system which ensures the closest our friend on the donkey will ever get to a car is to guard it for one thin dirham. All my high tone moralising was probably precipitated by food poisoning, an unpleasant affliction at the best of times, but made unbearable by the need to stomp large unkillable cockroaches every time I had to dash to the loo. It was unnerving to crouch gingerly over a small hole, knowing that half a dozen of these maroon armoured beetles were a matter of centimetres below and might emerge at any instant. I vowed never to eat again.

◆ *Chapter Three* ◆

Past Tanmeld, the odd banner was flying, bleached and faded, in the streets of small rural communities, where men on asses dragged haltered camels along behind them and small horse drawn carts carrying timber and vegetables clipped through stony, unpaved streets. It was not far to Safi, and the other end of the fish industry, canning and preservation, and the closer we approached, the wider the road, the neater the curbs and the thicker the road signs. It is obvious that the Moroccan tourist board is attempting to drag Safi onto the tourist circuit by creating this highway which will link it with already popular Essaouira. Safi is a powerful thing to behold, a shock after the docile nothingness of Essaouira, for here is raw energy at work, the technology of today and tomorrow overwhelming the skyline and the remnants of ancient history alike. The huge chemical complex with its enormous off-white mounds of phosphates, silos and chimneys lies to the south of the town, throwing a haze of thick fumes against the cloudless sky. Small goods trains park on sidings and a mushroom-shaped tower rears up through the filthy-white discharges. Up by the modern port, whose approach is marked by a red and white buoy, Shell Oil containers squat next to ammonia vats, grain silos, enormous ocean-going vessels, and still more white hills of phosphate. This is big business at work, not pretty sardine boats, and thus I was resigned to the inevitable refusal to allow me access to the port, the talk of police and permits, stamps, identification.

Unlike many other relatively small towns, Safi has chosen to plough back some of its wealth into upgrading its amenities. This is very visible in the new town, whose wide, clean streets, lined with willows and beautified with pots of flowers and shrubs, link this modern and expanding quarter to the medina and potteries for which Safi is renowned. Hundreds of neat villas nestle on almost empty boulevards, their heavily flower-draped outlines occasionally broken by a local tea shop or patisserie. The youngsters in this part of Safi, wearing fake Chanel and St Laurent logo T-shirts and the latest style in trousers, gather in ultra modern Place Mohammed V, a bandstand-shaped square with strange wooden benches sitting at the heart of half a dozen main roads and encircled by grand municipal buildings and armed sentries.

Everyone seems busy and the virtually deserted streets shelter no groups of chancers, while the cafés with their immaculate counters, marble floors, refrigerators, displays and fans, serve a purpose rather than provide somewhere to kill time. Safi was the only major town outside Rabat which actually had the promised ice-cream at its ice-cream parlours in August. Fez and Meknès and Marrakesh lied through their teeth! And what a selection. Orange, peach, lemon, chocolate, raspberry, almond, pistachio, some of which was served floating in complementary juices, others in thick cones or minute pink plastic tubs with child-sized rigid spoons attached. The patisseries here seem to favour savoury foods over sweet ones and sell pancake roll snacks filled with spinach, cheese and potato, as well as bite-sized olive pizzas, tartlets crammed with anchovies and mushrooms in a thin bed of pastry shell and crumbly quiches. Just looking at the spotless tables, the elegant baked morsels on this side of town, made Safi appear an odd spot, closer in ambience and aspirations to its coastal sisters, Rabat and Casablanca, than its geographical neighbours.

PART ONE

Change can only alter so much so quickly, though, and down in the central Place de l'Independence, remnants of the past, the old Portuguese port, remain. Foremost among these echoes is the bulky Château de la Mer, a stumpy, overbearing coastal fortress which housed the Portuguese governor during the forty years when Safi was an Atlantic stronghold for this expansionist sixteenth-century maritime power. When they pulled out in 1541, Safi went into a period of decline which coincided with the expansion and development of Essaouira, and since the Portuguese tried to destroy whatever they could in leaving, all that remains today is the Portuguese-built choir of the Roman Catholic cathedral. The Portuguese Chapel, as it is known, is down a narrow alley in Safi's small dingy medina. Apart from staring up in the dark at the roof with its spotlit bosses and making encouraging admiring noises for the benefit of the sleepy guardian, it excites little in the way of passion or reaction. Safi is not a flat town, and the climb through the medina to the fortress of the Kechla is steep. Endless, low-ceilinged, arched tunnels wind their labyrinthine way up and still further up. Dim alleys reveal patches of bright sunlight and children playing with spinning tops, and the breathless visitor is obliged to squat down on the wide flat steps for a rest. The medina stalls are not geared to the tourist and consist of vendors selling cheap plastic shoes, jeans, meat and vegetables, the odd kaftan and, right at the far end, a few piles of Safi pottery.

The relative calm was suddenly shattered by men running through the lanes yelling the call to prayer. Obviously, the acoustics of the public address system in the Grand Mosque down on the coast and by the Rue de Souk did not reach this far. Numerous shopkeepers pulled down their shutters as we walked by, but just as many merely glanced at the mouthpieces of Allah and returned to watching their portable televisions – which were broadcasting a German athletics meeting in unison. Khalid Skah, a middle distance runner, was the hero of the day and when I leaned over and asked about Said Ouita, the unenthusiastic response hung like a chill on the air. His thigh muscles were weak, they claimed: he was too old and injury prone, in short, a nothing.

By the time we reached the edge of the medina the bane of all shoeshine boys throughout the land, my talc-coated black suede pumps, had hit the dust. This trip was proving hard on the Imelda Marcos complex. I decided to buy a plastic pair like everyone else and chose flat white sandals, stamped with orange flowers, trees and leaves on the inside. They had a thick strap across the middle of the foot, no back, a peep-toe opening, and cost fifteen dirhams. I later learned that everyone else is charged ten! Moroccan women have narrow feet, which means that my own heels slipped over the back edges of the sandals and rubbed against the ground. Cracked hard skin which occasionally spurted a trickle of blood was the result. Overall, however, once I acquired the art of lifting and setting down my feet, making a sound like a wet fish slapping up and hitting the sole of my foot, these items of footwear excited a certain devotion. They were also seemingly indestructible, even though the flowering extravaganza started to wear off in a matter of weeks.

Inspired by the purchase I was easily lured into a clothes shop owned by Mohammed and Samir, two brothers in their early twenties who had just come back from, of all places, Katowice, Poland. Their grammatically shaky but enthusiastic grasp of Polish moved me as they described trips to the shipyards of Gdansk, the Hankas and Dankas they had met and the Poles they first knew in Safi, people they had recently looked up and stayed with in Europe. Our conversation was surreal in that these reminiscenses were punctuated by haggling over a plain black gandora which pleased me, since it had no gold or contrasting embroidery around the neck, hem or waist. At times I lost track of the state of play and quoted a figure which had already been rejected, or jumped too high, too quickly, only to plunge into a discussion about the appeal of Warsaw, (dull) and the forthcoming Morocco versus Nigeria football match, (difficult for the home team). Mohammed also had a TV, a small red one, in his shop and we ended up glancing at the screen, haggling, talking of foreign parts and Safi in a round Robin. Somewhere in the process, the gandora dropped from one hundred and fifty dirhams to fifty-five dirhams, at which point it was wrapped up and I was wryly congratulated on my persistence. Apparently, most tourists would have stopped at the magic figure of one hundred dirhams. I joked that it was my Jewish blood. The response was hostile and as I looked at them questioningly, the brothers realised slowly that it was a jest, a quip and gave a weak smile.

Once again, I was caught up short by the iron-clad hostility which emerges in a nation whose proudest boast has been that it saved all its Jews during the last war, and provided an open-armed welcome and shelter to any who made it to Moroccan shores after escaping the Nazis. But the foreign policy of the state of Israel had seemingly destroyed the traditional religious acceptance of the 'People of the Book', an acceptance which stretches back to the Prophet's time. When Mohammed received the message from Allah, his followers prayed five times a day facing Jerusalem, not Mecca, as Moslems do now. Jews were honoured, along with Christians, for having received part of the revelation of the God of Abraham. Even when it became obvious that they would not embrace Islam, the Medina Charter granted them cultural and religious autonomy in the expectation they would remain politically loyal. And here is the rub, for the original punishment for disloyalty to the Prophet was exile, but after the Battle of the Ditch, men were killed and children and women were taken into slavery for their political actions and allegiances, though not on racial or religious grounds, it must be stressed. Of course, these days the separatism within a community of the Prophet's era, which evolved to the point where Jews had to walk barefoot outside the mellahs of Morocco and convert on pain of death if they happened to wander into a mosque, has changed into confrontation based on the Palestinian issue. Political loyalty to the state, Mohammed's test, is no longer possible since it involves loyalty to the Arab world's stated campaign to drive Israel into the sea.

Samir offered to show me the Kechla or citadel, two crenellated Portuguese towers situated at the far end of the medina. To his surprise and mine, we discovered that it had been transformed into a half-empty ceramics museum as of 12 May. The guardian bustled out to meet us, immensely proud to have visitors, and shepherded us past two cannons and through a small courtyard with richly carved doors and a splendid cedar ceiling into a long corridor lined with large glass display cases. Unfortunately, his linguistic talents did not match his enthusiasm but he would not allow me to proceed unaccompanied. Instead, he walked a step or two in front of me, reciting, 'About eighteenth century, a couscous plate, an inkwell, a vase, a soup bowl, a vase, a penholder, a vase.' It was hot, as usual, and my attention began to flag. 'Look,' he virtually screamed, 'a vase!' I nodded dully. Many of the eighteenth-century Fassi and sixteenth-century Meknessi pieces had been Superglued together and he pointed to each crack, saying 'Repair,' watching for the nod which signified I had absorbed this wonder.

It was hard work and I was grateful when a Moroccan family materialised by the entrance and he scurried off to start their tour. Unwilling to be caught and force-marched round again, I crept to the top of the tower and looked out over Safi, straight at a scene out of *Blade Runner*. Up on the right, amongst the white koubbas and ramparts, the people and the asses, there were dozens of small fires burning under the darkening sky, kilns covered with palm-leaf roofs squatting in the nooks and crannies of the hillside. The potters of Safi, whose blue on white glazed ware is to be found throughout Morocco and Europe, were tending to their timeless craft, and seemingly in very large numbers too, for this was no mere cottage industry spread out beneath me.

Samir had disappeared and it was late afternoon, so I resolved to climb down and, after knocking back a drink, look more closely at what was being made. Just outside the thick city walls on well-kept Avenue Moulay Youssef, the main route to Marrakesh, a new café has opened with a large terraced garden. Disturbingly enough, a group of bored older children were smashing glasses against the walls. A well-heeled Moroccan bought me a coffee virtually before I sat down. Amazingly, uniquely and wonderfully he did not speak to me. I ask myself now how tired and bedraggled I must have looked to elicit such charity, but I had no mirror in which to assess the heat damage at the time. Instead, I decided to simply enjoy the coffee, and then stroll down to the main road to watch the crowds. Men were waiting for buses, squatting on the pavements (and how nice it was to see these again), playing chequers with small pebbles and using the flagstones as a board. The women seemed less frequently veiled than in Essaouira and were sorting through piles of second-hand clothing which had been dumped in large hillocks, according to age, on the corner of Avenue Moulay Youssef and was attracting feverish grabbing. Teenagers were spreading out their wares – greeting cards, tin teapots, chewing gum and watches – on the pavements, and behind them all, ever present and telling of the sea, the invaders and the riches of the deep sat the Château de la Mer, unmissable and curiously beautiful. One almost expected it to suddenly shake off its torpor and plod, tortoise-like, into the sea.

The pottery owners' co-operative had a scout squatting at the side of the road past Bab Khouas ready to ambush visitors, whom he neatly handed over to one of the owners, a seedy Algerian with a broken front tooth and a damp handclasp. Nevertheless, this man knew his stuff and was as eager to explain as I was to listen. So, we strolled up the road, snapping questions and answers back and forth, until suddenly he stopped and demanded, 'Why do you want to know so much?' I had no ready reply and muttered something about understanding processes. He was unconvinced and, stupidly, perhaps, I pulled out a notebook and pencil to show him it was a professional enquiry, that I was serious about really understanding how the potteries work. The Algerian walked stiffly up to a stone sink containing clay and showed me how this clay, washed down from the hills, can only be used for poor quality work because of its high salt content, while that taken from underground is pinker and better. The clay is left to soak for a week and is then taken to one of the two hundred and twenty potters who toil at the wheels inside dimly lit workshops I had to stoop to enter.

A group of Moroccan women were standing in one such hut watching an old man cast his clay. Within a matter of a few minutes his long stubby fingers had placed a mug, a tagine dish, a flower pot and a vase on the table before us. The women told me they were ordering a dinner service for a relative who would be marrying the following spring and had come down to choose the design and decorations. They wanted something modern, elegant but not green, since the girl's fiancé came from Fez and Fez green, a rich emerald hue, cannot be surpassed. I left them chattering excitedly about serving bowls and shapes to see what happened next.

Just outside the workshop lay rows upon rows of half cylindrical roof tiles with crinkly ends, most of which were destined to become green. Apparently, the potters actually make complete cylinders, then break them cleanly in half. Spoilage is high during firing, so twice as many tiles are fired as have been ordered, as a matter of precaution. It appeared a high margin of error, but when I reached the kilns, where the glazed porcelain articles were to be given their final firing, I was amazed that anything at all survives, given the picturesque but essentially risky technology. Huge trunks of wood are stuffed in the kiln, whose temperature is measured by a long hooked piece of metal which is thrust inside and probably wreaks its own damage in certain hands. If the vase or pot survives, it is decorated and, as a matter of simple common sense, anything that touches the mouth, such as plates or dishes, is coloured with natural dyes, while purely ornamental ware is chemically treated. The man feeding the kiln added that I should test decorative plates by pouring vinegar mixed with water on them and checking the bubbles (which denote chemical dyes) and remember that white patterns usually indicate chemical colouring. The idea of popping into a souk with a Thermos of this acetic solution and splashing it around was unrealistic but tempting, and I scribbled this tip down and thanked the guide for the tour.

He would not let me leave and my graceful exit line was ruined by his insistence that I come to see the goods, the shop. I was yanked across the yard by the shoulder and thrust into the point of sale room where a well-trained teenager immediately launched into a sales pitch. Just as he began to tell me their vases were made in one piece and did not have the weak long neck joined to a round body of medina ware, the owner silenced him. Surrounded by five men, all of whom seemed openly hostile, I barely held my ground and leaned against the wooden display case with what, I hoped, passed for nonchalance. There were mutterings in Arabic, an exchange of glances and shuffling of feet, and the owner, once again, asked me why I wanted to know so much. I tried the truth. When he heard that I was interested in regional differences and crafts, food and politics, the best I could come up with in the circumstances, he started circling around me, prodding my shoulder blades and upper arms, hissing. The jist of this venomous little attack appeared to be that there were no differences between Moroccans because all Moroccans are Moslems. There were no regional differences in cuisine or crafts because no Moroccan is hungry and God gives his talents as he chooses. The logic of this argument was poor but I was frightened and became increasingly uneasy when he gestured to one of his minions to half close the door. Leaning close to my face, the Algerian told me how it was, in his eyes: I was a spy for European ceramics manufacturers, the men who already drive their enormous lorries to Safi to load up the work of honest Moroccans and sell it at an inflated price as Spanish pottery. And if I was not in cahoots with the Spanish scum then I was surely a magazine writer putting together an article about artisans, an article which – at this point he thumped my shoulder for emphasis – 'will not only deny them credit and a mention by name but also cut them out of the fees and copyright.'

As has happened so many times in my life, whenever I am under pressure, I automatically, unthinkingly, but very efficaciously turned into a moron and came out with a singularly inappropriate response, which astounded my listener into self-doubt. 'But we don't eat tagines,' I answered, 'so there wouldn't be any point in copying the dishes, would there?' As a non-sequitur it was inspired, and slowly the atmosphere in the shop loosened up, the door was opened fully again, the group of men dispersed to sit down on the stoop and dust the exhibits, until only the Algerian remained upright, facing me. Unsure of what to say, he asked me if I had any Led Zeppelin or Pink Floyd tapes. Although I loathe that type of music, I swore that I had albums by both bands and not only that, but all the CDs and tapes they had ever produced, and of course I would bring them up to the shop on Tuesday, first thing, to swop for a pot or vase.

PART ONE

No one believed me and I sidled away, breaking into a run the minute I reached the first bend on the dusty path, sloshing through heaps of roof tiles and clay mounds, in my Safi sandals, as if the hounds of hell were after me. Later on, when the trembling had died down, I cursed myself for not having noted the first sign of paranoia and responding accordingly by toning down the interest. My blindness to the sensibilities of others had created a situation which had seriously worried me for a few seconds and it could all have escalated into a sordid little scene. I resolved to be more careful, little realising that far worse was to come, and the next day, at that!

After a night spent listening to fighting dogs, a turkey with indigestion and boisterous Moroccan youths at the Golden Fish Disco next door, who spent the whole evening slamming car doors, honking horns and shouting farewell, I woke to the sound of the 'nnyeep' man, a Moroccan version of the totter (Safi and Casablanca boast a disproportionately large number of totters). This character rode a bicycle, had a greyish-green carpet rolled across the saddlebar and gave voice every few minutes. I wondered where he would put anything else if he got lucky and won a sink or a rainwater barrel, such as his confrere in Casablanca had been blessed with. We waved to each other. Things were looking up. The 'nnyeep' man reminded me of my desire to look into garbage disposal, but the first cannery row beckoned.

Although it was a Sunday, groups of unemployed men were lounging outside the gates of the fishing port trying to pick up casual work and being harassed by officials attempting to keep the entrance clear, a sight reminiscent of black and white photographs of the Great Depression. Just past the still deserted Place de l'Independence, we stopped at the cliff edge to take in the view of Safi in the soft morning light before the sharp glare distorted outlines and images. My eyes were drawn to a group of uniformed municipal workers a few yards away who were carting metal trolleys to the cliff top. Luck, rather than judgment, was now answering my garbage disposal questions and a depressing, squalid system it turned out to be. As soon as the mound of rubbish was large enough, it was set afire and burnt off with much prodding and reshaping of the pyramid. However, anything which would not burn was simply flung over the cliff to land on the ledges below. Alongside, young boys dumped used brazier fuel, brought up from the local cafés in large baskets, and a group of women carrying green plastic buckets, leaning on the opposite side of the road, crossed over and started sifting through the salvaged charcoal for domestic use.

Peering over the ledge of the sea wall a foul smell and sight met our noses and eyes. Every available crevice, ledge and boulder was splattered with rotten fruit, bones, wet cardboard, broken old bottles and newspapers. Far below the débris, young boys in cut-off denim shorts were innocently fishing, their long thin rods complementing their long thin bodies as they swayed in the wind and dodged the spume, shrieking, showing off their prowess. The sea churned violently. Above them the older, care-worn generation, those who could not afford to play-feed themselves but for whom the business of survival was a deadly serious one, scavenged. Armed with bags made of sacking, they slowly and heavily picked their way over the slippery, filthy rocks, selecting bottles and rotten tomatoes, stashing away pieces of string and material. What had started out as a light-hearted comment, a barbed aside aimed at all the high profile ministries of hygiene which oversee neglected, garbage-strewn towns, had turned into a human tragedy. I couldn't watch the dozens of figures any longer as they poked around in the slime, and the beauty and freshness of the new town suddenly seemed both a blessing and a curse. How can one reconcile the immaculate tubs of jasmine and the well laid-out municipal park, entry one dirham, with this absence of basic foodstuffs?

Travel writers speak with admiration of the Moroccans' ability to recycle anything at all as if it were a clever, Simian trick, an asset within poverty. Have they never considered that the Moroccans might prefer to buy new objects, that they are driven to hone skills they might well resent and that – Oh revolutionary thought – they might enjoy a pristine bicycle and look upon it with pride rather than find themselves forced to weld together a collection of bent pieces of metal, even though it be so, so adroitly. We talk of recycling from the vantage point of abundance, but popping the old newspaper or Coke can into a collection point on the high road is no hardship, takes little effort and doesn't make or break us. The recycling I saw on the cliffs of Safi is born of naked need.

It is hardly the same activity and deserves sober analysis.

Chastened, and suddenly exhausted, I sped through town towards the south and the canning quarter, whose overpowering stench is pleasant at first, a little like a cup of Marmite held close to the nose, but then builds up to such a rich intensity that it suffocates the uninitiated. Car windows glided up hastily. The kilometres of long, narrow, white streets which have created and sustained Safi's fortune and population for so long are lined with tanneries, truck depots, tin and leather factories, canning co-operatives and refrigeration plants. There are crowds of men, women and children on the streets chattering by the impromptu roadside bars selling Fanta and grapes, reading the papers or eating ice-cream. The stench rises to an unbelievable crescendo of warm rot, salt and liver. The sardine may be king here, and it may well provide employment for a large percentage of Safi's three hundred and fifty thousand, but I cannot believe that people who six days a week gut, clean and pack the four hundred and fifty thousand fish Safi exports a year, enjoy chomping on their grilled cousins on their days off. But they do.

The high buildings of cannery row tapered off to reveal the phosphate plant of Safi, another major employer, a particularly beautiful belching chimney which was streaking the sky like an Impressionist on cocaine. This was photograph material of the highest calibre. Barbed wire surrounded the compound, but since it was so close to the road I thought nothing of it. I took two snaps, parking up hard on the right of the broad road to get just the right angle.

Barely had my finger clicked down on the button a second time when a silver Renault 25 screeched to a halt, at an angle in front of me, and a small, tight-lipped man rapped on the window. Three other cars, tatty Renault 4s drew up before I had time to wind it down, and a group of uniformed men leapt out and stood armed and at the ready. At first I failed to take any of this in. It was all a bit like *Miami Vice* but without the glamour, since the faces surrounding me were hostile and the man with the largest gun had huge biceps and a mouth full of steel teeth. Mr Renault 25 was slightly built, very angry and spoke French with a clipped correct accent. He demanded the film. I stalled. He demanded the film again and told me I should be deported that day unless I gave it up immediately. At this point I couldn't accept his reasoning.

'Surely,' I argued with him 'there could be no harm in taking a photo of a landscape. After all, I've got a reasonable camera, nothing more, and no zoom lenses and,' I added, inspired, or so I imagined, 'anyone who wanted close-ups would use a satellite or pay an insider for information.'

The mere mention of spying and satellites only infuriated him further as he leaned against the car and extended his hand. I dropped the film into his paw and inanely asked what would happen to the picture of the man on the donkey waving the flag. Renault 25 told me dismissively that he would develop the film and return any harmless shots to the place where I was staying, so he would like the address. Right then. Trembling fingers scribbled it down for him. I couldn't control the shakes and asked him, for reasons which I shall never be able to fathom, whether he wanted any money for printing and developing the non-seditious material, adding that, if so, I had better give it to him then as I might be out when he called to drop it off. An incredulous, fascinated expression passed over Renault 25's face as he stared at me with something close to wonder. 'Go!' he yelled, smacking the bonnet. 'Just go!'

I couldn't respond and finally snapped out of my trance in time to see the four guards break away first. In this frame of mind I was convinced that we were racing each other to get to my luggage and that deportation was still on the cards. I remembered my paperback, *The Arabs*, my notes, copies of the *Saudi Gazette* and, spurred on by the urge to hide them, eventually made it back to the flat. It was impossible to tell if anything had been touched but I feared the worst and threw all the copies of *L'Opinion* and *Jeune Afrique* away. The day was ruined. I thought about packing. One hour later he was back. Unfortunately, the film did not come out and, unfortunately, he was compelled to take down my personal details again and, most unfortunately of all, he was constrained to remind me of two things: One, this was not England, and two, the only thing you can photograph in Morocco is historic monuments.

He asked me if all this was clear. It was clear, extremely, dauntingly clear. My hands were shaking again as I repeated the mantra – 'I am sorry' – for what seemed like hours, gorging on humble pie and waiting for the axe of deportation to fall. With a final threat and reprimand the man looked me full in the eye and shook his head. Cowed, all I could do was repeat my apologetic refrain as he walked away. I was disturbed by this run-in, ashamed of my own lack of spunk, but sure that this type of authority was best met head bowed and belly up. Had I been more aggressive, I would have had to spend an afternoon at the police station, receive endorsements in my passport and been obliged to undergo interminable questioning. At worst, I might even have received an escort to Casa and the RAM plane. After all, from the authorities' point of view, every chemical complex, even if it does only produce fertilizers, is a sensitive site (as Farzad Bazoft proved in Iraq) and a source of almost magical power. I giggled. I was cast in the role of evil eye in this situation, the meddling outsider who came too close and was expelled accordingly. No amount of symbolic explanation made me feel better about the incident, however, for it underscored the foreigner's vulnerability when face to face with arbitrary power. Two unpleasant situations in the space of thirty-six short hours and bad luck is supposed to run in threes. It was obviously time to throw discretion to the winds and run like the clappers. For all its gracious sculptures and murals, numerous street lights, bushes and gardens, Safi remains wary of strangers and prepared to repel all boarders, albeit with warrant cards and permits rather than the rusting cannons of the Kechla.

◆ *Chapter Four* ◆

The date was 20 August and therefore the roads leading out to Safi were lined with flags. Every tin pot barracks, municipal building and square sported a long row of sun-bleached national flags, the background red splodged, the edges of the green stars faded. It was a race against time to return the car to Casablanca, a good day's drive away, and I was banking on light traffic and a fair scattering of petrol stations along the way. The ever present and immensely helpful traffic police urged us to take the old coast road not the P8 at Place Mohammed V, since the day promised to be hot – a concept they mimed with broad smiles, mock-wiping their brows.

As Safi receded, the coast became savage, the surrounding countryside dry and rocky. The occasional water trough testified to some form of grazing and old women, perched on minute asses, wove across the plain, firewood balanced on large panniers. From time to time cows wandered across the road and youngsters, sticks in hand, marshalled herds of sheep and played outside the low, whitewashed houses. There was no bird song, no raucous yelling or heavy traffic, just the rhythmic whoosh and slap of the waves battering the rocks of the steep cliffs and being sucked into the many caves and large niches, before being thrust out back into the tumultuous waters. On the horizon a long ship hung, immobile and suspended, for all the world an optical illusion or a latterday *Marie Celeste*.

Clearly it was hard to make a living on this stretch of the coast, for the groups of children stood on the roadside, flagging down traffic to sell cracked conches and sharp, tatty shell necklaces, threaded on thin twine. Stopping to take a closer look, out of a sense of curiosity, or misguided pity perhaps, I was attacked by a fourteen-year-old harpy who thrust half a dozen necklaces round me and shrieked 'Thirty dirhams each!' I demurred since this was a ridiculous price but she persisted: 'How much then, how much?' It was obvious from her frenzied salesmanship that no one had actually stopped to examine her baubles for days and the girl was desperate not to lose this sale. Her wild smile, thrusting arms and teeth thickly coated with plaque and a yellow film of goo all repelled me. I gave her ten dirhams as a gift and prepared to drive off, whereupon she reached a peak of frantic despair over the lost sale, grabbing at the tomatoes and cheese triangles on the dashboard, yelling, 'A cigarette, a cigarette.' The car refused to restart and a small group of children assembled to join in the fray. I threw handfuls of loose change and a packet of Silk Cut out of the car, tried to clear an exit, appalled by the torn clothes, eczema-covered faces, shaved heads and leathery skin blocking my view. This wasn't enough to please them, however, and they started to rock the car slowly from side to side, jumped on the bonnet, pushed their arms in to grab for my necklace, scratching my wrists and arms as I gently and then frantically pushed back. Just as the whole affair started to get totally out of hand the engine caught. I rammed the gear stick into first and thumped down on the accelerator, driving over a foot and throwing kids off the bonnet as the Fiat finally responded. I felt unrepentant. They spat at the car. It was all getting to be too much. In spite of the fierce heat I resolutely did not stop at the melon sellers with their luscious yellow fruit, ignored a cow eating a peeing woman's radishes out of her unattended basket and broke for the north.

These open battles over seventy-five pence did not bring out notions of compassion or superiority in me. I can't push children out of my way like certain other tourists or assume a high toned impatience and smug sense of being a benefactor when I throw them a dirham. Instead I feel ridiculously angry. Charity is one of the five pillars of Islam, but there is a sense of equality in the Koranic interpretation of almsgiving, unlike our notions of the 'deserving poor', and all the class-determined paternalism which passes for 'giving' in the West. In Morocco, those who give do so because it is their duty to do so. Those who ask do so because their place in Allah's scheme of things demands it. The blind men who chant 'Allah, Allah' over and over again in the medina are not cringing or aggressive, they are merely pointing out that they need alms. In a sense, then, zakhat, charity, is a natural transaction, not one based on pity but on obligation. It is also certainly a far cry from the assault tactics practised on the roadside, which have more to do with blackmail than a just redistribution of wealth.

The landscape gradually changed as the kilometres sped by. A lagoon with oyster beds and salt bands stretched out on the left, while rows upon rows of cloches and windbreaks made of gum and maize branches lined the right bank. Carts piled high with tomatoes, green peppers and fat, crinkly cucumbers clopped slowly through the paths separating the hundreds of market gardens. This was the Doukkala Plain, an intensively farmed, rich area where no cultivatable patch of land is left unplanted. Large metal hoops lay piled by the roadside alongside the sheets and bales of plastic which were being erected in the distance by a small group of men. A lorry sped by, its back covered by a tarpaulin under which nestled a heifer, a woman and two infants along with the man of the family, whose turbaned head was gradually being uncoiffed by the strong wind.

Off under a stumpy olive tree a man in a pink shirt was lying face down in the stubble, napping. A crucified white and blue djellabah was nailed to a low brick wall nearby, adding a macabre touch to the scene. Was he a tailor or merely a rural worker trying to earn a few pennies by selling his clothes? No chance to find out since, abruptly, the road was cordoned off to traffic and a veritable sea of national flags and serried ranks of local buses testified to the first true holiday celebration we had run into.

Oualidya, a small town renowned for its seafood, in particular its oysters, was en fête, and no one was allowed to pass through without joining in. The minute my feet touched the ground I was grabbed by the arm by a couple of pretty, laughing teenagers, who pulled me to the front of the crowd, smiled and disappeared. Directly before me stood a small stage, empty for the moment, and four tables stocked with umbrellas around which several exotically garbed women, their hair loose, their feet bare, were sitting, quietly sipping Coke. Amplifiers were balanced on planks of wood, a series of microphones were humming loud static, and the crowd was shoving expectantly, waiting for action. A matter of minutes later a seven-piece folk troupe uncurled from its table and strutted onto the stage and the singing and dancing began. The women were wonderful in their loosely tied, floor-length dresses, slapping their feet against the sun-baked earth, flinging their black hair over one shoulder one minute and then, the next, wailing, their throats exposed to the clear, hot sky. Then holding hands, they charged towards us, only to halt at the last minute, stamp their feet, circle and retreat. The men kept up a steady chant and knocked out a harsh rhythm on the drums, looking into space, caught up in their own tempo rather than the actions of the women. Twenty minutes later, the first set was over and I was clapping and shrieking with everyone, the tension of the morning forgotten. A young boy standing behind me told me that only loose women performed in public in this way and that they all, but all, came from

Azzemour, a town apparently renowned for its prostitutes. 'Are all dancers prostitutes?' I queried.

'But of course,' he replied dryly. There seemed to be no point in discussing this any further since Moroccan men are quick with the tar-brush and any unaccompanied, partially uncovered, attractive female, particularly if she is European, automatically falls into the loose woman category.

A tent had been erected on the edge of the square: a giant thing, its walls lined with cream-coloured foam seating embossed with a dark green pattern. Seriously important and affluent men were perched within, behind numerous low tables heaped with ceremonial silver platters and teapots, bottled drinks and cakes. The children had been penned in a separate section of the tent, where it was standing room only, and were being kept in line by their teachers who were armed with tin whistles. There were no women to be seen but a middle-aged official courteously asked me into the dignitaries' tent and everyone squeezed up to give me a perch. Behind the largest, most elaborately decorated table sat a group of religious leaders flanked by the chief of police, local administrators and provincial representatives. Half glasses of mint tea and small macaroons, a piece of Islam-green angelica poked into the middle of each cake, were handed round and we all munched happily. The plywood table which sat at the main entrance to the tent was loaded with cups, trophies and bouquets. The flowers were presumably intended for the dancers and, judging by the size of the other prizes, the children would be running races today. There was an atmosphere of relaxed geniality in the tent. A brown-clad, hooded figure was whispering sweet nothings into his companion's ear, a quick peck on the lips was exchanged, hands were clasped. This was not simply male camaraderie but sexuality at work, yet no one blinked an eyelid. An official photographer nipped in and out of the tent, his flash exploding. No one paid the slightest notice until the flag-hoisting ceremony was convened in the middle of the square and he was called upon to catch the assembled row of representatives of the powers that be in mid-salute, as the Moroccan flag slowly glided up the pole, to flap wildly, almost angrily, in the brisk wind. This formality dispensed with, everyone settled back onto the cushions and finish lines were marked out in the sand. Speeches commenced and the refrain 'Mohammed V, Hassan II,' lulled me off to sleep. Given the number of streets, boulevards, avenues, and squares which are named after the two monarchs in every town in the land, and the numbers still under construction, the time will doubtless soon come when it will prove impossible to give clear directions anywhere in Morocco.

It had been a joyous, uplifting morning for all that and I wished I could stay for the spit-roasted lambs, the Berber dance troupe and the feasting and just slump back in the tent and applaud the riot of obviously competitive children. The brain nudged me: Hertz, Casablanca. I paid my respects to the main table, thanked them for their hospitality and left.

Pressure of time notwithstanding, there were two spots on the road to Casablanca which I had long promised myself to see. The first, the small village of Moulay Abdullah, is the site of an important early August moussem, or pilgrimage, part religious festival, part fair, which draws hundreds of tents and visitors to its sanctuary founded by a companion of the Prophet who came to Morocco when the village was called Tit and still under Phoenician rule. Home to the only surviving Almoravide minaret in the country, Moulay Abdullah was a centre of orthodoxy during the struggles with the Berber heretics of the plains, the Berghouata and the Doukkala, but the population was forcibly moved inland to Fez by Abdul Moumen, the twelfth-century

Almohad sultan, to prevent tribute being paid to the Portuguese in nearby El Jadida. Time has not treated Moulay Abdullah kindly, and all romantic thoughts of graceful, Phoenician prows being battered against cliff faces; slim minarets and delicate pillars; elaborate mouldings and carvings; and thick comforting city walls, braving the harsh Atlantic winds, receded in the face of the all-pervading filth and flies which are the hallmark of this comatose spot.

One or two men lurked at a rusty table in the central square and the dogs scratched among the piles of rubbish which were heaped everywhere. Two dead rats lay in a small mountain of empty cigarette packets, Omo boxes and squashed fruit. The covered arcade which stretches to the left of the approach to the shrine was manned by two boys in dirty cotton trousers; an older figure, presumably a relative, lay at the back of the arcade, his head cradled in his arms, dozing against a pile of sacks. As I approached, the boys called out and plied me with small bottles of rosewater, for sprinkling inside the sanctuary, stubby candles to light and plastic and felt emblems decorated with sequins, metal leaves and symmetrical shapes which, if hung at home or in the car, would protect me against the evil eye. I preferred the stick-on plastic strips available at many tobacconists, whose Hands of Fatima, kohl-outlined female eyes, eagles and pointing fingers embellish every private and public vehicle in Morocco, glinting wickedly in the sun, the silver and gold backgrounds overlaid with Habitat-style primary colours, provocative and lurid. Nevertheless, I bought a bottle of rosewater for three dirhams and secured the boy's promise that he would offer it up for me. So, together, we pushed past the female beggars slumped in the sanctuary courtyard and went in.

A black bitch was sleeping just by the threshold to the shrine, occasionally twitching and scratching her flea ridden pelt, but nothing else stirred as the lad sprinkled the bottle's contents over the grass mats which covered the shrine's floor and handed me back the glass container. Looking around at the immobile heap of rags with their outstretched hands, the emptiness, I felt a surge of hopelessness and fastidious repugnance. Sacred or not, this backwater was sordid and yet another reminder that the simple rural life extolled by so many is hard, dull and thankless when all it leads to is subsistence and more back-breaking and repetitious labour. I couldn't live here for an afternoon, let alone a lifetime. Almoravide and Almohad relics notwithstanding. Just as no one raised an arm in greeting, so no one waved farewell – an appropriate lack of reaction. Let it slumber.

Five miles north of Moulay Abdullah stands El Jadida which, it being August, was crammed with local tourists from Marrakesh and Casablanca enjoying a traditional seaside holiday. The bucket and spade brigade, Bermuda shorts rolled up to tan knees, were fighting for a square metre of space where they might spread a towel on the long crowded beach. The cafés were doing a roaring trade as families strolled along the seafront boulevard and stopped to nibble sweet pastries, paddle or go for a leisurely walk round the ramparts. It all reminded me of Brighton on a hot Bank Holiday Monday and, after Essaouira (a smaller version of the eat and bathe philosophy), there seemed little point in doing more than beeping the horn to say hello, picking up a pile of newspapers and continuing, to reputation-besmirched Azzemour.

Azzemour was home to a large Jewish community until 1960 and its moussem celebrates the Jewish Rabbi, Abraham Moul'Niss, whose small sanctuary is shut these days, except for Sunday prayers, or for infrequent visitors. The hostel for Jewish visitors, the riverside synagogue, the neglected cemetery and the mellah itself are all deserted and falling apart, no longer used, and the thirty thousand strong population is now overwhelmingly Arab. Perched on the shore of the silted-up Oum er Rbia, whose waters run a murky red if it has rained in the hills, the town is approached by three bridges, or a narrow road which takes you one kilometre off the S 121 and straight to the sixteenth-century Portuguese-built walls which surround the medina. The ramparts and towers which the Portuguese erected during the forty years that they held Azzemour show no signs of restoration, yet there is a shabby grandeur to the town which twists the heartstrings as soon as one stands in the new square, staring up at what must be the Atlantic coast's most neglected little corner.

The medina is a mess of small white houses full of peaceful corners where weeds and wild flowers grow stem by stem through the cracks in the broken paving slabs and rubble. The roads here seem to curve and bow rather than twist, and Belladonna trumpets cascade over the broken walls, while surprisingly fat cats sun themselves in patches of searingly bright light. A few curious children were playing football with an old can, intent on their passes, for all the world as if this was Wembley on FA Cup day, but they broke off and ambled over to see who I was, what I was doing. The oldest, Amir, spoke more Spanish than French and, trailing two infants in his wake, set off to see the town through my eyes. His garbled, shy explanations were cut short by an apparition of such presence and grave beauty that, for a moment, I believed the Angel Gabriel himself had descended. The sun was obviously unhinging me. Framed within a stumpy, arched doorway stood a man in his late forties with the kind of features the Greeks would have killed for: over six feet tall, grizzled hair, Alexander technique posture and a deep voice. But, most remarkable of all, he wore a spotless white gandora and clean feet. Impolitely, openly, I gazed at his feet and marvelled at the clipped unbroken toenails, the soft shining skin, the lack of dust. After the squalor of Moulay Abdullah, I was his slave and would follow him anywhere.

This apparition shooed the children away, placed his right

hand on his heart in greeting and asked if I knew much about Azzemour. 'Nothing, absolutely nothing,' I replied, conveniently forgetting everything I had ever read which had brought me there in the first place. The apparition clasped his manicured hands behind his ramrod-straight back and glided forward, explaining that Azzemour was colonised during a relatively early period, since the Portuguese only turned their attention south after the Battle of the Three Kings and left as soon as they lost Agadir. Their arrival formed the cement which brought the Arabic and Jewish communities together, making common cause against the infidel, and allowed three wise men to be honoured in one town. When I asked whether the Jews were pushed to go or enticed to come away I was told that the second description was probably more accurate, and that Israel's call for assistance rather than Moroccan anti-semitism, though it was blooming by 1960, was the catalyst for the modern exodus. The religious struggles fought out behind the walls of Azzemour, home of the Berghouata tribe, were ever visible in a curious-looking mosque, which was once a Catholic church. When the Portuguese left Azzemour in 1541, they destroyed all the mosques, leaving only their own God's house standing, and the citizens promptly reversed its role. It is strange to imagine Moulay Abdullah and Azzemour struggling against each other's interpretation of the Word of the Prophet so many years ago, raiding each other's crops, destroying each other's property. Stranger still to see the vanquished prosperous; the victors half dead in their righteousness.

Strolling through the crumbling masonry of the former prison, the air full of shrill bird song, Azzemour revealed itself to be a quiet, happy ruin. The apparition, a professor of Arabic history no less, at Casablanca University it transpired, came there to relax and walk and forget the car horns of that most demanding of Moroccan cities, Casablanca. His English was flawless, his serenity enviable and I was not surprised that when our relaxed, disjointed conversation drifted to books he revealed a love of Virginia Woolf and James Joyce rather than KGB thrillers. If he could find work there, in his native town, he told me, he would never have moved away, but most of Azzemour's inhabitants work the fields or travel as far as Jorf, the new phosphate complex built with Japanese and Spanish money which has only been open for six years and is twenty miles away by local bus. It was, perhaps, the existence of Jorf that explained the limping, bald-headed boy who asked me for the bread I had just bought, his overbright eyes set in a thin face which seemed on the point of collapsing, his hands fidgeting and claw-like. I doubted whether he was much over twenty. Having taken the flat, seed-covered loaf, he shuffled off to a dark corner and started to eat.

Like so many well-educated Moroccans, the professor looked straight through the boy, making it too impolite to mention his existence. Moroccans are highly sensitive about their poverty and object to visitors focusing on it to the point that they chase away their own beggars so tourists won't see them. As for taking photographs, well, enough said. I said nothing, content to trail along past the zaouia or seat of the religious brotherhood founded by Moulay Bouachaid, the town's patron saint, and back to the square which divides the old town from the new. The apparition told me that it had been a perfect afternoon, so we mustn't exchange names or addresses. I knew exactly what he meant but I was tempted to run after him as he dissolved back into the medina, to touch the only man who had not pressed my flesh on this trip, to ask him how he kept his feet clean – anything at all to destroy the magic of the encounter which would tantalise me unless I reduced it to banality immediately. Too late. He had gone. And I was doomed to remember him forever.

◆

Berber Bob was waiting in Casablanca, unruffled, smiling and full of the joys of his new job at exclusive Ain Diab where he was running a night club. The coastal resort of Ain Diab, with its five star hotels, private beach clubs, restaurants and glitz, is the height of Western-style sophistication. Here, European women with blonde hair long enough to sit on dine out with credit card wielding Moroccan businessmen, playing with walnut and Roquefort salads, spinach hillocks and braised celery dribbling black peppercorns. Nouveau cuisine, stilettos and Tamla Motown tapes meet twentieth-century, Saudi-financed architecture. I was pleased for Bob, whose unbounded optimism, cheerful world view and kind nature allow him to glide through life untroubled and constantly content.

Sitting with him exhausted, on the edge of the Parc de la Ligue Arabe, fairylights blinking in the dark trees, the unspeakable traffic and suicide jockeys screaming past, it was difficult to believe that Marrakesh and Casablanca were on the same planet, let alone in the same country. The children's funfair was in full swing, hooters blaring, the strains of 'Reet Petite' mingling with the permanent cacophony of tooting car horns. Smart women wearing full sets of gold jewellery (necklaces, earrings, bracelets and rings), strolled past in their Ted Lapidus and Oscar de la Renta, trailed by servants entrusted with their mistresses' children. Men and women walked together unsegregated, young couples even held hands, or sped by, glued together, on noisy mopeds. The djellabah count had dropped below the horizon and turbans were definitely not visible either.

Casablanca is modernity personified. The fastest growing city in Africa, with its population of three and a half million, 'Casa' is a city of apartment blocks, office skyscrapers, glass frontages, plazas and concrete: Bond Street crossed with Birmingham's city centre set down by the sea. Its civic monuments are attractive in the same way as all fountain-focussed squares, straight, flag lined roads and huge government buildings are attractive, and neither the medina nor the parks speak of times gone by. The bidonvilles which earned Casa its notoriety have been stuck behind walls now and are not visible to the casual onlooker, although accommodation remains a problem as apartments are difficult to find and expensive to rent. The old French military housing complexes are now occupied by retired Moroccan soldiers, and cranes and excavation speak of efforts to bring supply up to the level of demand, to forestall the urban rioting and strikes which are Casa's response to inadequate resources, shortages and poor urban planning.

Out on the coast stands the new mosque, Hassan II's monument to himself, which promises to be the largest mosque in the world when it is completed, its lasers beaming forty visible kilometres out to sea towards Mecca (to the consternation of international air traffic controllers). Every brick and ounce of cement has been paid for by compulsory donations levied on all Moroccan adults, male and female. The mosque is a controversial topic and divides the population into those who feel the government should have other priorities, and those who believe that no price is too high if the end product glorifies God. The anti-lobby argues that Allah is not interested in the building but in the prayers which are said within its walls and that coercion does not glorify the Creator. They add that the mosque should be named after the Moroccan men and women who have financed it, rather than their monarch, and question the justice of the system of collection which has frequently forced members of families who work in different towns to pay twice.

In the other corner, *Le Matin du Sahara* runs a daily headline under its banner exhorting Moroccans not to forget to keep giving until the mosque's final stone is in place. The mosque's setting, it must be said, is superb, standing on the end of a long, artificially reclaimed promontory overlooking the sea. But it is difficult to gain any clear picture of what the finished building will look like since it is still encased in scaffolding and surrounded by heavy machinery and workmen. Apparently, the exterior will be covered in polished marble and over ten thousand craftsmen skilled in carving and mosaic work have been working on the decorative ceilings and friezes, the floors and walls, for the last ten years. The end does not seem in sight yet, and the murmurings of discontent grow as the budget of over three hundred million increases in line with the passage of time.

Bob found us a room above a men's public bath for the night, slap-bang in the middle of town. Downstairs, shower stalls were being swabbed out with buckets and mops, steam was running down the walls and groups of half-clad men were towel drying their hair on benches in the blue and white reception area. Large ferns, which obviously thrive in this sweaty atmosphere, poured out of terracotta pots which had been used as ashtrays by the passing clientele. An old, well-muscled man was washing up rags in a corner. Bob whispered that he was the owner and masseur here and renowned for his osteopathic abilities. This man had been manipulating necks, spines and limbs for twenty years and charged only twenty dirhams for the full treatment, plus hammam. The rags were used to scour the flesh which passed through these portals. I was fascinated by the gossip but equally eager for a bed of whatever complexion. The owner was finally satisfied with the state of his cloths, which he hung over a thin piece of string attached to a pair of stepladders, and gestured that the hammam was closed, the hotel open. A plain, clean room, a bed with thin cotton sheets and a nylon blanket, one shadeless bulb and a rug all spelled good night, and trying to avoid focussing on the rumpus below, the traffic outside and the dead pigeon, one glassy eye fixing me with a blank stare from the window ledge, I collapsed. Next door Michelle resignedly opened a now disintegrating copy of *The Ugly Duckling* and Caspian's voice cut through the wall, asking yet again, 'But why was he ugly …?'

PART ONE

Casablanca shrieks and brakes into life early, too early. I ate an expensive breakfast of orange juice, rolls stuffed with crème patissière with a thick sludge of chocolate on top, and coffee in the Hotel Washington. Then I took a quick look at the more impressive examples of French architecture, the many Catholic churches and mosques of the city centre before wandering back to the acres of municipal greenery which form the Parc de la Ligue Arabe. It was by then almost 3:00 p.m. and waiters were busy wiping down chairs and tables in the cafés in the semi-deserted fairground. The teenagers of Casablanca were prom-enading in the culotte separates, 501s and silk shirts, and odd nursemaids had started to trickle in with their charges. Ten minutes later than advertised, metal grilles slid up, the last broom swept the last path and loudspeakers came on as Kylie Minogue's, 'Je ne sais pas pourquoi,' set the trees aflutter. Most of the rides were geared to the younger set, and fading metal notices firmly announced which age group was permitted to go on which ride. There was no appeal. The newest and most daring offering, the Jet-Glider, drew a crowd of teenagers who screamed with excitement as the planes flew up at a steep angle and swooped down again on the other side, all to the accompaniment of heavy rock music. I was drawn to the prettiest of pink pigs with black spots, and green-shelled turtles with user-friendly faces and wide grins. Both accommodated the under-fives and moved fairly smoothly and quite fast in a long wide loop. The rides seemed to last a long time, three or even four circuits of the track, and beaming mothers in sharp suits or kerchief-waving minders smiled and waved, like adults at fun fairs the world over.

Plaques emblazoned with the figure of a slightly distorted Mickey Mouse were hanging from various tree branches and a poor, miniaturised imitation of the castle at Disneyland was set in the middle of a train track. Each time the train completed a circuit it passed under the castle opening and hysterical giggles echoed in the semi-darkness before it emerged into the light once more, every child thrilled to the marrow. Diesel-powered go-karts were doing great business with the queue stretching back into the side road lined with Eskimo and Pingouin ice-cream stalls. Most of the punters were over ten and apparently had no fear in their bones. Every ride was paid for in advance since tickets were bought by the book, two dirhams for a ride which didn't leave the ground; three dirhams for anything which ascended, and four dirhams for 'the show'. I wanted to see this show and tracked it down to a large white building which was plastered in pictures of air, sea and road disasters. Inside there were no seats, merely a thin ledge running round the outer perimeter. Suddenly, the lights went out and an old projector with high-powered amplifiers thrust into action as a 3-D picture of a truck careering down a steep mountain road spilled before, behind and around the audience to the accompaniment of jarring, braking noises and the roar of a churning engine. The truck snarled off the road. Another truck roared towards us, intent on mowing us down, flying inches over our heads. The volume of the sound effects rose another degree, if such a thing were possible, and the audience began to thin as women with babies slipped out, unable to bear the vertigo and noise any longer. I held out for another few seconds before bursting out through the bars into the air, finally defeated by the roller-coaster sequence. My legs were shaking and I needed to squat down. One of the streetwise, attractive café waiters bent over to see if I wanted some water, and hauled me to my feet. He couldn't understand how the show could possibly have frightened me, since he often watched it during breaks or if it was a bit cold outside. We were mutually amazed by each other's tastes.

◆

PART ONE

It was this combination of exhausting frenzy, of money made, invested, banked and multiplied, of high rises and overpriced taxis, of luxury and internationalism which drove me out of Casablanca to what people often contemptuously refer to as dreary old Rabat, the capital.

◆ *Chapter Five* ◆

Rabat is simply the most seductive, well-integrated, wonderful city in Morocco, and having planned originally to take others' advice and pass through, spending only a couple of days there, I fell blindly in love with it and put down roots for three weeks. In a perfect world, I would like to live in Rabat and be buried in Meknès, in Moulay Ishmael's mausoleum.

Why is Rabat so attractive? In the first place, the time comes on every journey when the traveller wants to live somewhere rather than clock up encounters and sights. We Europeans are still not the world's most relaxed visitors. We walk around wanting to do or see, to eat or swim, to talk or read. In short, we are generally incapable of just sitting and accepting or waiting to see what turns up (if anything), unless we belong to the kif-smoking fraternity, and I do not. The spectacularly beautiful villages of the High Atlas, the remote pise hamlets of the Middle Atlas and the innumerable one-garage, three café towns, there-fore, tend to unsettle us. And rightly so to some degree, since unless you are part of the community or economy, there is a limit to the number of coffees you can drink, swatting flies and peering at the local colour go by. An urban animal by birth and inclination, my personal energies are most suited to an urban rhythm, albeit not one as strident or demanding as Casablanca's. Rabat, which synthesises the old and the new with rare grace, provided me with a home, stimulus and a sense of partial acceptance by the large, mixed community which is impossible in smaller places.

Situated on both sides of the Bou Regreg, today, Rabat-Salé has a population of just over a million. Salé was first settled in the tenth century by the Zenata tribe, who subsequently built a fortress to house their monastic warrior community on the opposite bank, now the site of the Kasbah Ouadaias, from whose stronghold they waged war against the Berghouata, followers of the Khajarite heresy, who lived in nearby Sala Colonica. The Khajarites, or successionists, are an interesting rigid bunch of heretical purists who split from the main body of Islam in 622, a period when the faith was expanding under the third caliph Uthman ibn Affan, a member of the Umayyad clan.

Syria, Egypt, Palestine, western and central Persia, even Jerusalem had all fallen to the Islamic armies by the seventh century. The Khajarites, many of whom were the Prophet's close friends or relatives, were all descendants of the Bedouin tribesmen who first converted to Islam, and began to question the ease with which subjugated peoples were converting. (In practice, to become a Moslem, it was enough simply to recite the creed 'There is no God but God and Mohammed is his Prophet'.) The Khajarites maintained that a man's deeds should count for more than a chanted declaration and that anyone who broke Islamic law should automatically lose his status as a believer and practising Moslem. Uthman, a pragmatist with a large empire to run, responded by arguing that judgment was God's prerogative and, for his pains, was assassinated in Mecca in 656 by his opponents, who thought he was establishing a personal dynasty based on corruption.

His successor, Ali, the spiritual head of Shi'ite Islam and the husband of Fatima, the Prophet's daughter, was originally backed by the faction in its struggle against the Umayyads, but when he decided to negotiate peace in 658 after a costly civil war, the Khajarites declared him a non-Moslem too. In retaliation, Ali slaughtered all but a few hundred of the four thousand Khajarite members who had fought for him at the Battle of Nahrawan. In the eyes of the Khajarites, he had openly declared himself beyond the pale by this act and, inevitably, he too was assassinated not long afterwards by one of the survivors.

The traditional views of the Khajarites which held that breaking the law equalled apostasy, were suppressed by the eighth century, although their descendants, the Ibadites, Bedouin nomads, still live on the Isle of Djerba in Tunisia and attempt to live according to a more rigid interpretation of the Koran and Islamic law. Since they acknowledge no form of government save Divine Law, the Tunisian state, already feeling some pressure from fundamentalist groups, pretends they do not exist and ignores their living challenge to Tunisia's pragmatic interpretation of Islam.

Thus Rabat's original function was to serve as a fortress, whilst Salé was a port and centre of trade and, over the next few centuries, Rabat served as a base for military excursions into Andalucia. The city expanded greatly under the twelfth-century sultan Yakoub el Mansour, who built the walls which survive to this day, and the glorious Hassan Tower in his quest to turn Rabat into an imperial city.

The jihad against the defeated Berghouata evolved into a jihad against Christian Spain. Success was followed by defeat, for in 1260 the Spanish sacked Salé and, according to a chronicler of the time, one Leo Africanus, there were barely a hundred habitable houses left standing in Rabat by 1560. Rabat was on the point of degenerating into an empty hamlet fortified by thick twelfth-century ramparts when fate intervened in the shape of the Moslem expulsions from Spain in 1610. Many of the new settlers put down roots in the area and set up the infamous, independent Bou Regreg Republic which thrived on piracy, attacking foreign merchant shipping and roaming as far as the Caribbean, Cornwall, Ireland and the Canary Isles. One of the by-products of the piracy was the subsidiary trade in human flesh, the capture and ransom of prisoners and the auctioning of slaves in the Souk el Ghezel. Reverberations of those swash-buckling times persist to this day. The fourteenth-century Marabout Sidi Achmed ben Achir is aptly enough revered here for his ability to entice ships on to rocks, and Salé's patron saint, Sidi Abdallah ben Hassoun, protects sailors on their travels. His followers dress as corsairs and Turks on the afternoon of Mouloud, Mohammed's birthday, when they march in pro-cessions carrying lamps and religious candles, an event overseen by the Guild of Boatmen.

No successful, independent enterprise survives for long without state intervention these days, and the same was true of seventeenth-century Morocco. By 1666, the Alaouite Sultan, Moulay er Rachid, had captured Salé estuary, cut himself into the action, and when he came to power the indomitable Moulay Ishmael took a whopping sixty per cent of the profits in order to secure men for work at Meknès, making use of the Oudaia tribesmen ensconced in the kasbah to ensure his dues were fully paid and to police rebellious Berber tribes in the area. This backhanded encouragement meant that the strange, uneasy mix-ture of European refugees from Spain, France, Italy and Portugal continued to strike terror into the heart of merchantmen from Cork to Iceland until 1829, when a vessel sailing under the Austro-Hungarian flag was seized and the imperial fleet promptly raised anchor to bomb every Moroccan coastal town in retaliation.

Rabat had been diversifying its economy, and carpet making, wood carving and basket work had developed as trades, but with Casablanca monopolising coastal trade and expanding, it seemed likely that the city would shrink in on itself with the banning of piracy, and revert to secondary status. However, the French, who established the attractive new town here, as in all the imperial cities in Morocco, wished otherwise and chose Rabat as the capital over its traditional rivals Fez and Marrakesh. And it has remained the administrative, ceremonial, and political capital of Morocco since independence.

Rabat's role and importance is reflected in a number of high-speed trains which link it with its business partner, Casablanca. The forty-five minute journey is comfortable. Over-priced drinks trolleys pass through the corridors selling rounds of tuna salad; the first-class compartment has scenes of fantasia riders, and women in traditional costumes, etched on the salmon pink seat dividers.

Almost before we settled down, the train was drawing into Rabat Ville, a modern white building on Rabat's main artery. As I stood on the shallow steps looking across the wide road the flags of the next-door parliament building beckoned for attention. A low, unspectacular piece of modern architecture, it stands back off the road behind a large piece of lawn and is guarded by an insignificant number of khaki clad sentries. It seems too popular somehow, too accessible to excite awe, wedged between the post office and the main shopping arcades, just as Buckingham Palace would look distinctly odd if it sat on Oxford Street. At the top of the road the eighteenth-century Grande Mosque dominates the view, marking the entrance to the Mechouar, the Royal Palace complex which one is allowed to stroll through – no deviations from the central road. And it is this series of buildings which appeals to visitors most of all. I had decided we would stay in a tiny boarding house which accommodates Morocco's equivalent of the travelling salesman outside the Bab el Had, the city gate which displayed severed criminals' heads until the early years of this century when the French outlawed this, along with many other practices.

Two young men were sitting at the poky reception desk in front of an enormous cut-out of George Michael and greeted us with some warmth before casually asking for money up front. I countered with a request to see the room and was led into a minute, rectangular space with a plastic waste bin and a new pine bed with horsehair mattress. A shower stood just inside the door which was covered with 'Do's' and 'Don't's' all in Arabic. Ziggy Marley, a great star in Morocco, dangled on the wall, secured with three pink drawing pins. Outside, the hotel sign blinked on and off, on and off every five seconds and I wondered whether the thin white linen curtains would be able to smother it. Probably not. Somewhere downstairs, a clock was chiming 'Happy Birthday to You', one of its twelve tunes, I discovered in the days that followed, as I saw identical clocks in the next-door bakery, the newsagent's and the grocer's; some salesman or other had obviously hit the jackpot in this area. There were no hangers, no soap, no loo rolls and no desk or chairs, but the young men seemed helpful enough, taking pains to point out which local tricksters sold old water and yellowed cigarettes, which peanut venders' nuts had mould, and where not to buy fruit because of the fruit flies inside. Unpacking was out of the question given the absence of space, so we kicked our faithful luggage below the window and strolled out to reconnoitre.

The downstairs bar-cum-lounge was draped with men watching the Grand Prix on, of all things, Eurosport, the Sky Channel, and Hamid who lived in and undertook every task demanded of him was busy using the espresso machine to make steaming hot mint tea, which he served to the residents. There was only one woman in evidence, the wife of a slipper manufacturer apparently, and in the days that followed I heard but rarely saw her. Her children cried incessantly and she wafted up and down the narrow marble staircase clad in a full-length, pink nylon nightie, looking depressed, tugging along in her wake a black-haired squalling girl in nappies. We smiled, she threw her hands in the air or sighed, and continued her rounds of smacks and tears.

The guest-house was a fascinating place since it lived off a passing trade which, in its own fashion, typifies Rabat's function. Zachary was here because the passport office refused to issue him a new passport and denied having received his forms in the first place while arguing that, even if they had done so, they were the wrong forms anyway. Mefta was an out-of-work freelance journalist from Tunisia who had come to make contacts with the left-of-centre press and see friends at RTM, the government-run TV and radio company. He had fallen foul of Ben Ali's regime and, like so many Tunisian dissidents, had not been jailed, merely prevented from making a living. We talked about the strike which the professors had planned to hold in March to protest the isolation of intellectuals freed in an act of so-called clemency, when the current Tunisian president gained power. But the strike was quickly throttled without confrontation when Ben Ali declared the chosen day of protest a national holiday. As a foreign national I was in the position of being able to look at Tunisia with disinterested curiosity, but Mefta was less able to distance himself and more prone to blowing a fuse every time his government was mentioned. Seeing him slumped on a divan watching whatever flickering image happened to be on at the time, day after day, I often plopped down next to him to ask about progress, leads, and how the job quest was going. The answers were always negative and I felt that his heart and energy were miles away in Sfax and that, like so many refugees, he would live his new life at one remove from his surroundings, mourning the homeland he loved and despised in equal measure, obsessed and trapped.

The owners of the guest-house, a family-run concern, were failed northern entrepreneurs who had decided to approach their new business with knives drawn. Their locked office held all mod cons – an answerphone and telephone, tape recorder and duplicate keys to every room – but the receptionists were connected to an incoming-calls-only line and were monitored by random checks from dawn to dusk in case they made themselves a cup of tea or, crime of crimes, napped on duty. Given the fact that their shifts ran from 9:00 p.m. to midday, a cool fifteen hours, and then from midday till 9:00 p.m., it was obvious that the man on the night shift would have a great deal of free time and might, perhaps, be permitted to sleep on a divan once the building was locked and the central heating system turned off. Far from it. Every night I would hear one or the other of the brothers unlocking the heavy main door at 2:00, 3:00, or 4:00, however the fancy took them, to ensure that the receptionist on duty was vertical, awake and behind the desk. Cheapskates down to the last dirham, they stapled metallised wrapping paper to the reception desk and offered free leaflets produced by the National Tourist Board with ingratiating gestures, as if they were paid for out of their own pockets. An old, black, and badly bound visitors' book, hauled down from their last failed hotel, theoretically proved their great popularity on the coast, but the Rabat clientele was mutinous and would not be placated by gestures of appeasement, such as the materialization of vases of roses every Monday and the ever present efforts of servile bonhomie. The problem was a basic one, a matter of classification and prices. The board's tariff, a reasonable ninety-five dirhams a night for a double room, shot up to one hundred and fifty dirhams once supplements were added. According to the host's whims, the supplements were based on children, the floor occupied, bath or shower, the season and the view. It is, of course, quite illegal to charge for infants. The tariff specifies 'with facilities' and the view, such as it was, offered an old Renault garage yard or an alley overlooking a block of flats respectively. Since any complaints had to go in an official book and any mention of this book would result in luggage being slung down the staircase, everyone grumbled and no one rebelled, though I did manage to negotiate a tiny discount of twenty dirhams through charm and not confrontation, just for the hell of it. Battle lines were quickly drawn and a charged atmosphere prevailed in the lounge whenever the family walked through, surveying their domain and their thoroughly cheated but mute clients. Nevertheless, minor tensions were just that, minor tensions, and the convenience of the location kept me there. I managed to recoup some money too, since I was laughingly publicly promised a dirham for every cockroach I found. I made a point of handing over squashed corpses when the lounge was full, calmly pocketing the coins and smiling as if this were all just a sweet little game. Faced with an audience, the brothers duly handed over the lucre, fuming.

The greatest joy of Rabat is the way in which new and old blend together and, in the space of a morning, it is perfectly possible to start in elegant boulevard cafés selling yesterday's *Times*, and white, mouse-shaped, marzipan cakes with tiny chocolate eyes, and end up sitting on the edge of a tiled Merenid fountain, watching the water sellers (with whom Rabat is positively infested) pass out their shallow cups to the medina shoppers. Boulevard Hassan II sports couture quality shoe shops and modern bank buildings on one side, while a dash across the impossibly busy road brings one to the foot of the Almohad walls with their solid gates and the life of the bazaar within.

Walking across the gravel-strewn wasteland which lies opposite Bab el Had, where local buses pick up and drop passengers, I passed carts covered with chocolates and sweets to walk through an imposing gate into the Marché Central, an arcaded fruit and vegetable market with a fish and meat section next door. Prices were posted on blackboards and the goods were stacked in eye-catching displays: radishes and plums, seedless grapes and fat onions, thin avocados and huge bunches of bananas. A florist who sold enormous houseplants, presumably to the residents of Aguedal, the suburb favoured by embassy and expatriate staff, was arranging long-stemmed roses and rigid birds of paradise in narrow-necked green metal vases, heaps of background greenery and artificial and dry grasses standing by to make up bouquets. Opposite, a jolly mountain of basketwork stood twelve feet high: flat plates for kneading dough; pointed purple and blue covered baskets for storing bread; red, turquoise bangles; shopping baskets with string handles, wide tops and narrow bottoms; orange and lemon coasters and mats. I would have bought the lot if I could have, simply since it was all so cheerful and fresh looking, and had to force myself to look the other way to resist temptation each time I passed. The short alley north of the fruit market sold agriculture hardware, rusty chains, hobbles and dog leads at the far end, before switching radically to toys and baby clothes, giant party balloons and tinsel windmills and whistles. Rabat medina was totally hassle-free and wandering with the tide through the orderly wide streets, it was a welcome relief to be able to handle objects, even try them on, without feeling any sense of embarking on a life and death struggle over prices. Naturally enough, I spent more, too much, in this atmosphere, where the beckoning finger invited but did not insist. The main thoroughfare, Rue Souiga, had the usual ghastly display of severed heads, rams this time, the more repellent for being lined up by the dozen, noses pointing upwards, teeth bared in a death grimace, looking at nothing.

I bought an expanding hairnet, a triangular blue affair with tiny pearls attached by invisible stitches, all the rage, particularly the black and red sequined variety which would not complement Anglo-Saxon hair or complexions. There was no sense of being enclosed in this medina. Little music assaulted the ears, and the random nature of the arrangement, no grouping by trades here, meant that my eyes darted unconstrained from shop to shop. I lusted after elegant hide sandals with thin multi-coloured straps and medium heels, reached out to investigate brass lamps with glass insets. A few hidden junk shops selling kif pipes and mass-produced jewellery which did not pretend to be anything but tin, made it clear that Rabat doesn't draw souvenir hunters in anywhere near the same numbers as its imperial cousins.

Rabat caters for richer punters and, as one passes through the kissaria and reaches the eastern end of the medina, the elegant Rue des Consuls (so called because foreign consuls were once obliged to live here just as Jews were obliged to live in the mellah) stretches out a languorous arm. Past the fabric sellers, suddenly the antiques appear and then overwhelm all other products. Antique carpets and kilims hang on dark walls, discreetly illuminated by stunning brass standing lamps. The sellers are older here; the quality of the merchandise surprisingly good, particularly the Rabat carpets and the old wooden chests and jewellery boxes. Heavy gold and silver cloak fasteners, bracelets, Koran holders and necklaces crowded the chic windows and there was not even the slightest whiff of uncured leather on the air. This area is gold credit card holder territory only, but it does make one idly consider turning to piracy, twentieth-century style.

Tucked as it is between the new town and the coast, the medina's walls open out into a horrendously busy coastal road, Tarik al Marsa, across which towers the Kasbah of the Oudaias, with its richly-documented and lauded twelfth-century Almohad gate, the entranceway to the Andalusian town built by the refugees from Spain. Its beauty is simple, massive and beyond description. It dominates the skyline and is utterly impervious. A group of guides lounging on the steps nearby, half looking for clients but basically concentrating on comparing skateboard base decorations, waved cheerfully as I skipped past. The kasbah mosque is apparently the oldest in Rabat and blends in well with the narrow winding passages of what is essentially a nostalgic copy of a Spanish village. The human proportions of the kasbah were relaxing. It was all too easy to forget that the Sallée Rovers' prosperity was based on human flesh. Human flesh of a different variety was crowding the popular Café Maure which overlooks the estuary and is situated in the exquisite Andalusian gardens which surround the Oudaia Museum. A tall group of bronzed Italian women of a certain age and their cliché suave guides were taking up every seat as three waiters dodged legs and delivered trays of tea and pastries. Low-cut tops revealed lumps of Mexican turquoise, expensive snakeskin belts and bags abounded, cinching in minute waists and cluttering up the already small tables. The noise was phenomenal: a flock of budgerigars trilled in full throat as teas were sipped, almond and honey chewed and then picked out from between teeth. The guide stood up and seconds later the world reverted to normal. Those of us who had been lurking on the periphery, frozen in our tracks, thawed and cautiously moved to the tiled benches with their grass mat seat covers and roofs, took places and looked out over the estuary to Salé and the ever popular beach.

The Andalusian garden, a French creation despite its name, is simply too small, neat and fastidiously laid out to accommodate groups of this size. Its tiny mosaic paths, low stone benches and symmetrically planted flower beds, a mass of purple, pink and white, call for slippered feet and pensive, solitary strolling. The multi-tiered prettiness of the flower arrangements, the red, blue and gold cedar doors, petite fountains and structured calm and order of the spot complement Moulay Ishmael's seventeenth-century palace, now a museum housing pottery, costumes and weaponry.

After an afternoon spent wandering through the serene self-sufficient world of ancient Rabat, it was difficult to step out of the kasbah and face twentieth-century images again. Reentering the medina through the Bab el Mellah, the former Jewish quarter unfolded and, with it all the naked poverty signalled by the goods for sale: piles of old magazines, screws, jug cords, plugs, washers and plastic bowls. The lanes were quieter here, no one appeared to expect to make a sale, for the mellah is a backwater, and there is none of the compulsive, anxious panic of the central medina. Men were sleeping in doorways here, their heads covered with sheets of newspaper, mute old women held out their hands, and a young girl with four toddlers smiled and added her arm to the bristling forest of demands.

Foolishly, I squatted down beside her with a view to taking a photograph but a heavy hand, shoving me from behind, put me right. Accusations of racism assailed me and I recalled the Moslem belief that to take a picture of somebody is to steal a part of their soul. The medina seemed a threatening spot now and every face I saw appeared hostile. I suspected that stronger than their beliefs and certainly stronger than their concern for the woman was their objection to the fact that I was photographing a scene which, theoretically, does not exist: a Moroccan who cannot feed herself. Thus I was somehow denigrating the Moroccans in the street, in Rabat, throughout the country itself. Maybe Mr Renault 25 was right: visitors were only permitted to immortalise historic buildings, the stuff of ancient splendour and modern admiration rather than express any implicit or explicit criticism on the gulf that exists between rich and poor in Morocco and, by extension, the gulf between the developed world and the Third.

When an international report came out the following week

stating that three and a half million Moroccans now live below the official poverty line as defined by calorie intake and income, the press frothed at the mouth for two full days. Leader columns and banner headlines refuted statistics and methodology alike, screaming in outrage that income bears no relation to the amount of food bought and eaten, since mutual help is basic to Islamic society, families band together and no one, but no one, starves, ever, anywhere in Morocco. In Morocco, discretion certainly seems to be the key to survival and it, in turn, positively encourages stealing images by wide angle and zoom lenses.

Shocked, confused, I limped away, my tail between my legs and was only mildly soothed by a splendid scene just inside the gate itself, whose deep arches sheltered pairs of high-backed benches which enthroned old men – sorcerers and typists. The sorcerers lay on their sides, wrapped in their djellabahs, paper and ink at the ready, waiting for clients whose horoscopes they would cast or whose fortunes they would tell by means of numerology. The typists are Rabat's version of the Scribes of Marrakesh, though rather than calligraphic skills they display ancient manual Olivettis on which they knock out forms and personal letters. The typists were doing a brisk trade that day and the vigorous hammering of keys startled the starlings roosting in the brickwork, forcing them to fly around in crazed loops waiting for the amplified staccato tapping to abate.

Night was falling and Rabat's streets spilled out businessmen, secretaries, clerks and bank and insurance workers. Cars jostled with the plentiful buses, heading home, and the cafés and arcades switched on their lights, ready for the influx of diners. The medina was full of late-night shoppers, and cauldrons of mussel soup were being spooned out to eager customers on Boulevard Hassan II. The karate clubs down the side street opposite the central Balima Hotel were opening their doors to the desk-bound, keep-fit set and the two main cinemas already boasted queues which stretched hundreds of metres. *Fatal Attraction* and *Bad* were both drawing large audiences who waited patiently, holding onto raspberry ice-cream cones or cracking pistachios between their back teeth. The streets hummed.

There seemed to be a large number of European residents, judging by the specialist shops with their displays of imported Néscafe, Danish blue cheese, Knorr soups and Robinson's jam, as well as the huge selection of foreign magazines, ranging from professional photography to soft core porn, available at the kiosks. There were fewer replica designer T-shirts to be seen and more of the real thing, and babies were wheeled past in smart buggies and not dragged along by the hand. The affluence of the new town made the few Berber women who ventured down its broad, illuminated streets seem out of place, country bumpkins who should return to the bled or, failing that, the medina's back streets. The halt and the lame who braved immaculately tiled ice-cream parlours or café terraces were shooed away, and I sensed a rigid demarcation line here which was not so visible in other Moroccan towns. Perhaps my interpretation of Rabat's reaction to the beggar woman was right, after all, and this heavily policed, clean capital prides itself on sweeping the debris under the carpet.

The babies had spotted some lime green Kickers, a make of shoe I believed to have been long extinct. Kickers have resurrected themselves and are being made in Morocco. The prices reflected this fact. These colourful, well-made children's sandals cost barely eleven pounds. Emerging with two boxes from Derby, the shoe shop found in every new town in Morocco, I looked straight into the eyes of Colonel Muammar Gaddafi who was walking past, loosely surrounded by four men in blue. 'Good evening, Colonel,' I stammered automatically before the import of what I had just seen hit home. My God, Gaddafi must be confident of his popularity with the Moroccans to walk around Rabat without any protection. And popular he is indeed, for people on the pavements noticed him and started to run towards him. Within seconds I was swept up in an enthusiastic sea of admirers. The women were ululating, the men were roaring his name and indecipherable slogans, returning to the chant 'Gaddafi, Gaddafi'. In response, the Colonel lifted his arms in greeting but did not speed up his leisurely pace. Gaddafi was wearing Western clothes, a dark navy suit, a light shirt and maroon tie. Seen close to, his skin was deeply lined and his expression mask-like. As far as I could make out, he did not blink but smiled out of the corners of his mouth and looked straight ahead. The man had charisma and arrogance: he was being crushed by the throng but somehow remained aloof from us all. He certainly does not invite bonhomie, back slapping or physical contact, and although I was a mere twelve inches or so away from him, when he looked at me, his eyes were blank and prohibited any attempts at questions. All I could do was to bellow his name along with the rest as the walk turned into a trot, and then a half run, newcomers and stragglers pushing up the tempo as they tried to get near the Colonel.

By now, even if I had wanted to leave his side I couldn't, as the pressure of the crowd had brought us to a standstill. Gaddafi turned once more to raise his arms and one fist; the euphoria was almost concrete. Everyone was smiling, hissing and whispering 'It's Gaddafi', almost as if they couldn't believe it themselves. As we all stood there, I suddenly realised that the crush and temporary lull had allowed the groping crowd a field day. Fingers and hands were casually travelling over every inch of my thighs and bottom, and there was no way of knowing who was responsible. I jammed myself round and threatened to slap the middle-aged man behind me, who denied any culpability with injured fury. The discussion was cut short by the arrival of two black Mercedes, which inched through to Gaddafi. Doors slammed and with a final hail to the people, hail to the chief, Muammar Gaddafi drove off. The crowd milled around for a while, gossiping, smiling and shaking hands. Instant friendship. The sexual harasser sought me out and reiterated that he did not, emphatically not, molest women and, in the rapturous atmosphere, all was forgiven. We exchanged a kiss on both cheeks and a handshake. People were reluctant to drift away, to break the spell and, as I returned to the guest-house, I felt ridiculously high.

I can't think of many world leaders who would take the air, secure in the knowledge that they are beloved of the common man, if not the government, in a foreign country which is theoretically hostile towards them. A populist in theory and obviously in practice too, Gaddafi is a controversial figure in the Arab world as well as in the West, but here he is accused not of insanity or murder but of apostasy (which makes him a non-Moslem), or deviation from Islam, a charge precipitated by the publication of the *Green Book* with its Third Universal Theory. The scenes of book burning filmed in Tripoli, Libya's high military profile and Gaddafi's open sponsorship of various subversive groups do not precipitate the same shrill cries of outrage in countries where censorship is a fact of life, along with compulsory military conscription, and members of subversive groups end up hanging off meat hooks, while dissidents often simply disappear in the classical Latin American fashion. In the eyes of the Maghreb, Gaddafi is restoring Arab pride, a trait they believe he shares with that other twentieth-century Robin Hood, Saddam Hussein.

◆

Another far less controversial saint. Mohammed V. is buried in Rabat in a mausoleum which adjoins the Hassan Tower, all that remains of the great Almohad Mosque of El Hassan. Built by Ahmed el Mansour, the mosque was supposed to be large enough to enable the ruler's whole army to pray together. Work stopped on the day of Ahmed el Mansour's death and the earthquake of 1755 finally destroyed what had quietly and stealthily turned into an overgrown ruin. The Hassan Tower is a warming, friendly landmark, and identified with Rabat in the same way that the Koutoubia virtually means Marrakesh, and Bab Mansour is associated with Meknès, Bab Boujeloud with Fez. Since it stands atop a hill, perched above the river, it often ambushes the unwary as it looms around the corner almost glaring across at the now depressed suburb of Salé, once its great rival.

It would have been difficult to devise more contrasting styles of architecture than the tower and the mausoleum even if the builders had expressly set out to do so. The mausoleum is excessively richly decorated, reminiscent of Les Invalides, with its acres of Italian marble, twenty-two carat gold carved ceilings, tiles, mosaics from Fez and a bronze chandelier which weighs a ton, designed by a Vietnamese artist – for apparently Mohammed V had Vietnamese friends. It's the last word in opulence and pomp, from its traditionally garbed guards to the wide imposing staircase by which one mounts to the entrance. I went to see it just as it was closing and stood there with two other women in a flat silence just as the call to prayer rang out, looking over the marble balustrade at the white onyx tomb of the king and his son Moulay Abdullah which appears to float on a block of black marble. The devotion and love which has been lavished here by family and subjects alike over the years must be contagious, since leaning there under the vaulted roof I drifted into a trance-like state of contemplation and remi-niscence which had distinct overtones of melancholy – a mood which was shattered by the guard's gentle reminder that it was time to leave and contributions were always welcome. Much of this reaction was doubtlessly brought on by the fact that the mausoleum was vast and deserted. I subsequently passed it on numerous occasions and noticed coachloads of out-of-towners picking their way up the staircases. I doubt whether the interior would have evoked the same lonely wistfulness in me in these circumstances.

Another spot which exerts a strange fascination is the Chellah, the ancient Merenid and pre-Merenid burial grounds, located just outside the city walls. The quickest way to reach this semi-wild spot is to walk through the Mechouar, the current royal palace and administrative complex. The police are always highly visible here for obvious reasons, guarding the royal apartments, the offices of State and all the subsidiary annexes, paddocks, schools and offices, but appear to be very proud of their work and gladly explain the function of each building, their walkie-talkies crackling on their belts. The grass here is so green it must be permanently watered and the upright busy lizzies, whose stems collapse after the slightest drought, confirm this. Various individuals in spotless gandoras busily criss-cross the paths and national security personnel whiz about on mopeds or jeeps. It's a splendid and impressively kept area with its spacious roads, a pretty mosque which the king occasionally attends for Friday prayers in his capacity as religious leader, arriving outside astride a white horse.

The Chellah, the site of the Venetian, Roman, Berber and Arab port of Sallah, and home of the Berghouata heretics, is seemingly totally untended, although spluttering, twisting old hoses lie in ditches and gardeners doze and smoke among the overgrown fig and banana plants. Coming through an almost Gothic ornamental gate which has lost all its tiles but none of its presence. I stood above a series of crumbling terraces and surveyed a lush profusion of creepers, climbers, lilies and trees. Sitting on the top step, legs dangling over a broken wall, I looked out at a ruined Merenid mosque and zaouia thrusting up through the palm, bamboo and Pampas grass below, the mosque's minaret balancing a series of untidy storks' nests. It was peaceful here and the Merenid rulers slumbered alongside a young man curled up on a wall covered in hibiscus flowers. The occasional flapping stork stirred the air and the droppings and feathers on the saints' tombs, hidden among the abundant trees and bushes, testified to the fact that the Chellah has become something of an unofficial bird sanctuary. The usual graffiti abounds here but seems irrelevant, and the tombs of the black sultan and his slave concubine, Morning Star, crumble away peacefully in the heat, down in the ruined burial chambers of the mosque, protected by the djinn Abou Youssef Yacoub left here to guard his buried treasure. Picking my way over the blocks of stone and through the unstable arches, it was not easy to imagine this sun-bleached corner ever being anything other than what I now saw.

The gossip of the zaouia students, Koranic chanting, prayers – all these activities seemed too positive, likely to disturb the dead of centuries past, for the Chellah was an ancient burial site before being enclosed by the Merenids. It is almost compulsory to visit the ruins of the Roman hammam, now a sacred pool, in Chellah, for it is here that infertile women gather to feed hard-boiled eggs to the eels which slither about in the water. The eels were much smaller and thinner than I imagined, a mere eighteen inches to two feet long, with transparent gills, and seemed cute rather than phallic. Hopeful cats perched on the brick wall nearby, occasionally rubbing up against the guardian who had succumbed to the spell and was napping, his turbaned head wrapped up against the midday sun. Down in the water a ten-year-old boy was wading carefully out into the middle of the pool to collect the morning's offering of coins, avoiding the milling eels. I dropped a coin in the guardian's saucer and wandered off to look at the whitewashed koubbas nearby, and what remains of the mosque, the courtyard and mihrab, the prayer hall. Guards dressed in navy jackets leaning on spades were guarding nothing in particular. It required an effort of will to move at all, to leave, in short to do anything more energetic than relax in the heat, surveying the unbelievable, almost threatening vegetation with its blooms, spears and plumes all around. The Chellah was deserted as I walked up past the flocks of birds, the dripping hoses, aware of a need to eat immediately. The scarcity of city taxis in Rabat is scandalous and everyone has to plump for sharing, but I was at last dropped back on Mohammed V, after taking one woman to l'Ocean and another to the far reaches of Salé. The driver meticulously deducted their contributions from the meter and refused a tip. What a change from Casablanca.

The Balima Hotel had the usual raucous crowd of Hooray Henrys drinking on the terrace, nibbling hot almonds from paper cones and dropping coins into the hands of the itinerant black dwarf whose strong featured, bitter face almost commanded money. Inside, the limp lettuce, rancid grated carrot and bruised tomatoes of the salad they served me killed my appetite, but the central fast food shops were no alternative since foreigners are encouraged to go upstairs to dine in Lyons-style splendour rather than sit at the self-service counter downstairs. A young boy called Rasheed asked if he could join me and spilled out a tale of woe concerning the wonderful Italian friends he had made, how they came from Turin, spent all their time with him but somehow left without giving him their address. He was obviously distressed by the betrayal, an all too common story, and I pattered reassuring explanations or a series of excuses, cursing the Italians inwardly for their indifference, their inability to understand Rasheed's world. A poxy postcard from abroad would have meant a great deal to him.

My awareness of the frequent cross purposes and running estrangement between Europe and the Maghreb was further sharpened when I picked up a discarded copy of *L'Opinion*. The paper was full of inconsequential bits and bobs: photos of an exemplary villager painting the outside of his grocery store and a reminder that summer means repairs; letters from Tangier complaining there is nothing for the citizens to do; a report on the neglect in Taourirt and car accident black spots; another fanning-the-flames article reminding Moroccans of the anniversary of the massacre of the martyrs of Oued Zem, whose pet dogs and rabbits also had their throats cut by the French. *L'Opinion* is not given to this type of article on a daily basis and had been campaigning for government recognition of the fact that there was a cholera outbreak in Meknès – and not widespread gastroenteritis as the Health Ministry would have had us believe. In the month before my visit two hundred people were taken into hospital, and the admissions were currently running at five a day. Twenty-nine people died in one weekend alone. The government was being accused of a cover-up and the argument was still raging. Meanwhile, foreigners were being urged to get jabs by their own health departments and the Meknèssi seemed in no doubt as to what was walking amongst them. I worried about stopping in Meknès as cholera can kill unless treated immediately via rehydration therapy, and anyone who contracts it loses thirty per cent of their body weight through vomiting and diarrhoea. Injections are only twenty-five per cent effective, if that.

Cholera seemed unlikely there in central Rabat with its businessmen, health clubs, banks with marble columns and multi-coloured high tech rainbows, toy shops crammed with Fisher Price Puffalump copies, rocking elephants, Lego and crocodile lilos. Yet the human casualties of urban living abounded. A man, naked except for navy and white Y-fronts, was led away by three policemen to the amazement and consternation of all, and as I crossed opposite the post office to pick up my forty-minute development film (ready in two hours) a young, excitable man wove in and out of the traffic, twisting in a circle and waving his arms frantically. Everyone avoided him and I wondered if he was having a seizure and went up to see what he wanted. The traffic, always heavy, was at a standstill, yet no one else wanted to become involved. The man yelled to me that he was drowning in his own blood, self-evidently untrue, since an unspecified 'they' had cut his throat and he was 'dying, dying'. 'They have cut my neck, look at the blood,' he cried.

Acting on impulse, I forcibly told him that my rings, silver knuckledusters of the type favoured by Mr T., had immense healing power and rubbed a fistful round his neck.

'Has it worked?' he asked.

'Yes,' I answered solemnly. 'Yes, it has.' A ludicrous dialogue ensued as he assured me that the pain was leaving and I, in turn, gravely monitored and reported on the stemming of the flow of blood. Pacified and half dazed, he walked off and, for my pains, I was accosted by a grey-suited Frenchman who lectured me on the inadvisability of having anything to do with fools, not only on principle but also because there are so many in Rabat that doing so could end up becoming a full-time occupation. He tutted in exasperation at my stupidity. I nodded, agreed, nodded again but felt chuffed and exhilarated by the success of my anti-Dracula manoeuvre. A new career perchance? Moroccans seem to tolerate the numerous schizophrenics with their open flies, their vociferous delusions, and the legless who crawl along, their torsos supported on skateboards, so why should they discriminate against the poor?

All was calmer down by the shores of the Bou Regreg, where men were washing wool in the river and drying it on the shore.

PART ONE

A small tide of passengers flowed down the hill from the main road to catch the rowing boats, one dirham per passenger, which cross to and from Salé laboriously and slowly. Salé is being lauded as the real Morocco these days and Rabat condemned for its fast-paced affluence, but such statements are not only worthless but suspect. Rabat may have an embassy row with faded sentry boxes outside, mock Mediterranean and '50s villas, advertise Daniel Hechter bargains and low finance deals on Fiat cars, all emblems of the twentieth century, but I also bumped into cows being led by the ear ahead of a wooden cart holding a wedding party, en route to slaughter before the traditional feast at the bride's house. Similarly, the suburbs of Rabat are simply poor, and twenty minutes travelling on a Number five bus took me to municipal housing estates and bidonvilles which are homes to the unemployed, to the hopeless and forgotten Rabatis. I can't see any reason why Salé, with its deserted, dingy streets, partially successful attempts at municipal planning and general air of dereliction (bloated Alsatian rotting away, on the beach, abandoned metal pipes, barbed wire, bare ground) should gain kudos and authenticity due to this very neglect. Salé does have some exquisite architectural offerings, but common sense should prevail over sentimentality, and the European travel writer's insistence that the picturesque (for which read backward, or dead) is superior to the modern (for which read progressive, and efficient) should be scotched. Work gravitates to developed centres like Rabat rather than Salé's narrow streets, finger cymbal and gimbri-playing Gnaoui musicians notwithstanding.

It was an overcast day with heavy cloud banks and a choppy, unpredictable sea when I caught the Number One bus, Golfe, to the Royal Dar Essalem golf-course, one of the top fifty courses in the world and, presumably, where the other half plays. Tony had been on the course since 7:00 a.m. and Michelle and the babies were preparing for a day on the beach. To date, they had still not managed to find a path down to the water which did not involve scaling a four-foot wall below the Kasbah and trespassing through the Moslem cemetery. They intended to paddle and count the crabs, which pop out of the hard-packed sand at low tide and, as I slipped out of the guest-house, all three were busily applying thick layers of suncream to random parts of the others' bodies. The bus station was jammed with nut and water sellers, the latter calling out 'Water is God's gift' as they passed out mouthfuls in their shallow cups. One of the water sellers was dressed in green, the Prophet's colour; the rest favoured red, as did the smartly dressed ticket sellers, whose red hats and skirts, clipping machines and air of efficiency made them stand out in the milling crowds. The Number One Golfe is not a popular line and, as we left central Rabat, it was easy to see why. The bus passed through the expat and embassy belt, whose residents all presumably drive their own cars. By the time we reached the terminus I was quite alone and slightly nervous and, as the bus pulled away and I approached the gatemen, the only pedestrian visitor this joint had seen in months, if not years, I was inwardly prepared for a polite 'Sorry, we're closed'. The man on duty charged me twenty-five dirhams to look around, and pointed up a broad two-lane avenue fringed with conifers, rhododendrons and dahlias. He failed to mention that it was a twenty-five minute walk up to the clubhouse and I trudged along, melting in the muggy heat, for what seemed like miles, past lawns you could use to advertise *Home and Garden*, shrubbery which sheltered groups of workmen, and one immaculate flowerbed after another.

The interminable slog was eventually rewarded by the sight of a large parking lot which at first seemed a BMW forecourt, a notion dispelled when I noticed half a dozen top of the range Renaults. I hadn't passed a soul as yet, and the parking lot was deserted as well. Perhaps the king was playing and the course had been cleared for security purposes. But no, the clubhouse hummed with life as I entered, glad that I had chosen a reasonably uncrumpled silk suit for the jaunt, wondering if my hard-wearing but indisputably grease-stained Tunisian handbag had been spotted and already earned me a black mark. The staff at the desk were charm personified, however, and urged me to feel free, to look, to wander, to have a drink at the bar, watch TV in the lounge, whatever. The first thing I noticed there, apart from the beauty of the landscaping and the meticulous upkeep, was the absence of Moroccans – Moroccan golfers that is, rather than Moroccan workers, dozens of whom were out on the course and running in and out of the restaurant. Twenty or so caddies squatted in the shade of the clothes shop waiting to be hired. Deep carpets and pristine, well-stocked marble toilets were evidence of a brigade, if not a division, of cleaners in action behind the scenes, and the heavily glassed building was obviously a nightmare to keep free of fingermarks and sparkling. Inside the oblong bar several middle-aged French women were curled up in soft armchairs watching a large colour TV, complaining and chain-smoking. Their husbands were obviously away on the greens. The bar food was simple and French inspired – Croque Madame, Salade Nicoise, Tart aux Pommes, Croque Monsieur, Omelette aux Fines Herbes – and it did not take a leap of insight to realise that the Dar Essalem was the French equivalent of the British colonial clubs of India and Kenya's Happy Valley.

Leather-jacketed Libyans had gathered at one of the small glass-topped tables and were eating melons with all the confidence born of a GNP which surpasses that of every Arab nation outside the oil rich Gulf. The Libyans are gregarious and are keen to enjoy themselves when outside their politically correct homeland. Bored European teenagers called out to one another on the sun terrace and ordered beer and still more beer as the sun finally ripped through the clouds and started to bake everything in sight. There was an atmosphere of monied leisure here, and the portraits of the king prominently displayed in a variety of golfing poses, eight handicap, seemed to bless the players of his favourite sport, unlike grim-faced snaps of the monarch as soldier or hunter which were also doing the rounds. He seemed happy in these pictures and I remembered that over the course of the previous decade he had been adding golf-courses to every royal palace in the kingdom. Outside on the neat gravelled path, signs led to a clothes shop, the championship course, the practice range. The clothes shop was run by a man who slumped across the counter and could barely be bothered to return my greeting. The shirts and T-shirts on display were all printed with the course's emblem, a lion balancing a ball between his jaws, and were criminally over-priced but dashing rather than staid. I picked out one hundred and seventy-five dirham T-shirt in black with a white lion and a matching visor to stave off the dazzling sun before embarking on a swift look at the course which was, as expected, superb.

The thought of missing the bus was worrying me as I realised that it came only every hour or two and I had not checked the times. Perhaps someone would offer me a lift home? After all, I looked respectable enough and had obviously been seen in the clubhouse, since there could not have been more than thirty people there. An hour later, I had realised that respectable, female and white though I might be, I was doomed to squat beneath the pine trees watching elegant cars flying past, choking me with gravel and dust, reducing my suit to a rag. Everyone who left the club looked, but no one stopped. Irritation turned to anger and then resignation. If I could be made to feel like a third-class citizen, then what about the effect of French arrogance on the Moroccans? Finally, a staff minibus full of cleaners and groundsmen took pity on me and stopped. The down-trodden picked up the lightly-stepped-upon, and I bounced and fumed all the way back to the guest-house, partially reconciled to the press's anti-European campaign with its tales of the arms caches of 1952 and colonial muscle flexing.

The guest-house clock was chiming 'Home on the Range' as I marched in. Zachary was sitting by the round, badly inlaid coffee table opposite the reception desk, looking for company. Zachary was frantic because he had still not managed to secure his passport and he was due in Germany on 15 October to enrol in his engineering course. On top of this, he shamefacedly confessed that he had bribed the doorman fifty dirhams merely to get into the passport building, only to discover that since it was Friday everyone was off to midday prayers and the office he needed to visit was closed. Zachary came from Fez, and all this to-ing and fro-ing was costing him not only precious time, which he would otherwise have devoted to listening to his *Learn German in Three Months* tapes, but also money. He appeared punch drunk as he recounted the miseries of the day, but cheered up when he heard that I would be seeing Fez and immediately insisted that I stay with his family. I declined for two reasons. In the first place, I disliked his broad, smiling face, his grovelling, canine attitude and the way in which he explained the obvious such as 'Allah is God in your language,' as if imparting great wisdom. In the second place, I had set my heart on staying at the Hotel Amor, Rue de Pakistan, simply because it was such a ridiculous combination of name and address. The place might be a dive but it deserved a try.

Zachary was disappointed by my refusal but rallied immedi-ately as he launched into a spiel about Fez, the most splendid city in the world. I gave Zachary the benefit of the doubt at that juncture, but could not bear his countering any and every comment about my time in Morocco, and Rabat in particular, with the rejoinder: 'But in Fez ...' Listening to him, I was led to believe that Rabat and Fez were locked in mortal combat and Zachary was the cavalry personified. Ali, his older cousin, was glued to the pay-phone and muttering away while rhythmically kicking his already scuffed, bright yellow babouches against the wall. His voice rose and fell with the kicks, and a slammed receiver signalled the end of the conversation. He answered my unspoken query with a sigh and explained, cryptically, that Morocco was being ruined not only by drugs but also by the witchcraft practised by women who forced the evil men of their tribes and immediate families to the top. In Ali's eyes there could be no other explanation for the corruption of those in high places and the failure of good men (such as himself), to succeed. Apparently, he was waiting to hear whether or not he would be granted permission to take over a thirty-four kilometre stretch of Atlantic Coast, a camping site which was currently being badly mismanaged by a young Lebanese businessman. The problem was that the Lebanese had offered the minister in charge his daughter in return for securing the concession, and the minister, although presumably tired of the girl by now, was reluctant to break off the arrangement. Witchcraft and Panderus were mighty opponents indeed, and Ali was unlikely to get far on this one.

He and Zachary conferred and I wandered out into the night to buy water and relax. It was still warm although Rabat's ever-present breeze called for jacket, hot nuts and steaming coffee. The man in the local general shop seemed to be out at first glance, but was actually performing his evening prayers behind the counter, touching his brow to the ground in deference to Allah and His Messenger. I sat on the step amidst the empty crates and the plastic bottles, at peace with the world. Zachary and Ali might be stymied in their plans, the rich might have it too good, but God's purpose remained man's as well in other quarters. Submission to His will suddenly seemed not only a good thing in itself but likely to bring contentment too. Rachid, the day receptionist, came up and squatted on the steps, touching my shoulder in greeting and maintaining a respectful silence whilst the prayer ritual continued. I had grown fond of Rachid over the weeks in Rabat: this slim, feral-faced man with slightly bulging eyes and dark gums had a suppressed intensity and cagey manner which intrigued me. In our day-to-day dealings he had always been ironically deferential and, for reasons best known to himself, called me Maria, although the passport I surrendered into his care clearly stated that my name was Sylvia. Rachid's low voice made everything he said seem more important and confidential than it was in reality, since we were all obliged to strain to make out what he was saying and paid attention accordingly. On several occasions I caught him watching my hustling and bustling with quizzical amusement. His presence at the desk had somehow both embarassed me and deflated the exuberant mode I used for daily dealings, 'interviews', with everyone I managed to capture. We handed over our eighteen dirhams and six dirhams respectively for European and local cigarettes and hovered outside waiting for a break in the traffic.

'And so Maria,' he suddenly laughed, 'what do you want from me?'

'To talk,' I answered lamely and invited him for a drink.

As soon as we were seated (he angrily insisted on paying), he embarked on his tale unprompted. Rachid had recently been thrown out of university where he was studying economics, not because he had failed to work or deliver the requisite number of essays, but because economics was, for him, a subjective field, and since his own thesis conflicted with his tutor's expressed views, failure was inevitable. There was no bitterness in his tone as he explained this reality to me, merely a polite interest when I voiced outrage and muttered about impartiality, the benefits of a broad range of views. These were Western concepts and had no relevance in a State bent on preserving its status quo. Having been brought up a socialist, Rachid was an open opponent of the State and brought together a strange synthesis of Islam and Marxism in his views. He brushed aside my tentative questions about Arab/Berber divisions, a fiction created and exacerbated by the French Protectorate policy of promoting Berbers into the administration, a classic divide and rule tactic. He refused to accept regionalism as a problem either, arguing that the separateness of the Rif is a product of the fact that the Riffians fought the Spanish, while the rest of Morocco fought the French during the colonial period. In his eyes, Morocco is a nation-state seeking a new source of legitimacy. The old generation is slowly dying out and with it will die the blind allegiance to the throne, an allegiance born of memories of the battle for independence and the role of the last Alaouite, Mohammed V, in that battle. Nowadays, sixty per cent of young Moroccans are unemployed and gradually becoming capable of recognising and articulating their resentment. Soon no amount of Green Marches and reiterating of colonial hatred issues will suffice to distract them from comparing their lot with that of others and pushing for change out on the streets.

Rachid cited the Casablanca food riots as symptomatic of the turbulence brewing in the cities, if not the countryside, and reminded me that no photographs reached the world during that period; that Moroccan dissent, if reported at all, barely made a paragraph in the foreign press, let alone domestic newspapers. And of course, he added, the State apparatus should not be underestimated here or anywhere in the Maghreb. He told me of one Friday afternoon two years previously when he and a group of five friends from his neighbourhood were playing an impromptu game of soccer on a slab of wasteland near the main road. A police car drew up, and one boy, Ali, was taken away. He was never seen again, despite his family's enquiries at the commisariat.

'What had he done?' I asked.

Rachid hesitated. 'I really don't know. Perhaps he was over-heard saying something critical, making a joke about the king. Perhaps he was mixed up with someone else, or perhaps he was simply suspected of being "antisocial", of doing something anti-social. You can never know or even guess, and too many questions lead you yourself into the same kind of trouble. I expect he is either dead, blind, mutilated or insane by now. He was only twenty-two when they grabbed him.'

There was nothing I could say. I had no consoling words, wise theories or magic knuckledusters to offer. We all know the statistics, Amnesty International's reports on Morocco's human rights violations, the unchanging nature of human cruelty. Rachid did not expect ridiculous words of comfort nor did he want to dwell on the state of the country, taking it for granted that anyone who ventured off the main thoroughfares would need no convincing that being born Moroccan was the equiva-lent of drawing the short straw. He leaned towards me and lectured in his quiet, persuasive, almost hypnotic way, obviously repeating a sermon he had given before at party cell meetings. I felt paranoia stalking me and drew my metal-legged stool closer. To outsiders, we must have appeared desperate lovers rather than seditionaries as he continued explaining the party line in a near whisper.

According to Rachid, the revolutionary consciousness of the people must be combined with the 'correct' appreciation of the social, economic and political teachings of the Koran. Military coups and the rule of the imams were out since both were oligarchic rather than populist, in his sense of the term. Each citizen was charged with learning his or her rights and duties so they would know where to draw the line between the good of the self and the good of the body politic (echoes of Rousseau here). Only then could a collective consciousness push for the articulation of concrete demands for an end to economic inequality, the establishment of a moral society and a new guardian of the welfare of the nation. Hassan II was not such a guardian in Rachid's estimation, but rather a self-seeking corporate raider who preyed on the people and who could and should be removed on religious grounds rather than political ones. It was, he told me firmly, a mere matter of time, since a king who does not follow the Koranic precepts on good government was not a fitting spiritual leader, and religion must serve society as well as vice-versa.

I blanched when I picked these sentences out. Any criticism of the king, if overheard, would have us both clapped behind bars automatically, with no appeal possible. After the skirmishes of the last few weeks, I had a healthy fear of drawing the attention of the powers that be to myself and no faith in the relevance or pull of my British passport, with all its sweet exhortations to allow the bearer to pass without let or hindrance. I realised that Rachid was mumbling something about the cinema for some reason or other and I snapped out of my panic and tuned in again. He was saying that Morocco's lack of a cinema industry is proof that Moroccans are all aware of their current limited and repressed way of life and cannot find pleasure in seeing it writ large on the screen. The past had been hijacked by the government and was thus untouchable, and as for the future, any imaginative projection of what might be automatically ran foul of the censors, since it criticised the present by implication. As a result, Morocco was a favoured location for shooting exotic movies, nothing more, and a repository of those violent B movies which allowed the unemployed everywhere a bread and circuses escape from scraping by, waiting for another interminable boring day to end and selling individual cigarettes around the cafés. I listened and listened, interjecting the odd murmur of agreement, watching his thin frame tense and relax, his head sway towards and away from me, occasional smiles lighting up his plain features, transforming them in a time-honoured way. He was a persuasive speaker and I could easily imagine him organising away in his local meetings, painfully educating himself at home after fifteen hours of mind-numbing work, longing for change, looking over his shoulder, swinging between cynicism and exuberance. He excited my maternal instincts, but was obviously best accustomed to playing the male in all-female company, so I restrained my ludicrous impulse to stroke his intense face for fear of running into the usual rigid sexist misinterpretations of human contact.

I did ask him about his parents – he struck me as being unmothered – and heard that he had been living away from his family on and off since he was ten, but that I was welcome to come and stay at their home and see what life was like in a 'blue collar' area, well away from the glitz of central Rabat.

The next morning found me, Michelle and the babies on a bus heading for Rachid's home. Not knowing what to bring as a gift, we put together a spontaneous but random selection of objects: a black leather lead and collar for his dog, Laika; six long stemmed roses for his mother; milk chocolates; a cassette; and our much coveted, striped double buggy. The buggy was slowly disintegrating but as another six months were left in its frame, it seemed wasteful to cart it back home only to sling it away when so many women could appreciate and use it here.

Rachid was visibly amused by our offerings and probably surprised that we had actually come. He was waiting for us, nervously pacing up and down the pavement, and had put on a new blue cotton shirt in our honour. Hospitality aside, I hoped the family had not been cooking all day since I had left my appetite somewhere on the trail between Safi and Casablanca and it still hadn't caught up with me. I was living on water, bread and vanilla yoghurt and had lost over half a stone in the previous three weeks. I enquired who was home. Apparently, Rachid's father had gone fishing and his mother was shopping. I made the first gaffe of the day by enquiring how long his father had been out of work, a question which is never asked in a country where unemployment can mean destitution, and all mention of it is skirted around cautiously. Luckily, Rachid was hugely entertained by the novelty of such tactlessness, but reminded me not to repeat the query and, switching to a totally different topic, asked me not to reveal my Polish parentage on any account.

Before I could file these snippets away I had to concentrate on more pressing matters, namely pushing the babies through crumbling streets awash in uneven boulders. Winston & Kent covers perched on several of the larger rocks, marking out each individual seller's territory. The local market spread down one vegetable-strewn road, large mountains of spices piled up on plastic sheets, detritus lying inches deep next to shiny aubergines, peaches and wonderful new potatoes. The ladies' knickers here were a far cry from the cotton lace-trimmed minis of central Rabat and were knee-length white nylon affairs, lavishly finished off with rows of embroidery. They looked dismally scratchy and user-unfriendly. The second-hand clothes were even less promising and only the bright green plastic 'jellies' inspired admiration. The Berber women spoke no French but flocked to kiss the babies who had by now become quite used to the attention precipitated by their formerly blond, now white, hair. Caspian had only balked once, muttering 'God will punish you' (of all things) when a spectacularly draped and muffled bundle-with-lips sharply tugged a few hairs from his head in Essaouira. Groups of old men were playing cards and did not look up as we squeezed past; washing flapped from balconies and tiny kittens with sore, weepy eyes, played in the dust by a doorway. The paintwork here was neglected, the brickwork crumbling and two young welders lay on their backs under the chassis of a petit taxi, while their friends dragged large lengths of pipe across the impromptu garage forecourt, narrowly avoiding men slumped over giant mounds of fresh mint, half asleep in the heat. Rachid guided us past the activity to a row of houses opposite the mosque, a property which the late Mohammed V had erected for the urban poor. His rent was a pittance and apparently he had the right to inherit and sell the house. At one point, the owners of these narrow, three-storey homes dug small gardens outside, but the municipality flattened this effort at beautification, maintaining that the pavements, virtually archaeological sites as it is, had to remain clear.

Entering through a low doorway with half-tiled walls and steps, we walked up a narrow, steeply winding staircase. By the first turning, the orange, white and blue ceramics had turned into concrete and our shoulders were almost brushing the walls on either side. The first landing held three-legged pot stands crammed with cacti, but also marked the cut-off point for the wall tiling, which now reverted to whitewash. Finally, panting, the stairs ended at a lobby where three children were waiting to greet us with shy kisses and giggling. The lobby was clean but shabby, with its ornamental bellows, a cracked mirror on one wall and a Koranic tract opposite, while a low shelf held outside shoes and a miscellany of popular cleaning fluids. Rachid led us into his 'kingdom', a tiny room whose window overlooked the street. The mosque was a stone's throw away.

Almost on cue the Friday prayer began flooding into the room, bringing a gasp to my lips as the swell of voices muffled all the other noises, rising and falling, demanding attention, confirming allegiance to the one God, the life hereafter and paradise, the irrelevance of the struggle for economic survival unless it affected man's spiritual mettle. The mosque was packed and two little boys were perched up on the minaret looking out like sentinels awaiting the day of judgment. It was good to sit and listen to the perfect accord of men at prayer, and like most failed Roman Catholics who never quite manage to fill the gap left by moving away from the Church of childhood, my ever present and gnawing spiritual hunger, normally assuaged by doses of T.S. Eliot and Leonard Cohen, was temporarily appeased. Islam's tension between submission to God's will and the correct interpretation of that will prevents it from being a fatalistic religion, and yet there is an opiate element to all community life, community worship. Here and now I don't want to consider any of the arguments about Islam – the sexist, the aggressive, the dogmatic. All I know is that I would rather listen to prayer than analyse it as a social phenomenon; that it makes me feel uplifted.

Rachid is not a practising Moslem and appeared to worship the Madonna of the peroxide, not the rocks. Five pictures of the blonde bombshell were taped on his walls, while Annie Lennox and a ragged edged photo of a Harley Davidson adorned the door. Other Western influences were visible among the herbalist encyclopedias, hardbacks on military history and dictionaries which were piled up on the black and russet tiled floor: Dire Straits and Peter Gabriel tapes. All were Moroccan bootlegs, an excellent buy at twenty dirhams, as long as the cassette doesn't stretch and you don't mind an abrupt ending and beginning. The apartment was dauntingly clean. Clear whitewashed walls met a turquoise and yellow ceiling, and a globe light splattered in yellow paint testified that the turquoise had got there first. An unvarnished, hexagonal plywood table stood next to a heap of mattresses covered with grey blankets, and two or three velvet pillows lay on the floor nearby. An old multi-coloured glass partition had been smashed at some point in the past and the hole was partially blocked by a framed rectangular picture: a Koranic quote in multi-coloured metal lettering set against a black background.

I could hear frenzied barking somewhere upstairs and the babies' excited yelps and screams. The famous Laika, the only pet dog we'd met so far who didn't guard property or sleep on the streets, was obviously in residence. I asked to see her and climbed up past another small room with a cracked wooden door onto a roof terrace. Up above me, perched on the roof of the toilet and tied with a piece of wire to a low railing sat a fox-faced orange dog who was slobbering with excitement at all the sudden attention. A nipping, squirming bitch with a shallow cut on her neck from the improvised wire collar which held her in place, Laika slept on the roof when she wasn't being lured to play on the streets by the children who called her name. Rachid removed the wire and fitted the dog with her new leather collar, and Laika shot down the stairs barking with joy at this change of routine. The babies, who missed our own dogs, raced after her and, peering down a minute or so later, I watched them joining the local toddlers, in a game of chase, Laika zipping noisily between them all and biting the nearest arm, leg or bottom.

Rachid prepared tea in the roof-top kitchen, pushing past a washing line bowed down with cotton dresses and nylon nighties. The gas stove ran off a cylinder and worked erratically; the giant aluminium pans were spotless; the shelves held a collection of unmatching plates, cups and saucers. Tea was taken in the sitting room, and it was here that the display cases with their tea sets and glasses and dinner sets resided amongst a plethora of souvenirs, thin brass plates, the requisite wooden hand of Fatima with the eye in the palm and a sombre felt figure of Bambi. Rush mats lay before low divans, and a huge black and white television was the undisputed focus of the room. Almond fingers sprinkled with nuts were carted in by his twelve-year-old sister, who ducked out of the room as soon as she had put the sweets down, returning to her rag and washing down the stairs. The intimacy of the domestic setting, the raucous presence of the babies, turned my thoughts away from various stale conversations on the state of nature and visions of society and towards more personal topics. Rachid was twenty-eight and unmarried, and yet the house was large enough for him to introduce a wife and he was earning enough, just, to support a family. More to the point, he must have broached the subject with his family by now, and have some views on when he was going to choose a partner, or have one chosen for him. This seemingly innocuous line of enquiry was another unfortunate choice of chit-chat material since Rachid was, predictably enough, had I thought about it, totally opposed to being trapped by the dowry and bride price system. Given his belief that all men and women are equal in nature, he refused to pay the going rate of two thousand dirhams down, the rest later, to the family of a woman for the pleasure of sleeping with her.

Traditional weddings are still the norm rather than the exception in Morocco, and these are impressive and expensive affairs. A man must observe a code which establishes precisely what gifts he must give his fiancée upon betrothal and on specific religious holidays. In addition, he is responsible for the purchase of furniture and the construction or rental of housing. The wife supplies kitchen equipment, bed linens, curtains etc. In Rabat, where an apartment costs between twelve and fifteen hundred dirhams per month plus bills, an engagement is prohibitive, and not to be embarked on lightly, since a woman can divorce a man for failing to keep her fed, lodged and adequately clothed. The jewellery a bride receives on betrothal must be made of gold and comprises rings, bracelets, necklaces and earrings. In addition, she receives two sets of underclothes and two complete outfits, make-up, perfume and all the classic trinkets which comprise the trappings of a 'feminine' woman. The outstanding balance of the dowry can't be forgotten either and is paid off in installments. Luckily for the man, if the couple divorce, an agreed upon percentage is returned to the man's family. Marriage is serious business and astrologers and herbalists do a brisk trade in love potions and infusions (which are supposed to restore the woman's hymen on her wedding night by making her bleed whether or not she is a virgin) and the drawing up of personal charts. Of course, if you want to be doubly sure of restoring virginity, then any number of clinics in Casablanca specialise in replacing hymens as a side-line to the transsexual operations which brought them notoriety a decade ago. Virginity is crucial to finding a husband. Men, of course, get their sexual experience from prostitutes and, needless to say, from us, the European tourists, and are expected to spread their wild oats discreetly. Couples who attempt to book into hotels and cannot produce a marriage certificate have to take separate single rooms (unless they're foreigners) and courtship is still a regulated rather than a casual affair. The usual double standards, in fact, for while Rachid would prevent his sisters from going out unescorted with unknown men, he gaily declared, 'There is so much milk available, why should I buy a cow?' I found this a strikingly offensive statement and my face must have showed my reaction since he was quick to recant and qualify as I glowered at him from across the room.

The Koran teaches that when a man and woman are alone in a room, a third person is also present – none other than the devil. Moslem men fear women's sexuality, believing women, multi-orgasmic, have no capacity for sexual self-restraint, which is why they need to be protected from their own appetites by their male relatives. Men also fear women's menstruation, their powers to bewitch, and cast spells and curses, powers particularly strong during the monthly bleeding. Intercourse is forbidden when a woman is menstruating and men believe that their genitals and internal organs can be weakened and attacked by the blood. And this is not all, for every type of female bodily fluid is suspect, and frenzied ritual cleaning rather than a cigarette, a kiss or a relaxed conversation follows passionate sex in the Arab world. I remember buying tampons in a supermarket one day while I was shopping with Ridah, an old friend married to an Australian and thus presumably more in tune with Western views than the average Moslem male. To my horror,

Ridah stopped at a pharmacy soon afterwards and bought a brown bottle of viscous muck, a tonic which he preceded to drink in large gulps as we walked along to protect himself from my blood – which, I hasten to add, was hardly spurting out and on the attack.

It is rare to see teenagers out in pairs outside the large cities. It is rarer still to spot an embrace, tentative hand-holding or public kissing in the country, and yet sexual desires need outlets, here in Morocco as elsewhere. So what the hell do they do, I asked Rachid. Oral sex, he promptly and coldly answered, or early marriage he added, since both in their own ways allow a woman to display the blood-stained sheet expected on her wedding night. I felt embarrassed by this point in the conversation, caught myself listening out for distractions with half an ear. Dogs and children, anything would do. I felt I shouldn't be asking these questions of a man, that I'd bulldozed through taboos, the parameters of male/female interaction, and that Rachid certainly wouldn't have broached these topics with other women, such as his mother or sisters. The mere idea was ludicrous, for to do so would be offensive to them as women. I was out on a limb. Only the fact that I was a Westerner assured me the benefit of the doubt and protection from accusations of immorality.

Perhaps Rachid sensed my discomfort and my misgivings since he started to talk to me about homosexuality, thus putting me at ease again by removing the spotlight from women and, by implication, the fact that I had been so unwomanly and forthright. Out of the blue, he confided that he had once sold his body for one hundred dirhams and two packets of Marlboros. The two packets of Marlboros intrigued me. Why two? Why not one or three or even a carton? I shall never know. Apparently, when he was taking a hoteliers' course, his first stint of work experience was as a member of a room service team in a well-known upmarket American hotel. Fifteen, ambitious and unsure of himself, Rachid found himself being delegated to serve breakfast to a Norwegian businessman every morning. and every morning the Norwegian would sprawl out naked, watching Rachid open the curtains and position the tray. Eventually, predictably enough, he pounced, grasping the young boy to his chest and complementing Rachid on his beautiful eyes, unaware of the fact that the liquid gaze and stunning pupils were drug-induced rather than a gift of nature. For it was Rachid's wont to smoke two joints to calm himself before starting work. The affair lasted the week the Norwegian spent in Morocco.

Every day, he would place one hundred dirhams and the famous Marlboro packets on the bedside table. Every day, Rachid would signal acceptance of the offer by pocketing both items. Asked how he felt, Rachid said he considered the question stupid. Obviously enough, he had felt nothing. He qualified the statement – nothing but contempt for the man kneeling at his feet, vulnerable, and disgust at the quivering white, middle-aged flesh. I was interested by his reference to white flesh, and wondered if he would have felt so sanguine with a brother Arab. The very notion of a sexual transaction between Arabs angered him. If he had accepted a proposition from an Arab, he would have been demeaned, unmanned. Didn't I know that the only acceptable physical contact between Moroccan men was a slap or an arm around the shoulders? But no taps on the buttocks. These are forbidden and reason enough for a stand-up brawl. It all seemed odd and muddled to me but went some way towards explaining why Rachid was perfectly willing to marry a non-virgin. Anything else would only be the grossest hypocrisy.

Laika, Michelle and the babies were still roaming the streets. The mosque was quiet now and faint shadows were etched on the pavement as I sipped my fifth cup of tea and tried to make sense of a moral code which had so many delicate shades of grey. Tap the shoulder, not the buttocks, hide the tampons, avoid adultery and fornicate so that you remain a technical virgin. Humiliate foreigners for cash, but guard against all bodily contact with fellow Arabs. Somewhere behind all the rules lay an underlying truth: the community must be preserved, so family units must be preserved. Echoes of Maggie Thatcher in a djellabah here.

Eventually, as the streets darkened, we made our farewells and climbed back on the Number five bus. It had been a sobering day. We left Rachid in his kingdom with his painfully carved out views, to the care of his sisters. Chugging along through the late afternoon streets I realised he was the only person I had met who didn't want an exit visa to the West, but there again he had chosen to struggle on his own turf rather than pontificate from abroad. The image of twenty-two-year-old Ali being hussled away in a car haunted me. Would Rachid be next? No, inshallah, he would survive, inshallah he would remain unnoticed and unquestioned.

Reality smashed through anxiety when we reached the transformed boarding-house. Zachary had smothered the reception area in potted plants, dried flowers and rush mats. The George Michael cut-out had gone; new tin teapots and four glasses with gold rims sat on the espresso machine. Zachary himself seemed to have been bitten by a poisonous snake judging by the pained expression on his face as he cantered through the lounge, distributing tiny wicker coasters on every available surface. It was his last throw of the dice. He had decided to invite a man from the passport bureau for tea and give him an envelope. 'What envelope?' I asked.

'You know,' he snapped, good manners set aside for once. 'An *envelope*.' Aha, now I understood. Money, filthy lucre, was to change hands tonight; hence the new look downstairs. But what on earth was he planning to do with two or three dozen potted plants when this was all over. I asked myself, bemused. Had he got them perhaps on a sale or return basis? Would such a thing exist in Morocco? Zachary was not a large or tall man but the way in which he had positioned himself in the lobby vigorously suggested that we were expected to go to our rooms at once, and not disturb the flowers nor, God forbid, the coasters. I was happy to comply and curious as to how this would all turn out. Since I never saw Zachary again, his scheme must have worked.

Temara Zoo is home to the king's once private collection of animals and birds. I was not looking forward to visiting Temara, both because zoos are usually miserable places in Third World countries and because a popular guide-book I had flicked through for a description of the place led me to expect the worst. Forget guide-books. What a glorious, well-planned place this, the largest urban zoo in Africa, turned out to be. Temara, with its space and still more space, its enormous wooded paddocks, hills and ponds, is hard on the legs for the very obvious reason that the animals are not piled on top of one another, and getting from, say, the jackal to the elephant involves a very long walk. And yet it was so heartening to see how they lived that I ignored the heat, dusty paths and cryptic picture signs (which invariably led me half a mile east or west of the chosen animal).

The zoo was virtually deserted when we arrived, walking off the main road up a rough unpaved street which eventually swayed round to reveal a small gate and kiosk. A riot of hibiscus tumbled over the high walls and entrance and I noticed that there was no bellowing, moaning or yelping to be heard. I imagined the worst. Perhaps the zoo had been emptied or shut for the summer. Perhaps the animals had been stoned to death by bored teenagers. Far from it. Inside, they were all busy doing animal things and I was struck immediately by the fact that there was no tortured, disturbed pacing to be seen, since most of the creatures inhabit spacious enclosures rather than small cages. The big cats are usually a good litmus test for zoos and I set out to find them. I found the lions in a veritable paddock, high up on a hill top, and I could just make out their shelter, near which the corpse of a boar was being torn apart by a very large male. Two lionesses lounged under a tree, sound asleep, waiting for their stab at dinner. Gazelles grazed and ostriches galloped nearby in a heavily wooded enclosure. What can only be described as a herd of jackals next door had collapsed in the shade, having posted token guards along the perimeter. It was obvious that a real attempt had been made here to combine safety and privacy, space and visibility. Judging from the reaction of the gentle giraffes who pottered over to stand eyeball to eyeball with us at the low wooden rails, hoping for bread and a neck scratch, all God's creatures here had been well protected and knew no fear of watching humans.

Numerous trees and brushwood screens separated the public from the animals, and neither the half-submerged crocodiles nor the totally submerged hippos were reduced to performing a feeding ritual for our benefit. Apart from one recently bereaved, curled-up desert fox, everyone lived in groups, not merely pairs. Yet the odd, expansive layout ensured that there was also some degree of segregation between the various species, as well as between the residents and their visitors. Trees have been incorporated into the design to provide shade, along with water holes and sleeping quarters, which are located as far as possible from the paths, rather than half-glassed in at front and back so people can stare through. And everywhere but everywhere I saw the result of this approach: kids and cubs, fawns and pups, fledglings and foals. Out on the lake, dozens of those most peculiar birds, pelicans, were flapping on their island home, while nearby monkeys amused themselves doing handstands and playing at gymnastics. A ridiculous wild pig with short legs was attacking the groundsman trying manfully to muck out his pit and was being held at bay with a wooden handled spade and yells of fear. The pig was bound to rout his puce-faced enemy in the end.

Ostriches mock-charged shadows and sleek, fat goats neither feinted nor practised but simply attacked each other. A group of Moroccan women passed out food to their children. The picture of a leopard inspired me to pay a visit, but he had retired into the hillside undergrowth and was out to visitors today. Trudging over the bleached couch grass and the bare red soil, I was happy that he had the option to refuse, that even coachloads of tourists would be easily accommodated by the zoo and reduced to distant shapes from his perspective. No zoo is good, but some are far better than others and I hope the influx of fun-fair equipment (currently a deserted mini-bike circuit and two non-functioning baby rides) will not be encouraged and that Temara Zoo will remain a forgotten, sprawling haven for its furred and feathered families. Anyone who has been roughly licked by a leathery black giraffe tongue, brushed a trusting baby elephant's itch away from its whiskery trunk and leaned against a net fence back to back with calm antelopes can only walk away as enchanted as I was that September afternoon.

Coming here was a fitting climax to our stay in Rabat, which for all its failings and pockets of decay is inspirational as it strides confidently away from its well-preserved past into the twenty-first century and a prosperous future. All that remained to be done now were the farewells and the packing and then it was ever onward to Fez.

◆ *Chapter Six* ◆

Fez is currently divided into three distinct areas: Fez-el Bali, Fez-el-Jedid, and the standard French-built new town, constructed by that indefatigable visionary, General Lyautey. Legend has it that Moulay Idriss Al Akhbar, great-grandson of the Prophet through Mohammed's daughter Fatima and Ali, first came here in 789 and was offered a pickaxe, a *fas*, when he decided to found a settlement on the right bank of the river. It was left to his son (born after his father's death by poisoning at the hands of the caliph of Baghdad), Moulay Idriss II to expand the settlement on the left bank, where he built the el Aliya Palace and encircled it with defensive walls, praying, 'Oh God make this town a centre of science and jurisprudence, a place where people will read your book and obey your commandments, keep the population faithful to the Suma and the orthodox path for as long as you permit this town to exist.'

Over the next three hundred years Moslem refugees from Andalusia and Tunisia flooded into Fez, circling both sides of the river and building the Andalusian and Kairouine mosques within their distinct cities – mosques which survive to this day but which, like most religious buildings in Fez except the medersas, cannot be entered by non-Moslems. All I could do was hope for a glance through an open door, a lingering, stolen glance. By the eleventh century Fez was a large city and found itself fought over, brought into first the Almoravide and then the

Almohad empires. The Almohads reduced the Almoravide walls to nothing and threw up their own enormous perimeter wall around Fez-el Bali, much of which still stands today. As the population grew, so the city expanded outside Fez-el Bali (which is currently subject to a UNESCO preservation order as an historic site of world importance), and the Merenid dynasty, who chose Fez as their capital, constructed Fez-el Jedid, their imperial city, complete with mosques, palaces, gardens, baths and souks.

The Jews were moved here from Fez-el Bali to play their part in the financial administrative machinery which, through a system of delegation, oversaw matters as disparate as the health of numerous prostitutes, the leprosarium, divorce cases, the housing of students attending the Kairouine University, criminal executions and the running of the city's ninety public baths.

Fez bloomed for two hundred years under the Merenids who made it their capital in the thirteenth century and was one of the most influential centres of trade and Islamic culture during this period. The last Merenid sultan, Abdul Haqq, was executed by a mob in 1465, a mob bent on self-rule, but ironically, this spurt of optimistic assertiveness signalled not the beginning of prosperous times but the end of an era – for Fez declined rapidly from this point onwards. An earthquake caused wide-spread damage in 1522, the Saadians neglected the city and feared it, constructing a number of forts to subdue the population, and Moulay Ishmael, both suspicious of the Fassi and obsessed with constructing Meknès, taxed them heavily and moved west. In spite of Moulay Hassan's efforts at uniting Fez, through a programme of building and public works, and restoring the city's status, Fez only came to national prominence again in 1912 when the then ruler of Morocco, Sultan Moulay Hafid, signed Morocco over to the French protectorate with the infamous Treaty of Fez. Riots resulted and the European population fled for their lives, many failing to escape the mob.

Perhaps fittingly, an army was sent from the city of force, Meknès, to subdue Fez militarily once and for all and start building the new city as a safe haven for the French inhabitants.

Home to the world's oldest university and, without doubt, best preserved medina, Fez is not an easy town to visit, and even in the scorching heat of August it remains baited and ready to trap the visitor in its maze. As usual, hustlers are the real problem and do much to blight both days spent attempting to see Fez and memories of the place itself. Everything is a hassle, from finding a room to venturing out on the streets, from catching a bus to sitting down for a rest. Luckily, Fez-el Bali merits the effort in the end, though the four days we spent there were tense and oppressive. Fez lacks Marrakesh's joyousness and spontaneity; its sense of magic and open horizons. This city of the plains guards and protects its own as it has for centuries, and the walls which enclose Fez, plus its population's reputation for independence and turbulence, combine to repel the outsider, both physically and socially.

Pulling into the railway station in Fez new town, we barely managed to throw our long-suffering bags onto the platform before Tarik and Abdullah seized them, and us, in warm embraces. Two sets of official guide badges were flashed amidst the usual cries of welcome. I was flagging now, six weeks into the journey, eleven pounds lighter, constantly sweating and thirsty, sated of patisserie and unable to stomach the notion of hot food. In Rabat, I lived on bite-sized anchovy pizzas and pistachio ice-cream supplemented with peaches and apples. But I had reached the point of complete indifference to nutrition and I had been knocking back thick, black espressos and chain-smoking with shaking hands. My skin was dark for the most part, though old eczema patches stubbornly refused to change hue, giving my arms an odd piebald effect. My hair hung like a peroxide curtain of hay. My expression was wary and grim. I was surprised anyone would want to come near me, let alone welcome such a monstrous sight. Michelle was also suffering. Her cheeks had ballooned out into two golf ball-sized lumps of pus-filled chambers. Her eyes were bloodshot slits; her jowls hung distorted on her neck. She maintained a mosquito had bitten her. I suspect something uglier. I was surprised she hadn't been given any alms yet. It was only a matter of time. I shared the joke with her but she wasn't amused. Tempers were at breaking point.

◆

Tony, on his eleventh day of diarrhoea, had passed the point of knowing where we were or what we were doing. His daily routine was determined by the acuteness of the stomach cramps which doubled him over and the bed's proximity to the toilet. The babies, ironically and luckily, were bright-eyed, in perfect health and thrilled by every sight and sound. All the medicines I had compiled so painstakingly in London were pediatric-strength only, and looking at them, I wondered if we could risk wholesale pillage of the banana-flavoured antibiotics and bulk swallowing of baby-strength paracetamol in extremis. Probably not, for fate being what it is, we would all doubtlessly, inevitably and promptly fall into a coma.

Tarik and Abdullah were not what we needed right then, but their mystifying appearance took us by surprise. Each of us believed the others had arranged this reception committee and, as we pushed past the crowds waiting to squeeze on for Oujda and the Algerian border, our two new 'friends' took over. My booking at the Hotel Amor was relegated to history and, instead, we were taken to a two-star, B-class hotel which looked as if it hadn't seen a paint brush for thirty years. Cockroaches pattered up the walls and ducked and dived into the large, old free-standing wardrobes of the type sold second-hand in London markets for ten pounds. The floors were thick with dust, the toilets didn't flush, and old grey army-type blankets were bundled up on the metal-framed beds. Welcome to Fez.

In my frame of mind I no longer cared and lethargically agreed to everything – namely that the children would not wet the beds or make any noise after 5:00 p.m. – just to get the hotel owner out of the room. Two hundred and fifty dirhams for squalor. I wanted to weep. I noticed that the official star rating hanging above the reception desk had been defaced by a previous visitor and now I knew why. A trickling sound broke into my resigned consciousness and idly I looked towards the partitioned-off shower, only to see a rivulet of raw sewage and urine gaily dribbling across the floor. Simple anger, an anger born of exhaustion and a surfeit of harassment, propelled me downstairs to confront the owner. He shrugged, couldn't be bothered to listen, turned his head away in dismissal. After all, if I didn't want the room, then someone else would, so where was the profit in listening? Tarik and Abdullah sat ineffectually on the hallway sofa, pretending to be too engrossed in their own conversation to hear my tirade. The owner shrugged again as I repeated that I needed a bucket, that I had two rooms, hence two toilets, and neither flushed while both leaked. Stalemate. Suddenly, a large fist joined my dappled paw in thumping the reception desk. An irate Libyan launched into a harsh, fast Arabic spiel, and whatever he said must have been violent since the Moroccan dashed off to reappear with my bucket, a yellow handle-less affair with lumps of pink plaster stuck to the outside. I left the Libyan bellowing and smacking his fist, thanked him prettily and headed off with my treasure.

Upstairs, all was not well. The babies had discovered four dead birds outside and brought them in to 'wake them up'. Waking up dead birds apparently consists of popping them into bed to warm them, and Michelle was rabid with horror when I walked in brandishing my treasure, trying to ease lovingly squashed but unmistakably decomposing bodies out of the double bed without leaving a foot, wing or head behind. The babies were weeping at her cruelty, and Tony had collapsed, white-faced, in a chair and was staring into the middle distance as another series of stomach churning cramps attacked. He gamely and grimly assured us that he would be fine and that he would make his own way to the medina and resume taking photographs as soon as he could concurrently stand up *and* focus. Throughout the trip, Tony's cheerful demeanor and enthusiastic manner had charmed potentially suspicious people into agreeing to pose for him, not once but several times at that. To our general amazement, he had elicited smiles from jaded water sellers, indifferent shopkeepers and openly hostile farmers the length of the Atlantic coast. Threatened by a carving knife wielding barman in Chichaoua, for querying the accuracy of a bill, Tony ended up posing the aggressor (complete with murderous implement) in the café doorway, all grudges forgotten. If anyone was going to capture Fez-el Bali on film, then it was certainly going to be Tony. I was not even going to try to run the gauntlet. Michelle, judging on past form, specialized in decapitating rather than immortalising her subjects.

The temperature had hit thirty-nine degrees centigrade and the idea of a cold shower was enticing to everyone, but if a major crisis was to be avoided it was obviously best to get out of there immediately, and even the idea of our official guides was not as repellent as listening to street noises and the distant crash of breaking plates.

Downstairs, Tarik and Abdullah were sitting on the sofa, waiting. We negotiated a flat fee of sixty dirhams for their services and shook hands with some degree of insincerity on both sides. For my part, I disliked their pseudo-American accents and smugness and the fact that they had bamboozled us at the station and not lifted a finger during the bucket saga. From their point of view, I suspected we appeared a bad catch, since our cheap straw hats and plastic floppy sandals, not to mention the fact that we planned to walk to Fez-el Bali in the heat rather

than take a cab, made us appear cheapskates as opposed to high
rollers. Still, we were mutually saddled now and set off.
Abdullah brought his moped to the front door, and Michelle
and the babies rode off to the local municipal pool, perched
jauntily all along the frame, an accident looking for somewhere
to happen, as the saying goes.

I looked at Tarik, he stared back, and we pushed past the
alcoholic on the lobby step and the stoned Spanish girl with the
hennaed hair and a temporarily-tattooed forehead, to set out for
Fez. Tarik didn't speak to me as we walked out of the new town,
past the Place des Alaouites, but shuffled along, occasionally
throwing out statistics or pointing to hillside views. I didn't
answer him either, unless it was strictly necessary, and by the
time we had walked past the Royal Palace into Fez-el Jedid, the
parameters of the relationship had solidified into sharing the
disposable lighter (but drinking from our own bottles of water)
and our Q&A dialogue. Fez-el Jedid did nothing for me with its
acres of mass-produced plastic junk, Western-style clothing and
pots and pans. The sun was fierce and the Royal Palace with its
seven gates almost impossible to survey since the doors shone
so strongly and it was closed to visitors anyway. The mellah was
choc-a-bloc with jewellers rather than Jews who have moved to
the new town or left the country completely. Of the three palace
gardens which were constructed by the Merenids only the Dar
Batha was open, since the museum of that name is housed
within its walls. I perked up, but no, it was Tuesday, and the
museum too was shut to the public. The traditional entrance to
Fez-el Bali loomed ahead, the Bab Boujeloud with its two
minarets, which everyone photographs from the patch of wasteland just outside, visible through the arches.

I was drawn to a young boy with a churn slung over his
back. Popping out of the churn were a number of sticks topped
with plastic fruit. This was obviously a juice seller, no less. Tarik
was not interested in talking about juice sellers for, like a

clockwork soldier whose key has just been released, he suddenly barked into action, reciting the number of fountains, mosques, communal ovens, hammams and Koranic schools to be found in Fez-el Bali. I listened distractedly, but felt more inclined to flop down in a café adjacent to the gate and drink a mint tea while watching the world go by. It soon became obvious that, whatever else one might say of Fez-el Bali, it's a remarkably busy place, a working medina rather than a pretty setting for retailers and thus a far cry from Rabat's neat frontages and ornamental fountains or Marrakesh's fair-like ambience. Here, hundreds of asses staggered by carrying everything from gas cylinders to rubble. I counted one hundred and forty litres of Sim on one beast's back as it plodded past, eyes fixed on the ground, resigned, brown leather blinkers repelling flies. Men screamed 'Balek' in hoarse voices, urging the beasts forward, blocking the roads where the pedestrians pulled in stomachs and flattened themselves against walls or, eyeing up the width of the approaching load, quickly dived into shops and doorways. The occasional mule trundled past, swifter on his hooves, dragging a cart on which balanced dozens of chickenwire cages all full of hens, ducks, pigeons, cockerels or turkeys, flapping mightily to maintain their balance. A stream of traffic exercised a strong pull and I felt excited as Tarik led me up into the Rue Talla Kebira and into the heart of the medina.

At first it was difficult to focus on the activities taking place in the workshops, since I had to concentrate on following the flow and not causing a road block. Gradually, a rhythm of stepping aside, ducking and shrinking back established itself and I could actually relax a little and even stop, darting out of the stream to peek into the open booths. A young boy beckoned me over to look at the babouches, men's slippers, he was making. He and his friends were cutting shapes out of bright yellow skins while two other slightly older children sewed them onto thick leather soles using hole punchers and needles. A large wooden block held dollops of glue, and lining pieces were stuck together and tacked down with a rounded piece of wood. This production chain yielded four pairs a day on a good day, and the footwear was then sold to their outlet in the medina. I admired the slippers which were supple and had a polished finish and unscuffed soles. They sold for around fifty dirhams and I regretted having already spent seventy-five dirhams on a simpler, silver-grey pair. The boys were not interested in making a sale anyway but were happy to demonstrate their talents and discuss every Moroccan's obsession, football. I fear my limited knowledge disappointed them as I dredged up images of the last World Cup and memories of Tunisia versus Cameroons, the only vaguely relevant North African match I have ever watched.

Fez-el Bali covers fifteen square kilometres which sounds, and is, a huge area. Every inch assaults one or another of the senses. In one part we saw men working lathes with their feet, no mean task, producing cedar boxes and kohl holders. Next door, a couple of apprentices were hammering brass plates with tiny tools, heads bent over their work, tongues poking out in concentration. Large wooden advertising signs dangled on chains. There wasn't a rumour of wind in the air, so they stood immobile and silent. A sizeable proportion advertised dentists and laboratories which made false teeth. In one large window, artful displays of dentures rested on a branch whose twig-ends were decorated with metal and gold teeth, tubes of British-made cement standing to each side like sentries. The men at the counter offered me a tour which I hastily declined. The plates were too richly pink, the metal filed and polished, reminiscent of bullets and not suited for the more gentle demolition of chewing.

Tarik trailed me up, past boys bending over hunks of raw lamb, separating the muscle and fat with small sharp knives.

Children were washing their feet in the communal fountains, the babies tied to their backs wailing at the unexpected change of angle and position. From time to time I caught snatches of chanting as we passed a Koranic school where four- to six-year-olds parroted the Good Book, the girls' voices high in pitch and excited. Mosque interiors were visible round every corner – tiled courtyards where men were making their ablutions, or just sitting slumped in a corner, their eyes remote. It was impossible to absorb any of it, to think, let alone communicate with Tarik who was gaily striding ahead, occasionally shaking hands with other guides and embracing them, casually indicating my presence. I felt like a chained pet being dragged along reluctantly by a contemptuous master. Before I could work out how best to phrase my irritation, though, I was distracted by the sudden profusion of lace and ribbon-covered candles wrapped in cellophane dangling everywhere.

Ah ha! Nougat, incense and oils. This meant we were fast approaching a major shrine, and presumably that of Fez's revered Moulay Idriss. As the religious stalls multiplied by the metre, so did the number of the blind and beggars, and suddenly I was there on the threshold of one of the most sacred spots in Fez. Coloured candles twinkled inside the shrine, and leaning into the doorway I could just see the dark velvet-draped tomb which was almost completely obscured from view by kneeling women. Traditionally, Moulay Idriss is a particularly helpful ally in curing cases of infertility, and anyone who shelters here can invoke the right of sanctuary. Since he is patron Saint of Fez, and hence guardian of its prosperity, naturally enough trade guilds also gather here in August to seek his blessing, bearing gifts and making animal sacrifices. Tarik was full of disrespect and mocking contempt for the reverently kneeling women since he considered saint worship heretical and thus of no value, but although I felt no emotional response to this particular scene – probably, I reflect, because of its setting and my peripheral, barred view – it seemed harmless enough.

Of course, the very adjective 'harmless' is suspect in a culture where the forbidden and the sanctioned must be observed for the sake of one's soul and its eternal salvation or damnation. The arguments for and against praying at shrines, as well as in mosques, frequently crop up in the press, and the official line circa 1990 is that marabouts preserve Islamic orthodoxy in a changing world rather than deviate from it. Moussems, which honour local patron saints, are thus also harmless rather than a form of charlatanism, as more rigid interpreters of the Koran might maintain. Using a vaccination analogy, the powers that be argue that since Morocco is religiously united for twelve centuries, it is immune to all deviations from the permanent and changing path of Islam. Anyone who exploits Islam for political ends is a false reformer and debases the religion only temporarily, since politics change with the times but the Moroccan body politic remains true to the message of Islam despite temporary upheavals. In a way this argument begs the question, and throws up more questions than it answers. Blessing and sanctioning the strictly unacceptable by pretending that it is part of the state's foundations rather than an outbuilding doesn't make moussems and zaouias any more acceptable in orthodox fundamentalists' eyes, but merely underlines the government's fear of disrupting the status quo, its general lack of Islamic backbone.

The king is well aware of the uneasy truce he presides over here, and prefers to issue statements on healing the Sunni-Shi'a divide, the importance of teaching the spirit of the Koran rather than merely the form, and the need for comparative theology. It's probably wise of him to do so and, looking through a prospectus for the next summer university at Casablanca, which defines and resolves pressing religious issues, I was therefore not surprised to note that abstract themes prevailed. Here for example, 'The Symbolic Dimension of Religious Observances' (e.g. if you can't perform your ablutions because there's no water, wash yourself with a prayer) was on the agenda, along with an inquiry into whether the law is eternal or evolutionary, and methods for transforming religious teachings from semantics into moral precepts for the next generation.

Restoration work was very much in evidence in the heart of Fez-el Bali. The old fondouks, the caravanserai, were being repaired thanks to money pledged by UNESCO in 1980, and heaps of sand, wheelbarrows and a seemingly endless procession of asses carrying saddlebags of broken masonry, testified to the progress which was being made. I tried to sneak a look at what was actually being done at the Tsetaouyine fondouk, which was traditionally set aside for traders from infamous Tetouan, tricksters and conmen all, but a hairy man with furry arms waved me away. I barely had time to glance at the men's galleried sleeping areas and the enormous animals' courtyard before I was shoved back – none too gently, either.

Fez-el Bali is in crisis and epitomises the worst of rapid urbanisation run amok. Historically, its geographical position at the crossroads of Morocco, west of Taza, north of the Tafilalet, assured it an important trading role and turned Fez into a centre of economic power. It was here that European traders came to make their purchases, here that caravan routes intersected. Traditional hierarchies and social and political balances operated within the medina, along with a complex system of production and distribution based on the individual workshop. The twentieth century, and in particular the establishment of the French Protectorate, saw a gradual growth in tension between the new-style capitalism and administrative practices imported from abroad, and the traditional social structures and trade customs of the medina. The rural influx turned from a trickle into a wave as people flocked into Fez seeking work and housing, building indiscriminately, squatting on agricultural land and swallowing up what had formerly been rural communities on the outskirts of the town. Today, Fez is lined with unregulated and archaic housing developments. Villages such as Ain Chkef are no more, the population is growing at four per cent per annum and squatters, who numbered one hundred and thirty thousand in 1982, make up almost a quarter of the Fassi, their hillside dwellings spreading as far as the eye can see. Unfortunately, the problem is exacerbated by the fact that Fez has only some two hundred sizeable factories which provide employment for fifteen thousand workers, so the rest of the potential workforce is thrown back on traditional crafts as a means of earning a wage. Sixty per cent of the Fassi who do work, therefore, work in the overcrowded, crumbling, neglected and undermaintained medina, which now has twelve hundred inhabitants per hectare – a great strain on the water supply, the housing stock and infrastructure in general. Fez-el Bali is falling apart, bursting at the seams, for while it only takes up twenty-five per cent of the area of the town of Fez, it is actually home to fifty-five per cent of the population. To further compound matters, economic power has moved away to Casablanca and been defused regionally to Meknès and Nador, while Fez's population continues to grow.

Strolling through the streets, I wondered how it would all end and it was easy to imagine forced-march exoduses, perhaps to Dakhla and Laayoune to bolster claims to sovereignty of the Sahara, residency permits and the emergence of closed town status being applied in the not too distant future. What is beyond argument is the fact that Fez is out of control, that the city deserves its title of site of world heritage, and that its hydra-like smear on the landscape positively cries out for some form of that much loathed remedy, central planning, before it collapses under its own weight.

◆

PART ONE

No one who comes to Fez-el Bali manages to avoid two tourist spots, the tanneries and the carpet shops, so I was resigned to the fact that Tarik, in his guise as official greeter, would eventually add these to his unvoiced itinerary. To my surprise, the tanneries were visually exciting and smelled far better than the streets of Safi's cannery row. Having expected at least one pile of severed heads, and wooden frames loaded with fly-encrusted corpses drying out, as far as the eye can see, I didn't realise where we were going when Tarik started climbing up a narrow, stone passage, beckoning me to follow. I gamely marched up in his wake and found myself on a terraced roof. Down below, covering a far smaller area than I had anticipated, was a series of vats separated by a low narrow stone wall, each shrieking indigo, purple and green. School children ran nimbly across the wall whilst others squelched skins into the dyes, their torsos and feet bare, their skimpy shorts and aprons made out of what looked like dark leather. Tarik squatted down by me and pointed to a row of vats off to the side where the skins, which had already been stripped of their fleece, hair and fat, were washed and then preserved in urine. There was nothing much to see except for a gluey white and grey mess, but I bobbed my head politely after looking at them for a few seconds. 'How old are the children when they start work?' I asked.

'Five,' he replied sullenly, idly, throwing tiny pieces of gravel down into the work area. 'Five,' he repeated, adding, 'and it is disgusting work. They earn twenty dirhams a day, pick up eczema, cirrhosis and lung diseases. They're always sick.' Tarik had surprised me with this outburst and I suddenly looked at him with slightly friendlier eyes as he snapped, 'Let's go. I can't stay here any longer,' and gave me his hand as I stood up. Cautiously retracing my steps, I passed groups of children sitting in the shade, their feet and hands coloured with dye, eating what looked like slices of pie. No one was over twelve. Behind them, piles of cow, goat and sheep skins were being sorted by men, according to size and quality, presumably. I suppose it could all be seen as picturesque in a Dickensian way, yet being an eczema sufferer myself, the mere mention of eczema took all the colour out of the scene for me, the skill out of the craft, reducing it to a filthy, badly paid job which takes its toll on the health. Bring in the machines and conveyor belts and to hell with the fancy photographs and picture postcards of artisans at work, pursuing age-old crafts.

Tarik's humanity, such as it is, was submerged and forgotten a matter of fifty yards further on when he marched into a cavernous hall, muttering about having a mint tea and seeing someone. The size of the entrance way and the mention of mint tea immediately set off alarms in my head. 'My God! He's finally conned me into a carpet shop.' And indeed, he had. Now, anyone who has travelled in the Maghreb knows that sinking feeling in the pit of the belly which the Westerner experiences when entering a carpet emporium, the impossibility of beating any sort of retreat until at least an hour has passed and every item of stock has been perused, and the sheer helplessness of the traveller in the face of the carpet seller's courtesy and limpet-like insistence. I couldn't even bear the thought of enduring the opening moves, let alone the whole game, at that point, but it was far too late.

A small, sharp-featured man had, in a matter of seconds, clicked his fingers at his boys, ordered tea, introduced himself and firmly plonked me down on a cushion-covered bench, the more comfortable to be pressurised and tortured. I made vague protests, but he overruled them all. The ceremony began as dozens, nay hundreds, of kilims, rugs, runners, Berber, High Atlas, Middle Atlas and Rabati carpets unrolled soundlessly at my feet – a kaleidoscope of patterns, colours, sizes and impressions. I felt I might lose my mind – not for the first time – and glanced desperately at Tarik for help, for the white light, the exit. The bastard was sound asleep and the carpet seller was bearing down on me with more rugs, more exclamations, a hissing spume of adjectives. 'Do you like natural colours?'

'Yes, I suppose so,' I muttered lamely before a deluge of mint, antimony, cobalt and bougainvillaea-dyed rugs landed at my feet.

'Do you like High Atlas saffron shades?'

'Yes, enormously!' Giant cotton and wool carpets with elaborate Southern Cross motifs appeared as if by magic.

'The Southern Cross can cure infertility,' added the salesman, looking at me appraisingly. I rallied and told them I had three sons. 'Well, what about Saharan carpets?' he asked, beckoning to the boys, who were unrolling the stock as fast as I could blink. Before I could think of a fresh adjective, a new answer, Saharan carpets covered the floor and the man was telling me that he had personally wrestled all these priceless heirlooms from the walls of nomad tents, that the nomads were heartbreakingly reluctant to part with their treasures and I, Mrs Kennedy, was the luckiest woman in all of Morocco, if not the world, to be granted the privilege of buying such treasures.

Examining the saffron and henna dyed rugs I tried to transport them from here, this whitewashed, cool, tiled hall, into a large British drawing room with heavy curtains and solid furniture. It was impossible. The carpets would look disgustingly cheap and gaudy. Hesitating over my reply, I tried to distract him by asking about the images I could make out in the weave. Simple but charming symbols of desert life, two people on a camel signify marriage; birds with small spikes speak of patience; the eye motif asks for luck; the flame bird for liberty. A snake emerges at one corner to symbolise a long life, while gazelles with no feet, panthers and monkeys immortalise dancing after the hunt. The camel was here too, crudely stabbed into the thread, but when his head and tail were covered up, lo and behold, the triangular shape which remained was that of home, a moving tent. I was tempted to ask about tribal markings, the kasbahs, in short to get into the spirit of the thing but drew back wary of the lull before the storm, the chit-chat before the hard sell. The piles of carpets were now littering every inch of the tiled courtyard, rich royal blue splendid Rabatis with their cream borders and central flower motifs (which have purportedly taken over the void left in the market following the fall of the Shah), vivid pink and purple kilims dancing with black beasts and the subtle warmer hues of the Beni Mellal tribe of the Middle Atlas. Everywhere I looked – carpets. The man sat down now and the waltz began. I told him I had no money but deeply admired the work. He ignored the salvoes, rhapsodised about the cedar wood needles plied to embroider the kilims, the antiquity of it all, how small each carpet would roll up, how light they would be for the airplane. A bundle of plastic was brought over, along with string which had seen better days, so that a medium-sized rug could be rendered transportable before my very eyes. Tarik slept on while I looked and asked and repeated how poor we were these days, the English.

'Do you have no sympathy for your own sex?'

The question came from nowhere and knocked me back to attention. What on earth did the man mean? Seeing that I was piqued and, after all, from his point of view any reaction provided an opening, the carpet seller sternly told me that it was illiterate women who had made these carpets. Illiterate women who needed to express their creativity.

'This drive for creativity,' he continued, pointedly, 'will be dammed forever unless their sisters help by buying what they produce.'

Stalemate. Boys were still rolling and folding busily. Tarik was curled up on the bench but stirring gently. It seemed a good time to effect the great escape. As I once again reiterated regret, scooping up cigarettes, matches, handbag and a large pile of visiting cards, the carpet seller demanded which carpet I most admired.

'That one!' I gesticulated blindly towards a small runner and made to go. With each step of escape the price fell until eighteen thousand dirhams had descended to ten thousand dirhams and cash had given way to Access or Visa, then post-dated Access or Visa, split into four monthly payments. Battered, exhausted, I forgot all notions of an elegant retreat and ran for it, straight into the arms of Tarik's cousin, Abdullah.

Abdullah told me that I owed him fifty dirhams (or two days' wages) for the children's and Michelle's entrance into the swimming pool. He was smiling broadly, smug in his fake white Levi's, obviously keen to take up the tourist trail and convinced he would make a commission where Tarik had failed. I handed over five ten-dirham rags and followed. Without him I had little hope of getting out of Fez-el Bali very easily and it was surely around 4:00 p.m. by then, time for a glimpse of the sky, relaxation. Abdullah asked me about the medina, listened and slipped down alley after alley until we emerged at a most peculiar square embroidery shop. Seven girls in their early teens had been arranged in a spotlit niche under hot lamps and were supposedly spontaneously exhibiting their skills with the needle. Cotton squares and rectangles draped the tambour with which they automatically shielded their faces as I stumbled in to gaze on, amazed. It was a ludicrous scene, embarrassing for all concerned, exploitative and, anyway, I had only recently read a long article bemoaning the fact that girls no longer embroider and the age of the elaborate sewing machine has killed embroidery by reproducing it so flawlessly. The manager emerged, waving enthusiastically in the direction of the subdued, shy girls, clutching wads of cross-stitched napkins and cloths, yelling 'Nine dirhams the set, a twelve-place setting.' Four oval tables to the back, the wares had been set, with plates, cutlery and glasses – further adding to the staged unreality of this scene.

Enough was enough. I dredged up a trace of a smile and walked out into the alley to be followed by a miffed Abdullah who visibly took in a big breath and then tried to coax me on, saying it was hot, implying I was menstruating, neurotic, and offering to show me a hundred and twenty women working the looms to make mint and pink-striped silk djellabas. 'No looms,' I snapped. 'No looms, no carpets, no mint tea, no leather shops, and no more artisans.' I almost screamed the last words and reached into my trusted soft, old odour-free Tunisian bag for a swig of Sidi Ali. I was beginning to think of Tunisia as 'Heaven on Earth', a sure sign of shot nerves. Gulping down a mouthful, I promptly spat it out all over my black T-shirt again when Abdullah asked me if I was sure I was not Jewish. For God's sake, what was going on here? 'No,' I replied. 'My parents were Polish.'

'Jews then,' he mused. 'I thought most of you were killed by the Germans.' He added that he supposed I didn't enjoy seeing people work hard because Jews like to profiteer and, since I had a nanny, I was obviously a lady of leisure. This unexpected anti-Semitic outburst rendered me mute and at a loss. Let it go, my inner voice urged. Let it go and get out of here. You mustn't slap him, I choked down on my riposte and followed Abdullah out of Fez-el Bali, praying he'd fall down each set of steps we manoeuvred, hoping against hope that he would be trampled by mules or gouged by turkeys. Of course, fate is capricious and he emerged perky and unscathed, satisfied that his failure as a hustler could all be put down to the mysterious nature of the Jews.

The entire set of Jewish conspiracy theories which many Moroccans embrace as an article of faith is reflected in a wide-spread belief that the Jews are protected by the throne and, in exchange, have rendered the current king immune to bullets. This particular story has local variations but, essentially, it holds that the king turned to the Jews (traditionally feared for their dabbling in alchemy) after surviving the first assassination attempt. Purportedly, a rabbi was brought in to inject a piece of the Koran into the king's arm and sew the limb up. After doing this successfully, the rabbi committed suicide. In exchange, King Hassan II gave the Jews economic power and his personal protection, linking the continuing existence of his line with their prosperity. One variation maintains that the rabbi was executed, another that the king could still be shot through the head (and be killed), but everyone is in agreement about the bottom line: the Jews are the power behind the Alaouite throne, and dangerous.

At first it was a relief to arrive back in the very different hustle of the new town, to see the usual nut sellers doing a brisk trade, open-air cafés crammed with men and groups of children playing in the antiseptic, soulless squares which are a hallmark of this part of Fez. Souped-up cars were charging down the road and the local hustlers had lost interest in my face. Even the mosque behind its scaffolding looked fresh and welcoming. There was music and not a breath of wind in the air as I let myself back into the hotel to discover the Libyans were still at war with reception, that Abdullah had made an unwelcome pass at Michelle on the bike, and that the cockroaches were partying tonight. I offered the Libyans the loan of my prize bucket which inflamed the situation nicely, consoled Michelle and watched the beetles boogie. It was stifling, too hot to sleep, and as I listened to a dog howling at the moon, its piercing cry cut short by someone's shoetip, I realised how little I liked Fez, new town, el Bali and el Jadid.

It was not a night for roaming, sticky and static, and I flicked through the *Matin du Sahara* looking for distractions, light reading, chewing on a stick of bread as I turned the pages. As usual, there was nothing much to be found: an article on the

Built-in fridge, Berber-style, at Setti Fatma, Ourika Valley.

A striking example of contemporary Islamic architecture. Mosque outside El Jadida.

Men-only ceremonial tent, crammed with local dignitaries, Oualidia.

Bring on the dancing girls! Oualidia.

Rabati water seller. A welcome sight, with his cups and goatskin bag, during the hot summer days.

An old man weighing up the problems of a nation, Garden of Oudaias, Rabat.

Modesty overcoming pride. An embroidery workshop, Fez-el Bali.

*Artistically arranged hooves on the steps of the
Andalusian Mosque, Fez-el Bali. Many are still steaming-fresh.*

Dyeing vats, the tanneries, Fez-el Bali. Most of the
children suffer from skin and respiratory diseases and wages are low.

Gnaoua musicians, Salé backstreet. Their spirit-music
originated in West Africa and percolated into Morocco with the slave trade.

Market day, Moulay Idriss. The fish seller is
attempting to lure me off the vegetarian path.

Allah has not provided for this man in Meknès ... and Morocco has no welfare state.

Alexis succumbing to the heat and lassitude of Tinerhir.

Mid-morning at the Todra Gorge. Its cliffs reputedly house anti-European snipers, eagles and panthers.

introduction of twenty radio-controlled taxis in Casa, a letter from a teenager in Azzemour bemoaning municipal neglect and the state of the beach, another complaining about the lack of public toilets in Khemisset, which meant that people urinated indiscriminately. *L'Opinion*, with its double-page spread devoted to young readers' letters, was slightly more diverting since the poems about love and loss were truly dire and the continuing debate on the efficacy of sorcerers had now focused on why they can't foresee their own arrests if they are supposed to look into the future. Why, indeed? Perhaps the streets held the best source of relaxation after all.

The new town is expensive, its orange trees clipped to provide dark glossy pools of shade, its 1960s-style pedestrian precincts and over-stocked chemists speaking of Europe, European money and European visitors. A mere couple of miles away from Bab Boujeloud, with its secret inner world of dyes and blacksmiths, sheets of tripe, sweet-smelling communal bakeries and black smoking furnaces, you can buy a marble fountain, complete with doves and fishes, modern bronze lights, high couture separates and French perfume. The contrast is harsh and memorable and after sitting on a low concrete bench facing an out-of-work, sunken-featured garden, the adjacent video shop lights blinking on and off every two seconds, advertising a new Kung Fu production, my irritation with the day faded away and a romantic tinge crept over memories of Fez-el Bali, the medieval, the timeless. Surely it must be preferable to the sterile symmetrical concrete areas where patisseries and strolling groups of youngsters eating ice-cream attempt to infuse gaiety into a barren landscape.

Rabat also has a new town, of course, but that has been integrated into the city, squeezed within ancient walls, bonded to the past. Fez ville nouvelle is obscenely peripheral, a transitory place where you can find a cheap hotel, buy a gateau or a bottle of Jean Patou. The only functioning building is the Marché

Central and, peering through the sturdy metal gates I read *Lapin tué*, dead rabbit, and relished the words. Dead rabbit was meat and edible. The grotesque and elaborate mirrors in the furniture shop were redundant. In a country where the average monthly wage is seven hundred and fifty dirhams, who is going to spend money on gold-plated taps and minimalist chrome soap dishes if they can have rabbit stew? Any arguments about free choice and how to spend money depend on two factors: employment and wages. Morocco has sixty-plus per cent unemployment. Few people earn wages. There is no social security. No one has any choice in these matters. We should hide the mirror and the tap immediately.

An old man shuffled towards me, dragging a large, thin bag along the pavement as I morosely watched the video shop sign switching on and off. I was offered two cotton blankets and bought them without a word, without a struggle or vigorous haggle, silently handing over the six pounds he wanted in expiation for our Western sins, the building of such dreary streets. Taken aback, he shook my hand and whispered washing instructions into the neck of my shirt, dribbling gently as he emphasised cold water washes and no spin. The café owner emerged and demanded a twenty per cent commission for not chasing him off the premises. Oh, Morocco. The new ways may be cruel but were the old ways that much better? Nine-thirty came and gradually the streets started to empty. Soon everyone was gone, bar the odd, machine-gun toting policeman, home-ward bound bar staff and the omnipresent, invisible mass of howling dogs. I paid the bill and strolled back, two unwanted blankets richer, ready for bed. Fez had defeated me, made me think of home for the first time, refused to offer up its mysteries or reveal any beauty, any hope for the future of the Maghrebi town.

◆

Home was also on the Libyans' minds, for when I returned to the hotel with my black bin liner, a series of sleeping children were being ferried into a light blue Mercedes by elegantly dressed women. Inside, all was mayhem. Leather-jacketed men were throwing pigskin cases onto piles and room keys into a large flowerpot which one of them kicked into shards as they all stormed out, pausing just long enough to nod goodbye to me. A barrage of last-minute yelling and arm-shaking rent the otherwise still night, as they poured out and away. Mr Phlegmatic, behind the desk, was clutching the complaints book to his chest so it had obviously come into this argument somewhere along the line and he was cursing exuberantly at their fast disappearing tail-lights. This cacophony was the final straw for me and I found myself spontaneously telling him that we too would be leaving in the morning, news which seemed to cheer him up marginally as he turned to sweep up the pieces of flowerpot and retrieve the keys. I crunched a terracotta morsel under my shoe just for the hell of it and beat a retreat.

◆ *Chapter Seven* ◆

Meknès is a mere two-hour ride away from Fez by train and seemingly a popular destination since the station was crowded and stuffy when we arrived. People were sleeping on benches, on their bags, against one another's shoulders. Some had covered their faces against the sun with newspaper; others dozed, barefoot, in the concrete encased public gardens nearby. A smart Algerian woman in her early fifties nervously turned an emerald ring, near the ticket counter, while her over-burdened husband queued for first-class tickets to Oujda. Soldiers in uniform and concessionaires shoved through the mass of bodies and only the usual sprinkling of European back-packers reacted to the dearth of patience and manners. I still felt out-of-step in Fez and was relieved to be leaving. The children were chanting either 'There's cholera in Meknès' or 'We mustn't drink the water,' and Tony appeared to have collapsed in yet another toilet. As the hours passed a series of small flies drowned in my half-empty cup of coffee and I wondered whether Meknès the haughty would live up to its name, whether one man's dream, writ large in mortar and in blood, would move me in the way it moved seventeenth-century travellers, in short, whether Moulay Ishmael's town still exuded traces of his tyranny, strength and vision.

Over the years, I'd read a great deal about this contentious Moroccan ruler, the second Alouite sultan, the man who sired over eight hundred children, decapitated eunuchs at the drop of a hat, reclaimed Mehdya, Tangier, Asilah and Larache from their Christian conquerors, enjoyed both fornicating and inflicting pain, and restored unity in a riven land while isolating Morocco from the rest of the Sunni community. Like the legends surrounding Catherine the Great and Henry VIII, those concerning Moulay Ishmael have been both restricted and partially accurate. Thinking of him, as of the other two rulers, one immediately remembers all the startling statistics and excesses; the obscenity of his thirty-six thousand murders; the details of his rampant sexuality, slave armies and slave labourers; the fact that he brooked no arguments and did as he willed, pillaging and fighting the breadth if not quite the length of the land. And yet it would be too simple to say baldly that this man lived and killed to amass purely personal power, for much of his energy went into building Meknès, embodying his notion of the sublime, the Platonic form of beauty. Begun in 1672, the complex we know as the Imperial City, which housed well over fifty thousand people in its hey-day, was destroyed by the Lisbon earthquake of 1755. Yet to this day, clambering over the boulders and crumbling masonry of the inner walls and staring along or up at the stupendous encircling walls, all twenty-four kilometres of them, is an overwhelming experience. Meknès somehow diminishes ordinary mortals and after a few days of trudging through the ruins and absorbing the spell of the place, I was quite unsurprised in retrospect to find myself kneeling down before its creator's mausoleum, paying an uneasy homage to one of history's most driven, compelling characters.

Until well into the sixteenth century, Meknès was very much second in importance to Fez in the Middle Atlas. Fez, capital of the Merenid dynasty and the intellectual, religious and political heart of the nation, eclipsed its neighbour on every level and Meknès, founded in the tenth century by a Berber tribe, the Meknassa, remained a humble staging post for pretenders to the throne and a forgotten backwater, redeemed only by the rich agricultural lands which surrounded it then, as now. When Moulay Ishmael came to the throne in 1672, he resolved to establish an impenetrable base from which to consolidate his power, and rejected both Fez and Marrakesh on the grounds of tribal associations and historical allegiances. Just as he would form a new army drawn primarily from the descendants of Negro slaves (the Abids), so he would build a new imperial city, a city to rival and outshine the finest the contemporary world could offer, and this he did.

The magic of Meknès, its unique atmosphere is not immediately apparent in the same way as the light-hearted frivolity of Marrakesh. The first hint I had of its potency came at twilight, when the dark shadows of the looming hills crumpled inwards, enclosing the town in their deep embrace. The medina slowly sprang into relief then, plastered up on the hill against the sky, spreading across the horizon from east to west like a stage background. The odd gold and green minaret cut a harsh black line among the indistinct greys and browns, and the pale street lamps, which seemed half-doused, constantly on the point of flickering out, barely illuminated the tumbling maze of streets and alleys. Standing on the Avenue des FAR, the main road leading from the new town to the old, I gazed mesmerised at the gloomy, massive tableau stretching out on the skyline before me. Odd patches of white delineated wide cemeteries to the west, while way up high in the hills the sky suddenly seemed to reach down and swallow Meknès and then blur into nothing. It was dark and I thought of fairy-tales, of abandoned children spending nights in the forest ...

People were hurrying up the steep steps the like of which featured all over the old town, while buses careered up and down the darkening, narrow roads. Everything was piecemeal, difficult to gather together in a single frame. As I panted up towards Place el Hedim, the Oued Boufekrane valley dropped away on my left and I could make out the odd grazing horse, neat bushy mint patches, a group of chickens being herded into their shed. I tried to imagine finding apple trees, cows, and allotments running between Bond Street and Covent Garden. It was unimaginable.

Place el Hedim, the central square of the old town squatting at the entrance to the medina, had recently been completely revamped and bore no trace of activity. Ropes hung loosely from short, wooden stakes, keeping everyone at bay; square planters stood ready for miniature orange trees; modern lights, as yet not switched on, lined the tiled edges of what promised to be a pretty, rather than an original, modern addition to the hub of Meknès. On the western side of the square, the roads led into the covered food market and the fringes of the square housed barbers, ceramic stalls where workaday tagines, simply decorated bowls and braziers were piled up in heaps. Meknès does not expect tourists or pay much attention to us when we do arrive. No multilingual guides here, no students wanting to practise their English, no beckoning purveyors of bags, belts or painted wooden mirrors. The crowds milling through the narrow walkway around Place el Hedim were there to shop, not to squeeze dirhams out of foreign visitors, and there was a satisfying normality in queuing at the fruit stalls to buy fat pears and small, dark avocados, thin plastic bags at the ready.

The Meknèssi looked tall and adequately fed at first glance, Berber farmers who worked the fertile land, living reasonably well from it. The lavish displays of olives, pickles, vegetables and fruit testified to a short run between market and field and for once I was tempted to gorge, not just surrender to dull hunger. Towards the back of the market, round and oblong wickerwork baskets with sturdy handles hung from hooks. Some had floral motifs, others were criss-crossed with sharp black bands and rich purple circles. I bought one for the sheer pleasure of holding something which was useful, commonplace and spoke of domestic routines, not souvenirs. Swinging my bag, I followed the crowds round the stalls, popping the odd grape or proferred nut into my mouth, wincing at the distraught hens flapping on the scales, their eyes blinking, ungainly feet trussed together uncomfortably beneath their bellies. Rabbits in cages placidly swallowed large cabbage leaves, unaware of their fate until they were seized by the ears and held up, soft downy bellies visible for inspection. A mean-looking grey and white cat sat on a pile of brown sacks, the wrapping paper for the livestock I supposed, crunching a foul, knuckly lump of flesh, his ears back to warn off potential thieves, his eyes blazing and intent. I shuddered at the pinkness of his find, prevented myself from wandering too close to see where it had come from, and moved on.

Returning to Place el Hedim, I was struck once again by that peculiar blanket-like darkness which falls over the town, the way in which Meknès seems isolated from the rest of Morocco, a world apart. It was a comforting feeling to stand in the shadow of much-photographed Bab Mansour, a thick horseshoe arch, whose mass looms over the area flanked by two bastions; the heavy relief of the Koranic script and the tiles which remain speaking of strength rather than aesthetics. Bab Mansour separates the Imperial City from the old town and it is here at its feet that one catches all manner of buses and taxis for inner city and outer city journeys. Makeshift fruit juice and nut stalls have sprung up on the patch of wasteland, where grand taxi criers bellow out their destinations of the day and bedraggled groups of passengers stretch and loosen their limbs after enduring usually uncomfortable, fast and airless trips. Laden with bags and 'the bag', I scrambled onto a Number seven bus, mission accomplished, to return to the new town, first view of Meknès both complete and highly promising.

Over the next few days we all, for one reason or another, fell under the city's spell. The children had missed the routine of going to the park and running free. The immaculately laid-out sweep of the El Haboul gardens, which run along one side of the medina, parallel to the river, offered shade, bright flowerbeds, lawns, a park swing, alleyways and even a small zoo.

Unlike glorious Temara Zoo, Meknès's efforts in this direction were appallingly crude and the complex was badly maintained. Approaching the small gate, the first thing we noticed was the stench, a thick and rancid fug. Inside, the bird pond was a small concrete circle, the water stagnant and encrusted with algae. Monkeys sat in their own excrement, tearing newspapers into bits and chasing the strips, scabby and bored. Two lions were wedged into a cage which barely gave one of them room to turn around, let alone move. Their roars exploded on the still, scorching air as children poked at them through the bars with sticks wrenched off nearby trees, or pelted them with stones. Young men wandered around in groups, maliciously pulling the apes' arms through the bars, swearing indignantly and self-righteously if the animals refused to be grabbed or had the effrontery to bite. A man in a red parka with a distant look in his eyes was banging the golden pheasant's cage with his fist, startling the ducks, geese and flamingos nearby. He continued to bang away, satisfied that for one moment of the day he had existed, made a difference, an impression on his world. I decided that it would be unwise to say anything to him and reluctantly let it go. For some peculiar reason, the boars had welcomed a neglected porcupine and two tatty apes into their cage. Looking round at the rust, the misshapen bars, the cracked wood and the huge gaps in the netting, I was tempted to believe that the animals had staged this tableau themselves and got together to catch up on gossip or change their diet. A pack of dead-eyed jackals paced blindly in their iron rectangle, and the man in the parka moved on to flick pebbles at the tiny, suckling monkey and its mother. I pretended to trip, knocking into him as if seeking support, and ruined his shot. The face that surveyed me was wild and unfocussed. We stared at each other for a moment, each mirroring the other's dislike for what they saw, before he ambled off again. Mine was a minor and obviously temporary victory.

I decided that it would be a good thing to lobby for this particular zoo's sending its larger mammals to Rabat, filling their own enclosures with goats and pigeons so that the zoo, as such, remained, but giving it a thorough clean. Letters were duly written. Some two years ago I conducted a similar nagging campaign in Sousse via, of all things, the Tunisian Sub-Aquatic Sports Federation, the only government tourist body I could get access to. After a number of impassioned and cunning conversations with busy officials who were more interested in multiplying water-skiing and wind surfing facilities than zoos, a Mr. Mohammed Jomni promised a revamp of the zoo and 'a friend for the monkey,' his precis of my complaints, throwing in 'freedom for the camel,' something I hadn't even thought of, let alone mentioned, as a sop to persuade me to go away. When I asked when all this would happen, he firmly replied 'April'. In April, I rang the Sousse Tourist Office and was told that the zoo had indeed temporarily shut down for renovation. Home in London, I danced round the room, hugging myself with pleasure, calling down blessings on this nation which preserves its long-horned sheep and antiques with equal care, whose grass-roots representatives actually seem to do what they promise. I'll have to reserve judgment on Morocco for the time being.

Tony was missing Marmite, hot food and clean sheets and resolved to fly back to England immediately. The cholera epidemic which was still claiming lives daily in Fez, Meknès and Taza had broken his resilience since it meant that we could not shower, swim or eat and drink freely. Locals told us to use bleach in our washing-up bowls, avoid pools and fountains, fruit and vegetables and take our temperatures daily. This was a fairly simple regime to follow except for the ban on showers. Meknès was sweltering. Clothes dried in ten minutes flat on the balcony and I could feel layers of salt forming on my body virtually as soon as I started to move early in the morning. The babies' cholera chants had created a continuous mental loop in my subconscious and I found myself humming them round and round, over and over again, as I dived into different parts of the city. So now we were four. Luckily, the Panorama Hotel was a comfortable refuge from the heat with its huge, clean rooms, shuttered windows, terrace and separate WC and bathroom. Sleeping four to a bed was cramped. Three, however, with Blaise on the floor, was feasible. For once we had been granted both toilet paper and twelve hours of hot water a day. How tempting it was to use this. In the end we compromised. The babies washed in bottled water (eight litres between them a day seemed reasonable) and Michelle and I showered briefly, keeping our noses pinched shut and mouths and eyes firmly clamped against the bug. Did we cheat? Of course we did.

Armed with a bag of grapes, three litres of Sim (a cross between Fanta and liquid sugar) and the usual baguettes, which I was beginning to loathe by this point in the trip, we decided to tackle a sizable portion of the Imperial City, Dar el Khebira. Bab Mansour shimmered and expanded in the sun as we pushed through the crowd into Place Lalla Aouda, the twin of Place el Hedim. A kebab seller who poisoned dozens of Meknèssi by selling them donkey meat had his stall here until his recent arrest and as I watched the trestle-table grill supervisors turning their skewers, it was difficult to believe that none of the others was taking a similar short cut to profit. Poisoned asses and poisoned water, all within one city's walls. And what walls. According to the inhabitants it's quite common for pieces of skull and bone to occasionally emerge from the light yellow pisé, for slaves were immured as they fell from fatigue or the lash. The erroneously named underground Christian prison, just inside the Bab Filela, probably did not house Christian slaves, many of whom came from the Bou Regreg corsairs (since Moulay Ishmael had a sixty per cent interest in their trade) but rather acted as cellars for stores. As I gawped up at the walls, the street lights above shrank to Legoland proportions and I actually started to believe that Moulay Ishmael might have gone on to extend his ramparts to Marrakesh, as he threatened to do at one juncture, so a blind man could find his way there, unaided, as well as for the sheer joy of doing it, no doubt.

True building fever does not consist merely of constructing the better to admire, but also of constantly altering, demolishing and rebuilding what has just been finished. Using these criteria, the second great Alaouite sultan had it bad. Lakes, terraces and pavilions, palaces – nothing was immune to his restless frenzy of construction. Those who beheld the finished Dar el Khebira have left glowing reports of its beauty – which apparently surpassed that of its counterpart in the West, Versailles – of its gardens, menagerie, boating pools and lavish palaces, garrisons, pomp and ceremonies. Now, only the mosque-cum-shrine of the great builder remains on a square which once witnessed elaborate receptions, emissaries of foreign powers, eunuchs pulling coaches and convocations held to barter over the ransoming of hostages.

Moulay Ishmael's mausoleum is approached through a large wooden door, guarded by a stern, black sentry on the look-out not for treachery and assassins, but décolletage and revealing clothes. Passing through three courtyards built at angles to one another, loose wire mesh separating the open roof of the largest one from the sky for reasons I could not fathom, we entered the final courtyard with its grass mats, ready to remove shoes and sandals. There were no other visitors that morning. No one was in except for Moulay Ishmael, his marble coffin standing against the right-hand wall, in a slightly raised room with a bar discouraging further access. As I knelt down beside the bar, the two huge European clocks he received as gifts drew my attention. Dark brown oak or mahogany cased, they stand guard over the body of the man who once wanted to link himself to their home of origin, the France of Louis XIV, through marriage. Behind me in the Moorish hall, a small fountain trickled placidly and irregularly; the light green, apricot and blue painted plaster-work had run in places and there was a slapdash feel to the decorations which spoke of recent work. (I later learned the tomb had been restored as recently as 1959 by Mohammed V but that Islamic art had slumped to a low plateau in Moulay Ishmael's day and the eighteenth-century furniture, chests and ceramics which survive from that time are visibly inferior to both earlier and later work.) The cedar ceiling was magnificent, fiery in its red and green. The tiled floor reflected shafts of sunlight. An old man wandered through in a grey djellabah and pushed aside the metal barrier enclosing the tomb. He sat down casually on a pillow-upholstered bench, just inside, and started to read a book. The minutes ticked by and we stayed. The babies had fallen silent, partly because silence is as contagious as its opposite, partly out of exhaustion and partly, I suspect, because they felt some alien spirit there too. 'Is he going to get up?' I heard Caspian whisper.

'I don't think so,' replied Michelle in a voice edged with uncertainty. What was going on here? This was becoming ridiculous. We seemed to have been kneeling at the bar for hours and no one was moving, talking or even looking at the garishly bright decorations all around. The man was dead, God damn it, I lectured myself. You're not only creating your own illusions but also compounding matters by falling under their spell. I heaved myself to my feet and dragged my eyes away but could not resist a farewell, a closer look through the carved window outside which gave on to the shrine. Everything seemed bright and hopeful in the glare and I overtipped the guardian outrageously, eager to move on, to see the rest of the complex.

In this euphoric frame of mind, I gladly accepted the services of young Karim, a sweet faced sixteen-year old with straight black hair. Karim was on holiday and during the summer months I suspected he had lost his virginity. His conversation was single-minded and, over the next few kilometres, as we walked down past the gate of the wind, Bab er Rith, the only straight stretch of road past the inaccessible Royal Palace of Hassan II to the granaries and Aguedal Tank, Karim talked about prostitutes. Awakened to the possibility of, if not exactly the joy of sex, Karim saw prostitutes everywhere – on the street, in the bars at Azzemour (again) and at the hotel near his parents' house. Roundly condemning them in one breath, he circled back to how much they cost, how they found men, how to spot them, how old, ugly and alluring they were. I listened, non-committal, refusing to be drawn into comparing prices in Meknès and London, alternately sympathetic to his adolescent passions, and bored senseless. Like so many Moslem men, Karim sees purity or degeneracy, and nothing in between. He solemnly declared that all women must be watched as they have insatiable appetites and ought to be locked in the house, then switched tack to exclaim about probably apocryphal Berber villages just outside Meknès where Berber girls as young as twelve French-kiss passersby. I nodded mutely and asked questions about his home town, but Karim would not be deterred. The El Haboul gardens had to be locked up at night because of courting couples who came to enjoy the deserted paths and benches. Moulay Ishmael fornicated with mares; the price of food was exorbitant, so how was a lad going to put one hundred dirhams aside to buy a prostitute? Impressed by his relentlessness I tried a U-turn on the verbal road and asked about circumcision. Yes, he was circumcised, his mother kept his blue embroidered top trimmed with ribbons, and no, he couldn't remember anything about it but, more crucially, did I watch pornography? I was seized by a desire to scream and laugh.

It was midday and the light pisé walls were reflecting the heat with a hearty enthusiasm. The Aguedal Tank, which once watered the royal gardens and orchards, was now an oasis, but it was so polluted that it was forbidden to swim in let alone drink from its four-hectare expanse. Two youngsters were, however, dog-paddling after a plastic container at one end. The much-written-about terrace café which perches nearby, apparently providing an unforgettable view for miles around, was shut and the guardian of the Heri es Souani refused to unlock the granaries for another hour. Looking at the crude wooden cross-bars and beams which prop up the warren of tall, arched rooms which are all that remains of this, Moulay Ishmael's storehouse, the scale of his buildings once again rendered me speechless. The Heri es Souani was constructed to make it possible for Meknès to withstand siege indefinitely, indefinitely being the operative word. Now, centuries later, the decaying walls and gently collapsing rounded roofs conjure up martial images, quartermasters and campaigns, thousands of crack, avid troops milling around, ready to saddle up the twelve thousand cavalry horses kept in the nearby Heri el Mansour, grooms and eunuchs scurrying past with orders and messages, blankets and arms.

Karim broke in on my revery of Hollywood-type fantasy by bluntly saying, 'You shouldn't go in there. It's dangerous.' Running my hand over the uneven sandy surface of the granary walls, I had to agree. Whatever I touched seemed to move, and lumps of wall, showers of dust, gently pattered down to my feet. Meknès was neither preserving its heritage nor exploiting it. Instead of erecting the brown road signs which lure tourists into stopping to tick off another sight, thereby contributing the money to maintain it, Meknès has shut away its past and its riches, tossed them into the lap of Allah to preserve or erode as he wills. I asked Karim why this was so. He shrugged and told me that the king hated the city and its inhabitants alike, and refused to pour money into it or even encourage industry to invest there on any meaningful level. Apparently, Hassan II had not stayed at the Royal Palace since the time he was pelted with a tomato, early on in his reign, while driving through, getting to know the kingdom. Many Meknèssi swear that, in revenge, he's slapped down a twenty-year edict forbidding any form of building, excluding housing stock. Others amplify the tomato story and say that he was shot at, once, twice or three times (depending on who is telling the tale) in the area, and has therefore laid a curse on it.

What is indisputable is the atmosphere of desolation surrounding the Royal Palace, whose heavily guarded entrance is manned round the clock. A dozen or more storks perched on the buttresses, their straggly nests sticking out from the towers like badly chewed straw hats, their extraordinary, ungainly silhouettes bringing a spontaneous laugh to my lips. So, Moulay Ishmael's dream will die then, left to fall apart. Already lacking protection in the face of the Moroccans' tendency to recycle any available material, the Imperial City is beginning to blur and fade. Empty, scorched tracts of land with their overgrown and no longer recognisable walls, fragments of bright tiles and mountains of refuse cover former glories and combine to hide footprints and pavilions alike. Soon, imagination will have to suffice as the landmarks and tangible cues which help one to visualise now the seventeenth-century marvel that was Meknès, disappear.

Saddened, we retraced our steps to the Bab Mansour and the more recent past. The narrow row of grill kitchens facing the gate seemed garish, the cries of 'Take off your sunglasses,' 'Alone today, eh?' and 'Where are your husbands?' struck completely the wrong note. A woman in a pink caftan jerked us firmly back to the present when she shrieked as we bumped into her. In the ensuing excitement, Michelle trod on a man's foot and, attempting to apologise, trod on it again. The sun was beating down and combining nauseatingly with the smell of frying fish, warmed tomatoes and grilled kidneys. This simultaneous assault on our senses persuaded us to sit down for a while to gather our thoughts. I felt murderous towards Karim with all his sex talk and exhausted by the gamut of emotional responses this strange city had precipitated. Michelle's boil had doubled in size since the morning, assuming an odd, bruised, purple gleam, and the babies wanted a drink. We drank, sitting alongside the unemployed, those aimless and restless souls who pack the cafés of Morocco, sipping the glasses of water which accompanied their long-since drunk coffee. Our neighbours cadged cigarettes in broken English and watched the street: buses strained past; a pick-up truck full of revellers beating a drum honked up and down the road, presumably bound for Moulay Idriss and the moussem due to begin in two days' time. Shoeshine boys squatted under the awning, occasionally rapping brush against box to draw attention to their availability without having to do the rounds. Torpor descended and heads gradually slumped onto tables or collapsed onto upturned hands as we all listlessly waited.

The last thing I, for one, was waiting for was the appearance of a group of flash, giant, Honda motorbikes, fenders decorated with skulls and crossbones. As helmets were removed, tousled French faces emerged. The men looked distinctly affluent in their long-line, pastel linen shorts and casual shirts. The women hadn't got over seeing *Girl On A Motorbike* yet, and must have been swimming inside their leathers. The new arrivals picked their way gingerly through the unstable tables and chairs, avoiding the random puddles of grease on the tiled floor, obviously repelled by the crude facilities they found on offer. Michelle and I exchanged glances and slumped back onto the table, uninterested. This waft of Europe reminded me of how hobo-like we had become over the previous two months. My clothes had been perfunctorily washed and badly dried, over and over again, and were permanently damp and creased. Michelle had given up on fashion entirely and was now wearing the same floor-length, wafting, pink skirt and white broderie anglaise top every day. We were too lazy even to swap garments and I frequently ended up sleeping fully clothed, rather than covering myself head to toe in Autan insect repellant. The most pressing fashion issue we addressed was whether or not we had dry, clean underwear every morning, for nothing was more uncomfortable than facing a new day with wet knickers, sweating skin and filthy jeans encrusted with dust and flecks of mud. The French group had apparently not seen us as kindred spirits either, for they knocked back bottles of soft drinks and left. I noticed they hadn't left a tip. Michelle had been galvanised into philosophical statements by their appearance, for she murmured that we were too rich for the poor and too poor for the rich. I made a mental inventory of our funds and told her we would soon be much too poor for the rich, but quite at home with the poor. We now had £10 a day left, for accommodation, travel and food, and the Panorama was costing us £8.90 a night, the babies' constant cold drinks at least another £2. It was deficit time already with nine days to go.

Since the financial situation looked grim, I elected to cut short my twenty pence tonic water binge in the interests of an economy drive and arranged to meet Michelle and the babies outside the Dar Jamai Museum in two hours' time. They continued to slump on tables and in our arms respectively, as Karim and I headed back for the medina and a visit to the shrine of

Sidi Ben Aissa, the eighteenth-century founder of the Sufi Aissaouia sect, whose followers gaily eat scorpions washed down with broken glass, trip the light fantastic on hot coals and generally pursue their particular road to oneness with Allah in this life, and revelation by a personal communion, chanting music and entering trance states. The French were not overly keen on the Aissaouia, for Catholicism in particular, and mainstream Christianity in general, have always held ecstatic practices at arm's length and tended to see them as forms of possession rather than insight, a threat to the structure of the Church and the role of the priest. During the Protectorate, therefore, the Aissaouia found their rituals of self-mutilation proscribed and their teachings suppressed, for all central government fears local pockets of influence and power and the Aissaouia certainly had, and continued to have, a wide following in North Africa. On the pragmatic level, their indifference to the realities of this world carried within it a potential for martyrdom which the French did not wish to trigger into action, particularly since the Brotherhood, like most Sufi mystical movements, owe their primary allegiance to their sheik and not the temporal powers.

Surprisingly, the amenable Karim did not want to go anywhere near the zaouia of Sidi Ben Aissa, but reluctantly agreed to guide me as far as the nearby cemetery. The Bab Jdid area was 'bad', he pronounced, spitting out the word with great emphasis. It was particularly bad when the Aissaouia gathered at the tomb, usually on Fridays (it was Friday), and unbelievably bad if you were walking with a Christian who, heaven forbid, happened to be a woman. Persuasion failed to move Karim from his compromise. Bab Jdid and no further. Once this was agreed, we plunged into the northern medina and the second-hand clothes market, with its ironed suits and shirts hanging off tent poles and on rails, its jumbled up T-shirts and underwear lying on long plywood tables, its sewing machines humming.

I bought a checked cowboy shirt with no buttons for a few

dirhams and the man attached neat transparent replacements on the spot, pulling at the seams and cuffs for a perfect fit. Karim laughed and told me that no Moroccan woman would be seen dead in an old, not to mention a man's shirt and, of course, he was right. A rigidly defined definition of femininity rules in Morocco. Mules and wedge-heels, patterned headscarves and gaudy caftans still clothe ninety-five per cent of Moroccan women on the street and no one wears track suits or joggers and trainers. Where Western clothes have been accepted, in Rabat, Casablanca, Tangier, then it is always in the form of power dressing: businesslike blouses and suits with split skirts and stilettos. Jeans are occasionally seen, but on younger girls, and leather jackets beat their denim counterparts, no contest. Karim's remarks made me feel self-conscious, and the warm smell of beef dripping and unwashed armpits, which the shirt's former owner had passed on with his cloth, made me falter for a second, but only for a second. God damn it, Meknès was chilly at night. I needed a shirt and this one was as good as any I had seen. I tucked it in determinedly, took a deep breath and strolled outside the stall. No one blinked an eyelid.

Just round the corner the strains of Bad Company jolted through the air as we passed cane weavers, heaps of old mattresses, plastic bowls and chunky transistor radios. The streets were crowded for this was where the Meknèssi, not the out-of-towners, shopped. Huge cooking pots and ceremonial serving dishes with red and green cloth covers were stacked in doorways, and tethered donkeys blinked in the sun, sneezing whenever a cloud of sawdust spewed out from the carpenters' and joiners' workshops. As the medina petered out into a tatty second-hand street market, so the crowds thinned. From time to time men and women muttered at Karim, and he was warned repeatedly that I must not go into the cemetery or enter the zaouia which materialised on our right, a green roofed, impressively solid building on the edge of the cemetery, approached up a wide path. Scaffolding cloaked its outer walls but the steady trickle of people going up the path reassured me that Sidi Ben Aissa's earthly remains were not shut away from view. Karim sat down and told me that he would wait there and I must be very quick, and very respectful in my demeanour.

I removed my straw hat and ran my fingers through my hair, pushing it firmly back on my head, and crept behind a couple of young women dressed in dark green caftans. An old man wrapped in a blanket offered them herbs to burn and candles to light at the shrine, but offered me only a frown. My face impassive, I walked on slowly. Somewhere just behind the wall Koranic readers were chanting over a grave. It seemed desolate there, worrying, and I remember being warned that the Aissaouia loathe the colours red and black, which supposedly excite them to a frenzy of self-mutilation. My new shirt was red and white checked. I drew my jacket tightly across, buttoned up and continued a tentative approach. A man in his thirties clicked his tongue irritatedly as he walked past me but did nothing. So far, so good. And there it was, the zaouia door, closed to non-Moslems. The side window was just accessible if I stood on tiptoe and I hesitated, torn between discretion and curiosity. Just then a hand dropped on my shoulder: I feared turning round and seeing someone garbed in black chomping on scorpions or banging a nail into his head. The hand pressed still more firmly, twisted my shoulder to the left and so, cautiously, I turned. A bearded, lined face smiled, offered me a wooden box to stand on, put a finger to his lips and hobbled off. Quickly now. I hopped up and gazed at the second religious rite of the morning. On first impression, the coffin seemed somehow small, heartbreakingly small. The rush-carpeted floor was awash with squatting women and babies, their faces partially lit by wavering candle flames. The women seemed pensive and sat, immobile, in front of the dark, draped tomb. The deep colours, the stillness and the low light cast a sheen of reverence over the tableau. I've often suspected that all lapsed Catholics suffer from a deeply developed sense of worship which lacks a focus and are thus vulnerable to the quest for an altar throughout their lives. Their yawning emotional void and the habits of childhood create a deadly combination of prophets, causes and ideology – and tombs, in particular, at least in my case, spark off a real need to kneel and then follow. How else can I explain away my genuflecting, of all things, in front of Moulay Ishmael, of all people, a reflex Michelle, another lapsed Catholic, saw as quite natural as she proceeded to do the same.

Karim had had his fill of sights and follies and felt cheated of sexual titillation. The European connection had failed him and it was obviously time for a parting of the ways. Leaving me at the Dar Jamai he waved his black US baseball cap in the air in farewell, refused a tip and sauntered back into Place el Hedim, doubtlessly eyeing up ankles, his prostitute antennae flapping widely.

This may have been a wise move, since the museum was cursed by an euphoric maniac who shoved me from one room to the next, switching off lights before I was able to focus on what the display cases held. Decaying carpets were barely visible where they hung in narrow, shaded corridors, and most of the ceramic work and wooden objects were of fairly recent vintage. I gazed at my two-hundredth couscous bowl of the trip and smiled broadly, encouraging him to leave the light switch alone. No, we plunged back into the murk yet again.

Suddenly I saw a distinctly English face one room ahead, realised the curator had been trying to transform me into 'a group', in short, to rationalise his task by herding us together. Adrian, a medical student from Southampton, his sunburned neck strained from peering at the typed, descriptive slips, was as confused by the museum as I. Exchanging a few words, we agreed that back-tracking or, oh heresy, starting again at the beginning were probably out, and resolved to crawl through what remained in order to see something, anything, for our pains. The guardian sensed an impasse and played his trump card, declaring triumphantly that the entire first floor was closed for the day. Luckily, the jewellery and ironwork sections were good and blessed with natural light. Koran holders, more suitable for mastiffs' than for human necks, shone dully in their cases, their frayed red and gold cords hanging limp. Monstrous, crescent-shaped earrings, thick enough to precipitate a brain clot on the spot, made me recoil. Just the idea of pushing one through an ear lobe was numbing. Pretty, brash, enamelled silver rings and fibulae added a note of fun and frippery to the sombre displays of silver pendants and brashly decorated wooden boxes. Adrian and I chatted as we gazed idly at the booty.

The Dar Jamai (a former vizier's palace, which belonged to the brothers who built the Palais Jamai, Fez) dates back to the 1930s and is a gracious, airy, nineteenth-century building, with worn tiled floors and an attractively laid-out Andalusian garden in the central courtyard. Meknès seemed many miles away as we perched on the edge of the tiled fountain, surrounded by banana plants and an explosion of brilliantly coloured orchids, hollyhocks and geraniums, talking cholera and swapping grill café hints. Adrian swore by Café Bab Mansour, while I pressed the virtues of its near neighbour, whose coffee had less sludge at the bottom. Adrian was in Meknès by default, and thanks to the Gulf crisis. Originally, he was heading for Syria to practise his classical Arabic, but the invasion of Kuwait had deterred him from going and now he had two weeks to kill in a strange land where his classical Arabic cut no ice. Armed with a tent and a guide-book, and laden down with a veritable ton of medicines, he was camping by the Aguedal tank, suffering broken nights thanks to the proximity of the military academy and its band's love of early morning rehearsals of mutilated classical pieces. Dressed in sensible trainers, navy T-shirt and green army boots, he looked competent, but his batty, flustered manner, burnt neck and vague plans added a boyish vulnerability which instantly brought out the maternal in me.

We made plans for a trip to Moulay Idriss and did a second tour of the ironwork rooms, whose whopping nails and grossly studded hinges and bolts spoke of a general Meknèssi siege mentality, not solely confined to the sultan. A pick and shovel on one wall, and the keys it would take both of us to lift, let alone manipulate, were impressive but did little to reverse the general impression that the Dar Jamai, like Meknès itself, was being allowed to slumber gracefully into decay rather than testify. Perhaps it would gain a new lease of life when Place el Hedim was reopened to the public and coachloads of visitors directed through its heavy doors. I doubted it somehow, but this was August, prime tourist season and the Moroccans were on the Atlantic coast, unimpressed by door bosses and ink holders, oblivious to miniatures and sweet-smelling courtyards of bygone years.

Adrian departed for his deserted campsite after loudly bemoaning the state of Michelle's cheeks, throwing silver foiled yards of antihistamine tablets in her general direction, and eyeing the now vocal babies highly dubiously. I could see him calculating how long he'd have to sit on a bus in their company and weighing it up against another day alone, trying to discover a city using an out-of-date guide-book. It was a close contest but the trip to Moulay Idriss won – just. We repaired to an Arab café to try a mint tea flavoured with 'sheba', a bitter herb formerly used in Pastis, and apparently banned in Germany and France, which is supposed to act as a stimulant in the heat. The café was hidden in a medina back-quarter, a vine-trellised courtyard with a small whitewashed room off to one side. An old man stood behind a boiling kettle, chopping various herbs with a small bone-handled knife and gesturing that we should sit. Peering into the room I saw a fridge with a playing radio balanced on top, two foam-covered benches and three wooden chairs. Two men in their forties were chatting quietly in one corner and barely looked up as we entered. Glasses were rinsed in the bucket; the tea served. Sheba seemed innocuous enough although its greeny, mauve-feathered leaves left an unpleasant aftertaste when chewed and I was just beginning to share the absence of Aissaouia brethren, blood and gore with Michelle, when all thoughts of tea-drinking and refuge were banished.

One of the Moroccan men strode towards our bench, gesturing that we had to get up. Bewildered, I rose to my feet and stood there as he fished around under the foam before pulling out a handful of wooden kif pipes with clay bowls. I have few views on drugs but I do detest the smell of dope and observing the smacking of bowl against palm, the emergence of plastic wrapped leaves and the elaborate lighting and puffing ritual, I could virtually feel the men looking round ready for conversation. After making sure that we were not French and therefore could not change francs into dirhams – a minor digression – we were subjected to a full-blown diatribe on Britain's role in creating the Gulf situation by re-drawing Kuwait's borders. Saddam Hussein would be assassinated, they argued, since he does not crawl to the West, and the scandalous presence of the Yanks in Saudia Arabia would finally unite the Arab world. What did we think? Michelle and I blustered sweetly that we knew nothing about politics or the world, that we were simple tourists. Unfortunately, since we no longer either looked like or spent like tourists, the men were dissatisfied with our answers and, drawing deeply on the copiously replenished pipes, quipped, half-seriously, that we were probably communist spies. Now this was not a train of thought that should be encouraged in the Third World, and I started to panic, talking quickly in a tone which lacked credibility even in my own ears about the benefits of comparing cultures.

'Oh. what other Arab countries do you know?' barked out the chief interlocutor.

'Tunisia.' I replied. glad to be on solid ground. 'I know Tunisia well.'

This was a bad choice for these Moroccans felt that Tunisia was nothing, nay. worse than nothing, a dull expanse of beaches which knew only how to sell itself. In contrast, their beloved Morocco had a great deal to offer. A list was recited, but no one cared. Maudlin now. and gradually losing their vehemence, the men turned back to each other, disgusted by our lack of savvy. Michelle picked up our glasses and moved towards the café owner's bucket. She was interrupted by a loud shout.

'You. you over there! You take too many lovers and drugs! Where is your family? Where is your man?' The accusations hung on the air as Michelle turned to face the temporarily enraged Moroccan.

'My husband.' she gravely declared. as if saddened at having to explain, to reply, 'is an Arab.' (True.) 'He is with Saddam Hussein.' (Quite false. He is serving dinner at the El Mouradi Hotel.) Apologies rained down and we made a dignified exit.

Overall, Menkès had been very good to us. Here people waved hello and did not follow you, said welcome without inviting you to do a grand tour. beeped their horns and smiled rather than kerb crawled, yet a point comes in every journey when places recede and people come to the fore, a time when individuals in turn flow into a chorus of faces, desperate teenagers, idle men. spoiled, rich women and their worn-out, poor counterparts. I was gradually losing heart, losing hope for this country's peaceful transition from under-development to riches. I could not bear to read another sycophantic editorial commemorating some speech or other made by Mohammed V in 1939, or reminiscences of Hassan II's visit to Dakhla in 1980, features extolling the wonders of whale song and music as therapy. The gulf between the press and the people was truly immense; that between government and the people, wider still. Articles on losing weight seem obscene in a country where the prices, not choice, determine diet. There is so much mass powerlessness and large-scale destitution all around that even the sublime beauty of Menkès, a city at peace with itself, is finally irrelevant.

In neighbouring Algeria, social changes, segregation by sexes on buses and in schools, fines for using French instead of Arabic in official documents and the end of bilingualism per se, are being fabricated as a smokescreen for economic problems. In Morocco, the population explosion continues to swamp the government's will or ability to expand the economy, and the panacea of Islamisation, à la Algeria, has not been applied. Urban unrest grows as the exodus from the countryside gains pace and the status quo maintained by the security organs and the army will, surely, eventually give way and catapult the country into turmoil. Moulay Ishmael's walls and palaces may not survive into the twenty-first century, but the struggle he faced to hold onto power bids fair to be replayed in the near future.

Moulay Idriss, a mere half hour away from Menkès by bus, was founded by the great-grandson of the Prophet, thought by many Shi'ites to be the rightful sixth caliph. Until relatively recently this small town discouraged non-Moslems staying overnight (and, indeed, I saw no hotels), and Christians and Jews were forbidden entry until 1912. Part of the reason for this cordon sanitaire was the belief that five pilgrimages here, spiritual home of ecstatic cults and Sunni orthodoxy alike, equalled a pilgrimage to Mecca. In short, Moulay Idriss was too sacred to be profaned by the presence of non-Moslems, and to this day a thick, polished, wooden bar prevents asses and non-Moslems from approaching the mosque of Ali's and Fatima's grandson.

PART ONE

Looking at Moulay Idriss's brief career, it soon becomes apparent that he was a man of great charisma, with an unshakable faith in his own interpretation of Islam and opposition to the Abbasid caliphate of eighth-century Baghdad. Fleeing the east in 786, after the Battle of Fakh saw the rebels defeated just outside Mecca, Moulay Idriss made his way to Morocco, and then took shelter in Volubilis. The Berber Auroba tribe proclaimed him imam. Five years later, he was dead, poisoned by the caliph Harun er Rashid's agents, leaving a posthumously born child, Idriss II (buried in Fez) to carry on the first Moroccan Islamic dynasty, the Idrissids.

As arranged, Adrian met us at 9:00 a.m. outside the sparkling Bab Mansour, his royal blue cap signifying a new day and an alteration to his basic gear, eager to get on. The barracks band had blasted him into wakefulness very early and he was seriously considering moving to Azrou, home of the Barbary apes, within twenty-four hours, in order to escape their pitiful and wholehearted practice sessions. His neck raw from the sun, mini back-pack filled with sensibly chlorinated and unspeakably foul water, Adrian epitomised the nineteenth-century explorer, right down to his baggy, khaki trousers. Mindful of the strictures against unduly exciting the Aissaouia, Michelle and I had ransacked our pathetic bag of clean clothes and were wearing off-white from head to toe. The mere sight of the local bus, its diesel engine clucking and growling erratically as it shook in the sun, only patchily full, encouraged us to get a grand taxi – a sort of communal taxi which leaves whenever it's full – and preserve some degree of dubious cleanliness for yet another few hours. The majority of this morning's traffic of bright blue Mercedes was heading towards Moulay Idriss, and since we were five already, it took seconds to agree the price of forty dirhams and slide onto the already piping hot, leatherette seats. The countryside just outside Meknès is beautiful and visibly cultured to good effect: olive and fig trees, long feathery carrots being washed in the stream by groups of women, baby lambs dressed in T-shirts against the morning chill and awkwardly scampering across narrow irrigation ditches. As we purred up and down the hills, the severe black and white stripes of freshly turned-over soil and post-harvest stubble positively begged for a photograph, and I'm not surprised that virtually every picture I've seen of Volubilis includes this view, snapped with the Roman triumphal arch in the foreground.

It was market day in Moulay Idriss when we were turfed out at the bottom of the steep hill which signifies the beginning of the town's main thoroughfare. Large, air-conditioned tour buses were crawling up the bunting-festooned street, and before we had even got our bearings, an officious, grey-uniformed policeman tapped Adrian on the shoulder and, pointing at the zoom lens equipped square of photo power hanging round his neck, said emphatically that he did not want to feature in any pictures and then, almost as an afterthought, asked our nationalities. British, Australian. The policeman considered our national identities, rolling them round in his mind, looking for a connection or a spark of reaction and drew a blank. Tapping Adrian on the shoulder and glaring meaningfully, he walked away. Naked authority in action. Cameras swinging, gripped by a devil-may-care mood born of being a group and having jumped the first hurdle, we were swallowed up by the procession and swept up the hill. Animals were highly visible here, both slaughtered and vocally alive, lambs and goats being pulled down flights of steps by lengths of string, or pushed, like wheelbarrows, their faces frantic and confused. Donkeys staggered past, draped in panniers, each pocket containing the curious, peeping face of a kid or lamb. Buckets of intestines stood nonchalantly next to tethered, hobbled cows, and light, temporary tents, set up against the beating sun, sheltered old women with their silky-haired billy-goats and trussed turkeys.

I took a shine to one thin-skulled, black goat, the classic

Capricorn of a hundred horoscope columns, and asked the five-year-old girl who was supervising, if I might touch him. She smiled, uncomprehending, but loosened the twine. Two blunted horns thumped into my belly, my hipbone and, as he retreated, he delivered a few high kicking paces for a real charge. I fled humiliated.

Moulay Idriss is blasé about summer tourist visitors. Everyone wants to be paid two dirhams for a picture, and when I tried to focus on the popcorn seller to check the light meter, a stone was instantly hurled, followed by its twin, missing me by inches and not feet. Michelle, meanwhile, had attracted a young follower of her own, a pickpocket, and was weaving erratically through the mountains of melons, peppers, potatoes and carrots, trying to shake off her shadow. The babies tripped along behind her in their straw hats with red ribbon ties, enchanted by the chase and eager to join in this good game. I watched Caspian (who fell over his own shadow) tumble over a small wooden crate and collapse into a display of sardines, luckily not head first, scattering dozens of silver corpses into the gravel. He laughed and tucked a fist around a pole which was supporting the fish seller's tarpaulin shelter. Immobile, I waited for the whole bloody thing to collapse, separated from him by a mere nine feet of ground but tons of carrots and a wide display of herbs. The fish seller gave Caspian a sardine and waved the incident off. Another puzzle. Moroccans seem to believe bringing up children is a communal concern, and swiftly intercede when boys fight in the streets, shaking them apart like puppies, but are equally happy to castigate foreigners for imaginary crimes. On one occasion, an old man walked up to us in Fez and screamed, 'Why are you carrying the children?' when both babies were exhausted by the heat. On another, in Casablanca, we were soundly berated for smacking little hands intent on smashing the cake shop glass frontage which prevented them from helping themselves to the pastries behind.

Children were wandering through the food markets selling narrow banners and Moroccan flags on sticks, straw hats and bottles of cold drinks in buckets of shaved ice. A middle-aged man, yelling in the best market tradition, offered me a pair of natty, flared corduroy trousers for ten dirhams and was hurt by my refusal, pantomiming a broken heart and grinning from ear to ear. Somewhere over by the livestock square, I spotted Adrian's blue hat focussing on a long row of donkeys, mainly plump rear ends, unfortunately, since they were all facing the wall. Climbing gingerly down from the produce terrace, I joined the great throng pushing up and down the main thoroughfare and went with the flow, past the most hideous display of ornaments imaginable, plastic pots containing straight-backed plastic roses and carnations, all made in China, of course. Heaps of the by then familiar brushed nylon blankets, mattresses and occasional tables signalled the end of the road and I spotted an empty café table and claimed it unceremoniously. It was at least forty-five degrees centigrade today – and rising. Peering round through the café doorway into the murk, I saw that this was another kif-smokers' hideaway, for the men were puffing away and did not talk, a radio soothing already anaesthetised breasts. It was fairly obvious that this would not prove to be the home of fresh orange juice – far too much trouble – and that black coffee, precisely what I did not want, was the most I could hope for from the bartender. Resigned, I asked for a double and knocked it back, hoping it might wet my lips before the sun honed in on me. Abdul leaned across from the neighbouring table and told me that coffee was bad for the heart. I looked at the cigarette he was smoking and replied that nicotine was bad for the chest. Gesticulating, I revealed my own nicotine-stained right hand, thereby diluting my response and making this crinkly-faced man in his late thirties feel that it was perfectly acceptable to table-jump and chat.

PART ONE

Abdul was a teacher and lived permanently in Moulay Idriss, never having seen any point in leaving his parents' home. The youngest son, he had inherited a simple whitewashed box of a home, three stories high, its open courtyard choked with thick vine roots and branches. The sky was barely visible through a heavy curtain of dark blue grapes and bright green leaves which parted where a ladder broke through onto the roof which linked the two houses. His work was fascinating, he enthused, for shaping the minds of the young was important and children were closer to God than adults, so he learned from them too. In his prime and still (just) single, Abdul had recently become engaged to a nineteen-year-old girl who lived in Meknès, but he was having second thoughts about the match. Whenever he rang her out of the blue, she was tired or – classic, this – washing her hair, so their courtship was confined to the bearing of gifts of high quality, and family gatherings at which they discussed their wedding ceremony, where they might live and what furniture to buy. Abdul was depressed by the fact that Miriam had no interests in life, in art, God damn it, in anything really bar the trousseau and the kitchen equipment. To make matters more fraught, Miriam's mother's wishes had to be respected, on every topic, since the woman would be living with them and, he confided slowly, as if the very words were treacherous and dangerous, he was not sure if he actually liked either woman.

Break it off then, I advised, firmly. The idea horrified him. The shame of breaking an engagement would be unendurable. His own family would ostracise him and, he lamely added, he had already ordered the ceremonial chairs and booked the woman who would henna Miriam's hands and feet and help her in and out of the numerous garments and headdresses she would be wearing over the ceremonial fortnight. We racked our brains. Abdul volunteered the information that his sister-in-law was an ally and might perhaps be persuaded to consult an old woman up in the hills, who was reputedly skilled in making magic potions, and thus might conceivably make an antidote to love. He could then slip this into Miriam's food. This was grasping at ultra-short straws indeed and judging by Abdul's face, none of the family, who welcomed the fact that he was finally becoming a householder, were about to help him scupper the advantageous marriage connection. In short, he was doomed. To distract him from following an obviously well-worn and terrifying train of thought, I asked Abdul to show us around, which he agreed to do with alarming alacrity.

Separated into two residential quarters, Tasga and Khiber, which seem wedged into a frame of volcanic rocks, seen from one of the two main terraces that overlook the town, Moulay Idriss is breathtaking. Whitewashed houses nestle behind green-tiled roofs, the forested hills and lush plains spreading around as if clutching everything to a spiritual bosom, crushing Moulay Idriss against nature. The town's famous minaret seemed smaller than I had imagined. Based on a Meccan design, it was maintained and restored by a short old man who had recently died, and now no one knew how to repair this curious cylindrical protuberance. We climbed and climbed. Moulay Idriss was exhausting on the calves with its narrow streets and constant, totally unexpected, flights of stairs, and as one hammam became ten, I started to cough furiously. 'We're almost there,' said Abdul. Where, I wondered, and panted on. Turning a sharp corner, suddenly we reached a noisy, packed square and hence the entrance to Moulay Idriss's tomb. The nougat was very good here, the candles and incense standard, and the religious bits and bobs tacky. Having read so much about the famous wooden bar which marks the point of segregation between the Peoples of the Book, I was keen to touch it and pressed through the crowd of men, women and children, eventually to find myself staring at a courtyard at the end of which lay the mausoleum cum mosque of the eternally revered Idrissid. Apparently the bar is only raised when the king comes on his annual pilgrimage, since, as the Prophet's descendant, he is Moulay Idriss's equal and should therefore bow to no man. Less exalted persons slip past reverentially. To the left of the approach, it was possible to make out the pilgrims' sleeping quarters; to the right lay the king's rarely used but ever-ready apartments, where he rests after his yearly one-hour-long visit of homage. Apparently, Hassan II had recently decided to demolish the main square and finance a complete revamp, so soon the numerous stalls, cafés and tobacconists would disappear, to be replaced by another tiled rectangle lined with miniaturised trees, similar to Place el Hedim and the royal palace forecourt in Tetouan. This sanitisation of human activity and demolition of overcrowded squares may well be symptomatic of the king's assassination phobia, rather than evidence (and an indictment) of his aesthetic preferences, for cramped lanes are difficult to survey and an eddying mass of bodies could conceal a pistol-toting protester. Broad boulevards are, of course, the hallmark of all Morocco's French-built new towns, and underline the Protectorate's awareness of the need for crowd control and a clear line of fire – as well as a certain nostalgia for a less alien urban environment than the medina. It seems tragic, however, that such mediocre uniformity should end up swamping a functional communal meeting place, yet another step on the road to ensuring easy surveillance and gutted communities whose voice is stilled through being denied the opportunity to exchange views and eventually reach a grass-roots consensus.

The visual joys of walking through Moulay Idriss were dampened by the absence of the Aissouia, who had not been involved in the moussem's opening ceremony, an official affair composed of parades and speeches, but were expected to arrive the following Thursday. Abdul pressed fresh figs upon us, commiserated, urged us to stay today, tomorrow, however long we wanted to, and would not hear of allowing us to leave, unescorted, when we demurred and persuaded him that we really had to leave Moulay Idriss if we were to see the nearby ruins of Volubilis before sunset. His escort duty consisted of throwing us into an already tightly jammed flat-bed cattle truck, the restraining mesh bursting outwards from the crush, and paying our nine-dirham fare. Barely able to breathe, I clutched Adrian and Michelle with one hand, and fished around with the other to reassure myself that the babies were somewhere in the vicinity of my knees. The truck coughed, bucked and died, then coughed again and we were off, uncovered heads festooned with dust, nothing to grip onto, racing erratically out of Moulay Idriss's patch of car park, round and down a tarmacked road. Abdul waved his kif pipe, and then doubtlessly returned to his debate on love, honour and arranged marriages, worrying away at his misgivings over another coffee, as our truck chundered along, violating the still air. We passed stagnant pools covered in mould and animal excrement, and in the bright light the black and orange strips of the Zerhoun hills shifted and started to swim before our eyes. There was not a soul to be seen against the cloudless sky, no waving children, foraging hens or clopping asses. The truck juddered epileptically once, twice, three times and stopped. Everyone was looking at us expectantly and I realised we must be at Volubilis, although this road juncture seemed to be the very back of beyond. But there it was, the Roman city where Moulay Idriss first settled in 787; the former capital of Mauretania Tingitania under Juba II, King of Mauretania and husband to Cleopatra's and Mark Anthony's daughter, Cleopatra Silene.

Between the third century BC and the fifth century AD, Volubilis was the Romans' administrative capital and after their withdrawal north it remained a thriving town with a population which reached twenty thousand in its heyday under Emperor

PART ONE

Marcus Aurelius, during whose reign (161-180 AD) most of what we saw now was constructed. Moulay Ishmael and the Lisbon earthquake of 1755 were no respecters of history, however. The former looted Volubilis as and when the need arose for extra materials in Meknès (indeed there are columns from Volubilis to be seen in Bab Mansour), and the latter reduced villas, bathhouses, temples and libraries to dust. The contemporary visitor is treated with marked suspicion here, too, and seen as yet another potential agent of destruction, ever since art-loving Italians and their Moroccan accomplices brazenly bore off a statue of Bacchus a few years ago. The statue was never recovered, in spite of the fact that the accomplices were tortured by the authorities into revealing the little they knew.

Trudging up the hill past dozens of jettisoned bottles of Sidi Harazam, which had magically appeared from nowhere to litter the roadside, we reached a large car park. A cross-bred dog fastened to a thick metal chain leapt out from under the souvenir table, which took up the far left corner, the only living creature to be seen. Negotiating a cautious path past his broad jaws, we found an attendant sleeping on a wall near the ticket kiosk. The setting was magnificent: gaunt columns perched over forty-five hectares, a huge area, looming over a low valley dotted with scattered hamlets. Haymaking was in progress for huge lorries rumbled past, far below, loaded perilously high, children's shrill voices scoring the dull, scorched air. Adrian, guide-book at the ready, set off alone, determined to see every stump, every wall. I paid and walked in, past the colourful low rectangular flowerbeds, too hot and exhausted to do more than peer vaguely and stumble along one path after another. Old men armed with tin whistles and straw hats were milling around on the hillside, their 'weapons' giving off piercing metallic shrieks every time visitors approached a roped-off area, or leaned too closely over a mosaic which was so thickly covered in dust that little remained visible to the naked eye. I thought wistfully of

Tunis and the Bardo with its reconstructed Roman mosaics, well lit, cool corridors and dainty stucco ceilings. The Tunisians have spent millions of pounds on gathering together their Roman heritage the better to preserve it. The Moroccans post a few geriatrics on a merciless, exposed hillside to play dictator. Half an hour passed and boredom nagged at me. Where was the grandeur? It all seemed so far away and long ago, so irrelevant. Oil wheel. Basilica. Arch. Grindstone. Ballroom. Kitchen. Forum. Basilica. The mosaic portraying the Labours of Hercules and reasonably preserved House of Columns retained some vestige of life, and the odd red geranium provided an attractive touch, but Volubilis was a deserted, frustrating site for the layperson, an exercise in creative visualisation, repopulation – of filling in unmistakable voids and overlooking neglect. I realised that I was not happy there and Adrian, too, seemed to have lost his fever of exploratory curiosity as yet another whistle blew, twice. He returned to my side and we stood there, gazing at the walls and the remains of arches, temporarily puzzled as to why we were there at all, looking round as if for a clue. Nothing obliged and, as if by magic, the murmur of activity in the valley carried to our ears, beckoning us to come back to the present, to come, come away.

And so we did – in a lorry – jolted and jerked back to mainstream Moroccan preoccupations by the need to avoid the gas cylinders which rolled back and forth across the bed of the vehicle, narrowly avoiding crushing toes and bruising legs. Standing there in the lorry, flushed, two babies in my arms, my clothes a murky shade of grass stain, sweat and grease, I welcomed the flexibility of the present, its potential, the very possibility of change. Volubilis disturbed me because, there, the story had already been written, fixed for all time. I need to believe in options, in action as a force and not a memory – particularly in Morocco.

PART TWO
(November 1990)

TRAVELS WITH A BLONDE

◆ *Chapter Eight* ◆

Tangier was wet and windswept as Sheila and I stood in the Grand Socco, trying to fit the image we'd carried across the miles to what climbed and sprawled before our eyes. Being of an age, we'd read broadly the same cross-section of books, seen the same films and come to the same conclusion: Tangier, former home of spies and contraband dealers, world famous gay heaven, promised a seething hotbed of raunchy sex, arms deals and flippant extravagance. After all, was it not here that Malcolm Forbes had thrown his famous birthday party in 1989, co-hosted by Elizabeth Taylor: here that the Woolworth's heiress, Barbara Hutton, held soirées complete with camels, desert tribesmen, guedra dancers and every delicacy known to the human palate; here that Brian Jones pursued the drugs trail and captured the Pipes of Pan on tape for his Joujouka album? The list of Tangier's admirers is endless: Ian Fleming, Delacroix, Churchill, Marlene Dietrich, Gore Vidal, Humphrey Bogart and Tennessee Williams are but a smattering of the souls who have come here to paint and write, escape or find themselves. During the period 1922-56, Tangier was an International Zone, and hence a haven for tax exiles, dealers in currency and contraband of every complexion, as people were drawn to its lawless, duty-free shores. Intelligence agents, brown trilbys pushed firmly down against the strong winds that blow across the Bay of Tangier, gathered here to trade off and buy hard information. Social misfits found not

PART TWO

only a cheap home, but also an acceptance not vouchsafed them in more rigid, organised and censorious lands. And so they came. They came to gather at Madame Porte's, or lean back in the sidewalk Café de Paris, to speculate, people-watch and gossip. For then, as now, Tangier has always had a village mentality and every street urchin you meet today can tell you the current whereabouts of Paul Bowles, precisely when Mick Jagger last walked off the ferry and how the wife of the former French ambassador is coping now that he has died.

According to official statistics, six hundred and ninety thousand foreign tourists passed through Tangier in the first ten months of 1990, yet this staggeringly large figure does not seem to have held down unemployment in any meaningful way, since urban joblessness has been rising by twenty per cent per annum (twenty-four per cent in the period 1989-90) and, predictably enough, has taken its greatest toll on the teenaged to mid-twenties generation. The town's reputation for harbouring the worst hustlers, the most persistent drug dealers and opportunistic thieves thus has its basis in worsening social conditions, but few people who have run the gauntlet from the port gates via Rue es-Siaghin to the new town will feel much sympathy for their plight. In short, Tangier represents a hassle, and we had to struggle to remain unaccompanied, to be allowed to stop and look, simply to walk the streets. We had only been there for a couple of hours, and Sheila and I had already resolved to do the only sensible thing – take a guide to keep the others at bay – hence our walk to the Grand Socco, to put ourselves in the firing line.

Enter Aziz. His tentative approach appealed to both of us, for he materialised, out of the blue, half a dozen paces away, his hands clasped nervously behind his back, his dark eyes casting sharp, anxious glances in our direction. What could he be thinking I wondered, how did he see us? Sheila, petite, was immaculately turned out, Kensington-style, her elfin face framed

by a Vidal Sassoon bob, her make-up as discreet as her personality was open. She is barely five feet tall and looked seventeen
and in need of protection – but, more to the point, she is also
peroxide-blonde, a distinct plus in Tangier. From the moment
we stepped onto the plane, I had vaguely resented her size and
her tidiness, since it placed the onus on me to be the capable,
assertive personality virtually by default. I kept repeating to
myself that Sheila was a successful, professional, divorced
woman in her thirties, but an inner voice added a mocking
litany: she doesn't speak French, she is here for you, she doesn't
know Morocco ... all of which precluded my shrugging off an
infuriating sense of responsibility for her, something Sheila
herself would have resented.

Did Aziz realise that we were watching him follow us through
the Grand Socco, formerly the hub of Tangier, entrance to
kasbah and medina, both meeting point and take-off point for
new pastures? Apparently not, for as we took a blind left turn,
he picked up speed and announced gravely: 'The Malcolm
Forbes Museum is shut today.' This innocuous remark marked
the beginning of what turned out to be a close friendship which
burst the boundaries of the working business relationship
between visitor and guide, to the point where *he* was buying *us*
tea and lending us dirhams for souvenir-shopping in our final
hours. Little did twenty-seven-year-old Aziz imagine that he
would end up heartsick and lovelorn, that wet November afternoon, as he stalked and sized up his prey, assessing how best to
approach us and state his terms.

A tomato splattered against my bag just as I realised that we
were walking in conspicuous circles. The prospect of Aziz's
company suddenly seemed pleasing and we finally stopped our
pointless meandering and took the plunge. Half-Spanish on his
dead father's side, Aziz had a Hispanic face from the tightly
curling greased hair on his head to the goatee (and moustache)
he compulsively fingered, stroking it to a point only to ruffle it

up again. His features spoke of spurs, the Alhambra, courtly gallants and Andalusian ballads. We trusted him on sight. His grasp of English was peculiarly his own, a blend of up-to-date contemporary slang (of the 'it's wicked' variety), mixed with a faulty knowledge of tenses and an anachronistic vocabulary. Apparently, he owned five hundred books which he kept in a suitcase under his bed, attended Tangier's American college for three years until his money ran out, and had just narrowly avoided being sucked into signing up for a Christian Bible study class which was masquerading as English lessons for foreign students. Recounting his narrow escape, Aziz's mouth split into a huge grin, revealing chunky white teeth, and the goatee was whipped between thumb and forefinger for a few seconds. 'Life is life,' he stated, a phrase we were doomed to hear daily in Tangier, where the recording of that name achieved huge success two summers ago. A banal and infuriating remark, it stuck like a burr and soon, all too soon, Sheila and I had caught the Tangier bug and found ourselves succumbing to ending monologues with this Riffian full-stop: 'Life is life.'

Over the next fortnight, we poked through Tangier and came to the conclusion that, whatever it might have been in the recent past, this town had burnt itself out. The most attractive elements, the most moving architecture and the juiciest gossip all related to bygone days and not this wet November in the Year of Our Lord 1990. Having devoted seventeen years of his life to working as a self-styled hustler, Aziz had a methodical approach to sightseeing, so when we told him that we were attempting to track down the heart of his home town, he reduced our poetic quest to an itinerary: medina and kasbah, new town, rich and poor areas, port and beach. 'And,' he added, 'when we've done it once we'll do it again, so maybe you will be lucky and find this heart you speak of.' My mind boggled. Did he think it was a person, a deer, perhaps even a street that we were seeking? Like so many conversations held at cross-purposes, further delving would only muddy the waters more dangerously, so we agreed to a modest twenty-five dirhams a day for his services, and arranged to begin pounding the streets the following morning.

The Chellah Hotel keep-fit squad and bridge players were already in action at 10:00 a.m. as we braved a savage wind whipping in from the countryside and rendezvoused at the Place de France. The coast of Spain was a lumpy grey outline just visible through a mutinous dark sky which lashed down arrows of rain from all angles. Large sheets of plastic, with holes cut out in the middle, covered many a besuited Tanjaoui on his way to the office, and everyone had dug out Wellingtons and woollen djellabahs. It seemed unlikely that the sun would emerge all day, for the air was dull and heavy with pressure; for the first time, we had the strong sense that Tangier was truly a port and thus totally exposed to the elements. The medina promised the best hope of consistent shelter, so we dashed into the Grand Socco (now renamed Place du 9 Avril 1977, to commemorate the pro-independence speech delivered there by Mohammed V) and through the arched entrance to Rue es-Siaghin, silversmiths' street. Aziz pointed to what he called 'the king shop' on our left, a picture framer's which sold a large variety of posed royal snapshots and portraits, ranging from postcard-size to four-foot efforts geared towards the hotel reception market. We entered and bought two sets. One portrayed the royal family on holiday in the Middle Atlas, leaning on a fence whose wooden panels were hidden by a thick curtain of dead, bleeding partridges. The other card showed the leaders of the Arab Maghrebi Union striding down the road, all dressed to kill in their best ceremonial bib and tucker, yet all marching alone and refusing to glance at one another – a bad omen for the unification project, one might be forgiven thinking. Sheila and I sent off all twenty cards that night – not one arrived. A double standard seems to be in operation here: you can buy the images but they must not leave the country. God alone knows why.

Music blared from a cassette seller's stall and we lounged in the doorway, listening to Tunisian pop and traditional Moroccan tunes. Nothing caught our fancy on the basis of a series of ninety-second blasts but, just as we had prepared to move on, I decided to purchase the new Nass el Ghiwane tape (there is always a new Nass el Ghiwane tape). This popular, left-wing band has a wide following amongst the urban youth of Morocco, and I was astounded to hear that the lead singer was no more, assassinated on royal orders in Casablanca – or so the story goes. 'Was he shot?' I asked

'No, run down by a car.'

'So it could have been an accident?' I pressed.

'He was murdered,' the cassette seller bluntly replied, 'as a government warning to others to keep music non-political.'

Conspiracy theories abound in this town of contraband smuggling and drug dealing, where groups of West Africans sit in cafés, clutching their cardboard suitcases, waiting for nightfall and the seven and a half thousand dirham trip by fishing boat to a new life in Spain. If they are very lucky, they might actually cross the Straits of Gibraltar, but all too many are taken on a five-hour coastal tour, then dropped on a beach in northern Morocco and told to lay low until the morning. Aziz took the fact of state assassinations for granted. He told us that many singers and political and religious figures were removed by the government. Some of his friends had not seen their fathers for five, ten years and still had no idea what had happened to them. At first, they searched, going from prison to prison and making enquiries. Eventually, the police told them that it was a pointless quest, and nothing to do with their own departments or the jails, but rather a matter of state security. And thus, the men effectively disappeared in a plain white Ford one bright morning, never to be seen again.

I am aware of the Moroccan state's poor record on human rights, have read the Amnesty International reports, met Algerians who were electrocuted into deafness, the soles of their feet burnt raw, their fingers amputated inside Rabat's Laalou Prison. I know that Aziz was merely stating facts, but something in his tone reflected resignation rather than outrage, which seemed out of character, given that he had a volatile temper and was constantly reproaching people for minor crimes – showing 'a lack of respect' (pushing); or 'badness of tongue' (swearing). I asked him why, if everyone believed that the king was responsible for ordering deaths, no one had recently tried to kill him. Aziz looked at me as if I was brainless. 'Because of the Jew.' He shrugged and walked on.

'Which Jew?' we yelled at his departing back.

'Do you mean that you don't know about the Jew?'

'No,' Sheila and I chorused, exasperated. 'Tell us about it.' It transpired that Aziz was another firm believer in the Koran-implant story I had first heard the previous summer, and accepted the close relationship between the throne and the Jewish community, with its reciprocal benefits, as unbreakable. Before we could frame a response or question him closer, Aziz added, with a degree of what might be pride, 'Of course, our king is crafty and has tried to cheat the Jews by forcing them into co-partnership with Moroccans. The Moroccans only have to pay for fifty per cent of the business' original valuation, even if it is decades out of date, to get their hands on half the current profits.' He shook his head in wonder and asked us if we personally practised magic in England. Sheila bravely tried to reduce the question to a specific form – was aromatherapy magic? What of Tarot card readings and reflexology? Did they count? No, they did not. Aziz was only interested in cause and effect; spells and results. He maintained that magic was mainly the preserve of women and most commonly used to lure husbands away from their wives and children, but that holy men were also known to send people to 'magic shops' (presumably the herbalists) to make up potent recipes. These would, he stated, not work in a positive way unless they were combined with prayers, but since unscrupulous people had been known to poison others for their patrimony or to be rid of them these days, the most dangerous herbs were always kept in a safe.

I had been sporadically following the press's anti-charlatan campaign in the Maghreb for years, and had noted with some glee that it had recently been changing tack. Where the papers once spoke of stamping out anti-Islamic activity on the part of soothsayers and healers, now they had taken a more pragmatic approach and were attacking practitioners on the grounds of tax evasion and not declaring income. Out in the countryside, in particular, the evil eye remains as much a fact of life as the seasons. Sorcerers are said to be capable of making an entire field infertile, of causing men and beasts to sicken and die, chickens to collapse, their legs aloft and stiff, cabbages to develop thousands of holes in their leaves and children to fall prey to seizures and periods of melancholy. The best strategy to adopt if you find yourself under attack is, of course, to get as far away as possible from the spell-caster, but this is often impractical. If you can't move districts, then you can achieve at least some degree of protection by wearing clothes inside out (to confuse the sorcerer), hanging horn-shaped amulets on your neck (these will break the moment the spell is lifted), and hiding your coiled thumbs in your fists. Children should wear a piece of coral around their necks from an early age, just in case of attack. And, of course, the Hand of Fatima door knocker does its bit to safeguard the family.

Sheila raised wonder-filled eyes to Aziz, began to reply, then reconsidered, clamping her lips tight once again. Faith is beyond discussion. After so many months in the Maghreb, I had unleashed every superstitious instinct my Catholic upbringing stifled for so long and was quite happy to ball fists, wear T-shirts with the buttons hidden and the label hanging out like a white tongue, if it might assure me a poison-free, benevolent environment.

The topic of magic cropped up again as we wandered through the old mellah and ran into an obviously disturbed individual swinging an enormous, working ghetto-blaster through the rain, a camera hanging around his neck. We watched him stop, shoeless, and harangue a framed portrait of the king, then move on again.

'Now there you are,' Aziz exclaimed. 'His father, Larini, owned twenty shops in town and he, the son, was poisoned when the old man died, so that his brothers could inherit the bulk of the family wealth and cut him out of the will. He is now insane and his percentage is held in trust and administered on his behalf by the courts. Everyone in Tangier knows who did it and why.'

'How does he live?' I asked, 'and why doesn't anyone rob him of his cassette-player?' Aziz was outraged by this comment and subjected me to a long, repetitive lecture on the nature of the inhabitants of Tangier, who are, he emphasised, *people who look after their own*.

'The beggars you see in the streets,' he added, 'are not our people. They come from Casablanca or Rabat. Our beggars don't need to ask. Everyone knows who they are and gives if they can. Some shops even look after ten or twenty beggars from year to year and give them a little money every Friday morning.'

I apologised ... And, indeed, it does seem likely that everyone here must know who everyone else is, where they live and what they do, for the longer we stayed in Tangier, the more the town shrank before our eyes, until we also began to recognise the odd face, started gazing longingly at Spain and sensed the claustrophobia of living in a town you could not leave. Aziz himself had no desire to live elsewhere and was immensely proud of his home town. An unstoppable source of gossip in general, he took particular pride in the rich and/or famous people who had passed through and gave us the run-down on their generosity and personalities alike.

Mick Jagger came top of the list, because he distributed money to the poor, bought objects he did not want to give others pleasure, and refused police protection, preferring to frequent Arab cafés and relax, secure in the knowledge that he was accepted by a population who felt honour-bound to keep him safe. In contrast, Elizabeth Taylor earned poor marks because she surrounded herself with bodyguards and would not give autographs on the street – part of me could see her point of view. However, her fellow American, Oscar de la Renta, was admired both for his undoubted charm and for the purchasing power of his wallet. Going down market, the network of information spread its tentacles into every nook and cranny, every doorway. Here lived a Spanish family who made money by buying, doing up and reselling houses. Next door belonged to a middle-aged English couple, the husband retired, while over the way were the French absentee landlords, renowned for the bad wages they paid their workforce.

Sheila and I followed Aziz around the medina. The man loped like a wolf and assumed a protective stance, constantly scanning passers-by, checking the zips of our bags, warning us against recently slopped-out doorways and approaching mopeds. The city is built on a hill and as one whitewashed, curved alley spilled into its steeper twin, I realised that the medina contained few craftsmen and many retailers, a sure sign of a booming tourist trade. Leather goods, brassware, carpets and plated jewellery poured out from doorways; the craftsmanship seemed poor, the prices high. I looked with horror at the latest leather jacket collections: a mixture of black and purple and black and orange patches and stripes. Tangier is reputedly the last resort for shopkeepers who fail to move their stock and it is here that they bring the unsellable and the ill-made, outdated or badly fitting. Judging by the fashions on display in the souks, which seemed stuck in a mid-1970s time-warp, and the poor-quality silver and enamel work on display all around, this could well be true. Only the ceramics had escaped the bargain basement touch, and cheap, cheerful candlesticks, plates and bowls in glorious combinations of green, blue, white and yellow lay in large baskets or leaned, higgledy-piggledy, outside low shop doorways.

This was the Rif, home of kif, clay bowls and crudely painted wooden pipe stems sitting in the bottom of most window displays, keeping company with tin slave bangles which were growing green from the damp, snap-together plastic necklaces, cheap hairslides and spider lapel badges. I spotted a flash of exuberant colour in one bin and pulled out an extraordinary object, a red, gold and green knitted hat with black dreadlocks attached. These were made in Marrakesh, I was informed, and I wanted to buy two immediately and haggled gently. Aziz intervened. 'Too expensive. I'll get them later, myself.' His gesture surprised us. Aziz had no reason to be generous with his time or to turn his back on commissions. After all, he had not managed to find any clients in the fortnight preceding our arrival and, in his experience, foreigners reneged on established fees and turned him away at the end of the day with a ten dirham bill to his name. We talked about the great Arab-Westerner divide and the guide-visitor relationship and I argued that the classic Moroccan reply of 'Give what you like' to a query of 'How much?' was a dangerous one, for Westerners are then inclined to take the guide at his word. Aziz replied that he had always banked on the foreigners' generosity and that anything at all was a good fee in the winter, when trade was slow and only four ferries a day docked in port, in comparison with the daily dozen of the summer months. Since he did not have the corruption money necessary to smooth his way past exams to assume the status of official guide, he could not afford to worry about the future and was doomed to pick up what work he could by loitering at the train station, outside the main hotels or at the port gates. His sisters were luckier, being girls, since they could quietly leave school to help the women in the garment factories and gradually work their way up onto the bench, progressing from running errands and sweeping the floors to sitting at the sewing machines with an assured future.

Our hit-and-miss stroll through the medina had led us back to the mellah, whose unusual tall, thin houses are built so close to one another I got the impression that neighbours had to take turns opening their windows for fear of a mid-air collision. The Sephardic community has long been appreciated for its talents in Tangier and many have prospered and settled on the edges of the new town, taking over the huge, elaborate Spanish buildings which line Boulevard Pasteur, close by the large, well-attended synagogue. The small synagogue near the Petit Socco was shut that day, but a woman in her early fifties, wearing an incongruously short nylon frock, with pink flowers and a Peter Pan collar, which barely covered her substantial thighs, gladly threw open its doors for a peek. The building is minute when compared with the vastness of the brass-domed Spanish Catholic church nearby and probably holds only a couple of hundred worshippers. Yet it retained an aura of continuous reverence, lamps suspended, ready to burst into light, pews polished and gleaming. It seemed slightly inappropriate to find two places of worship so close to the Petit Socco, a small square lined with cafés which, during Tangier's time as an International Zone, was renowned for its numerous gay brothels, pornographic films, cheap rooms and the rent boys who plied their trade nearby. Now, and particularly in the drizzle, the Petit Socco was merely an innocuous coffee-stop, decorated with tourist shops and haunted by the ghosts of Kerouac and Burroughs.

Tangier's medina is attractively open to the sky and has a light, airy feel when compared to the labyrinthine secrecy of Fez or Marrakesh, the sprawling bustle of Meknès. The Andalusian architectural heritage – solid white mansions with splendid elaborate balconies – is breathtaking in its arrogance and its romantic flourishes. The clean, broad steps which all eventually lead up to the kasbah and the sea also speak of confidence and accessibility. Walking up and down, only to be forced to walk up again, we passed pastel patches of housing in shades of buttermilk, apple green and pink, punctuated by shady corners, but there were few ornamentally tiled fountains proclaiming the Islamic message, no sense of mystery or discovery around every corner – in short, a lack of passion, a dilution born of syncretism, perhaps?

Nowhere is the current blandness of Tangier more evident than up in the kasbah, the former Roman capital, held and fought over successively by Byzantine and Christian forces, home to viziers, princes and governors since ancient times. Entering through Bab el Assa, we found ourselves in Place de la Kasbah, site of the old Islamic court of justice, an unspectacular gravel rectangle where criminals were once sentenced to prison or execution, or set free to return home. A few arches and a tiled, crumbling wall marked the spot. To the right sat another of Moulay Ishmael's seventeenth century testaments to what will-power, money and slave labour can achieve, the Dar el Makhzen Museum. Nowadays, all the better and more important archaeological exhibits have been sent to Rabat, and entire wings here remain shut, since the Spanish curator previously responsible for running and safeguarding the museum resigned in disgust at the way in which it was being systematically looted and emptied. A tatty mosaic from Volubilis, a few copies of bronzes, a small collection of rifles and halbards, and a number of passable ceramic pieces from Fez, Meknès and Safi are all that remain within the traditionally decorated walls of this attractive palace. Wedding clothes moulder in one room; nearby, we found a meagre and unprepossessing collection of silverwork from the High Atlas; a few samples of embroidery followed and then we found ourselves peering into a room devoted to the art of Fez – a vulgar, bright body-blow to the senses and system with its raised pink, gold and blue bed. No one was at work in the now rampant Andalusian garden, which was going to seed, untrimmed and out of proportion; the upstairs rooms were out of bounds, the inner courtyard surrounded by large, locked, gates.

Despair struck when we took in the decay all around us, noting the contrast with the care lavished on St Andrew's Anglican Church, near the Grand Socco, where Walter Harris, the fearless and eccentric *Times* journalist, kidnap victim of Asilah's bandit chief Raisuni, lies buried. This corner which is forever England holds the earthly remains of, amongst others, the nineteenth century British consul Sir John Hay, various self-styled 'friends of the Moors', 'beloved wives' and RAF pilots who died in the skies above Tangier during the Second World War.

Walking down its slightly seedy, peaceful lanes, noting the sweet Victorian names on the gravestones, passing banana plants and conifers, we saw a curator gently and slowly sweeping away the pine needles and leaves which covered cracked marble tombs, tombs with slowly eroding names and eternal sentiments. A short moment in Tangier's history was being preserved here, by a dwindling expatriate community. Up in the kasbah, a vast heritage was being allowed to crumble away through indifference ...

The Detroit Restaurant, founded by writer Brion Gysin, sits just next to the Dar el Makhzen and reflects more recent influences, as well as boasting the best view across the Straits of Gibraltar in the whole of Tangier. We arrived in this modern Lyons-style café with its elaborate stucco ceiling just as the management was preparing for a tour group to descend. Squeezing onto a plastic-covered seat by one of the three glass walls which lend so much to the restaurant's charm, we watched a large metal trolley being loaded with thirty-six glasses, sprigs of mint at the ready. A postcard seller, cigarette dangling from cracked lips, was shuffling his wares into groups of ten, and two middle-aged men were arranging their fezes, preparing to perform the obligatory eruption of Andalusian music which would accompany the tea and cakes ceremony. Heavy footsteps and loud conversations on the stairwell signalled the off and, for a split second, we all sat and stood, respectively, paralysed. I for one wanted to bolt. And then they walked in, two obviously separate groups who were presumably sharing one coach, each led by their own djellabah-clad guide complete with fez and carrying, of all things, a shepherd's crook. The brown wooden crooks moved forward and, in single file, the groups followed their leaders, picking up glasses and plates, complete with pastry, finding seats and buying postcards. They were barely aware of the presence of serenading musicians who, legs akimbo, had now hit their monotonous, wailing stride up by the cake display. Five minutes later, we were the only people left in the Detroit yet again and sat, peering through the rusty windows at the dozens of seagulls which floated and swooped past on the choppy air currents, hovering from time to time, just in case someone emerged from the riot of TV-antenna-strangled buildings below to throw out scraps.

Not for the first time, I realised how Western tour operators demean their own clients, and why a recent article in *L'Opinion* queried the usefulness of half-day orientation tours run by the major European companies, noting that tourists might prefer to be shown landmarks such as banks, railway stations, post offices and churches, rather than carpet emporia and ceramics workshops. And of course, the feature writer was right, yet Tangier is not for the innocent and the unwary, the single traveller or the credulous, and the predominantly middle-aged package tour crowd might well need the security blanket of guides, coaches and sheer numbers to insulate them against the 'chancers' and the silver-tongued 'friends' they might make on the streets.

PART TWO

Aziz was becoming attached to Sheila in an obvious, endearing and fiercely protective way. His face beamed with delight every morning when we emerged onto Rue Allal Ben Abdellah to drink carrot juice in our local patisserie. He changed clothes with a determination which smacked of courtship and lurked outside the door, just in case, every time Sheila went to the ladies'. The yellow moccasins of our first encounter had given way to macho Cuban heels, and the mustard and black fake Levi's he formerly favoured had been replaced by blue denim jeans with a sharp crease running down from the knees. I was worried for Aziz, but Sheila thought I was reading the signs perversely just to amuse myself and declared this particular subject closed. We argued fiercely one night, lying on our twin beds, heads turbanned, moisturised faces gleaming in a room lit by two twenty-five-watt bulbs – the standing lamp had died a permanent death by explosion. Like many Westerners, Sheila is familiar with the tradition of courtly love which has inspired so much Arabic art and poetry, but thinks of it as an historical phenomenon, a curiosity rather than an indication of symbolic systems at work today. Having received more than my fair share of 'My dreams are ravaged by thoughts of your absence' letters, inspired by a ten-minute conversation held on a bus or in a post office queue, I am far less inclined to believe that simple warmth and friendliness will not, by some mysterious process, be reinterpreted as passion on the basis of cultural differences. Mutual misapprehension reigns supreme. Sheila had been damned friendly, and Aziz had made the quantum leap from 'She is polite and pretty' to 'I love her and why is she being so cold after leading me on?' in the space of five days.

I tried to persuade Sheila that each time she spontaneously showed Aziz affection, in his eyes she was not simply being appreciative but declaring her attachment to him in clear terms. In short, her openness was working against her, and now that Aziz had decided to accept her love and make her his damsel, he was making life-long plans for them both. This was bad timing on his part, since it coincided with Sheila's growing sense of irritation at what she viewed as his fawning adoration. Sheila snapped my head clean from my shoulders with denials, and yet the seeds of doubt had obviously been sown for, the following afternoon, I watched her being uncommunicative and off-hand with a totally bewildered Aziz as we all sat closeted in a new town café, watching thirty-three millimetres of rain fall on an already saturated Tangier. I isolated myself behind my Walkman's wall of sound and observed them, amused despite myself by her floundering ambiguity, unable to repress the odd smile and snort, which Sheila interpreted correctly and stifled with a withering look.

As minutes turned into hours and the opposite pavement was blotted out completely by a wall of water, I lost myself in the café ambience and felt a surge of love for the unemployed all around me, love for the slumped forms who stared aimlessly out of a window at an indistinct, empty street. The lethargy of a lifetime spent waiting was numbing, and after four hours I no longer wanted to think, talk or move. Occasionally, I watched my hand go through the ritual of bringing the cup of cold tea to my lips, but I tasted nothing as the world simply drifted away. Perhaps this was why my neighbour was mouthing the words of the paper he was reading, why the young boy opposite seemed to jerk involuntarily from time to time. Perhaps years of café sitting had taught them how to break the spell and thus reduce the anomie, reintegrate.

I made an effort to sit up straight and doodled with a red biro. Stick men and women emerged, all walking in a goose-step in different directions – the story of the Oriental male/Western female encounter encapsulated. After all, looked at coldly, most Maghrebi males have no work, no money, few prospects. A European wife offers a ready-made solution to their dead-end futures, a chance to escape, secure a higher standard of living and enjoy all the technological trappings they are aware of but cannot afford. The economic divide between Western women and Moroccan men is unbridgable and immense. I felt ashamed to buy anything which cost over thirty dirhams while in Aziz's company and snuck away to purchase what, to me, seemed a ridiculously cheap shirt at two hundred and fifty dirhams, in order not to feel profligate or belittle his earnings. For when I considered that a modest slab of Edam cheese cost half his daily wage, it became restrictive and uncomfortable for me to shop with Aziz around. In addition, misplaced generosity offends as often as it gratifies, for all too frequently it is seen either as condescension or as stupidity, and I had become resigned to being criticised for tipping too well (forty pence) or not bargaining hard enough. When this happened I felt torn between apologising to keep the peace, and ridiculing the sum of money in question, and thereby once again treating their currency as toy money, their hard-won wages as unimportant. As if this economic minefield weren't problematic enough, long-term unemployment leaves Moroccan men with too much time on their hands and the most casual encounter with a European woman is dissected and tested for its potential; its usefulness, in short. When one is desperate for change and release, any spark of hope fans into sheets of love at will.

Sheila was at a disadvantage in this arena because of her amiable temperament, her shortness and her bleached hair. Even if she tried to rearrange Aziz's interpretation of their friendship, she would not be taken seriously since, physically, she resembled a child, and thus a dependant for whom arrangements could and needed to be made. I watched Sheila gesticulating wildly, trying to make a point, her arms fly-swatting away in the air, while Aziz looked on adoringly, with shining, accepting eyes. She could be reciting the multiplication tables, backwards, for all he cared. Unfortunately, like most people who have put together an education without structured, outside guidance. Aziz tended to jump disciplines without logic or progression and come to what I consider wild, untenable conclusions. It was impossible, on the basis of a week's acquaintance, to undermine the shaky edifices he had so slowly and painfully constructed without, in the process, denigrating his efforts and destroying his confidence. Sheila had thus doomed herself to perpetually holding criticism in check and taking part in quite artificial, self-censored dialogues. Naturally enough, this further restricted an already narrow range of topics which could be navigated in a relaxed, natural manner. As communication degenerated, tension grew apace, for neither party's expectations of the relationship could be met within these parameters.

The Western woman becomes confused by the direction the friendship seems to be taking, reassuring herself that she is only being polite when she takes an interest in the Moroccan's life, views and family. The Moroccan man starts to feel cheated. He has been offered a chance of achieving intimacy on the chatty, personal level and sees this as proof that the woman has designs on him. Why else would she prod and enquire so thoroughly? A hurt stand-off inevitably degenerates into dislike and a sense of betrayal on both sides. Tourism has further exacerbated the problem on both the sexual and emotional planes. Huge posters warning Maghrebis of the high risks of catching AIDS (SIDA) through sleeping with women from Paris, Amsterdam and London are plastered over airports in the same way as anti-rabies warnings blanket Gatwick and Heathrow, for we are seen as promiscuous, available and therefore dangerous. The first time I spotted one such three-foot square warning against contaminated flesh, I died of shame and embarrassment on the spot and had to restrain myself from defacing the thing on impulse. The irony struck home immediately: AIDS accusations from within Europe all point to Africa, and thus it is virtually inevitable that an outraged Africa should reciprocate and, if Moroccan statistics are to be believed, since there are currently only sixty HIV-positive citizens 'registered' in the whole country. women from the West are indeed more likely to pass on than contract the disease here.

On the other hand, in a galling reversal of the traditional male-female roles, Western women, however suspect sexually, must be pinned down emotionally to some form of commitment, for without their help, their letters of invitation, the Abduls and Samirs are stymied and helpless, reduced to letter writing. It is the women who have the money to buy plane tickets, to decide if and when they may visit, when they must leave. The men hope and wait. I cannot believe that this bodes well for either party and, should the affair blossom, and a visit to the West actually materialise, then all too often this ill-fated experiment signals disaster. In the Western woman's eyes, the confident, omnipotent protector from Tangier's hustlers and souk touts becomes the badly dressed, helpless foreigner, an embarrassment who knows no one and can't even work the dishwasher. In the Moroccan man's eyes, the uncertain, glamorous creature of shorts and bikini metamorphoses into an impatient, domineering female who persists in leading her own life without deferring to him or granting him any autonomy or power. All things considered, it was high time for me to take off my Walkman and blunder onto the stage, suggesting a change of milieu and scenery.

And this is how, that afternoon, I found myself walking into the Malcolm Forbes Museum, with its collection of one hundred and fifteen thousand miniatures to halt, amazed by the scope of the man's obsession.

I knew that Malcolm Forbes liked toy soldiers and all the accompanying paraphernalia. I knew that in his home he had recreated battles from all four corners of the globe, and that he'd willed the museum to the State on his death. What I had not imagined was the sharp contrast between the man – Forbes of *Forbes Magazine* – and the boy of the display cases. There was something distinctly embarrassing about knowing that the same hands that had gripped the handlebars of those two whacking great motorbikes which leant against the left-hand wall of the entrance hall had carefully arranged plastic palm trees and trickled sand into glass boxes to recreate all this desert scenery. The theatricality of the posed scenarios was hard to digest: an assassinated plastic John F. Kennedy being transported in a hearse, with a plastic Jackie dressed in black, complete with hat and veil, standing on a nearby hill, tightly clasping the hands of John and Caroline; Hitler waving from a staff car; Marilyn Monroe, all two inches of her, assuming a classic pose, her skirt lifting in an imaginary breeze. I had expected all the soldiers to be made of lead, but many were of base metals or plastic and, second shock of the day, there was no uniformity of size. Medium-sized, cardboard operating theatres held bandaged World War One wounded, tended by smart, wavy-haired nurses in spotless uniforms. Nearby, plastic monkeys ate oranges perched up in tiny palm trees while, below them, an alligator was swallowing a screaming black man.

Moving from one ridiculous, simplistic set piece to the next, I felt pity for Forbes, and repulsion for the racism he exhibited in his recreation of the Africa campaigns, the careful precision of his vision, his apparently wholehearted allegiance to a clear-cut set of values he could not enjoy in his private life. Admittedly, once the miniatures were dismissed as manifestations of a need for a controlled environment, what remained was fascinating – albeit in a macabre fashion. The museum boasted a wide-ranging selection of prints and posters, including a memorable bloody handprint captioned: 'The Hun, his mark.... wipe it out.' World War Two recruitment posters for the marines; advertisements for Liberty Bonds; and the famous 'Deserter' picture, whose shame is only equalled by that of his weeping wife. The photographs of the Green March of 1975 were excellent, comprising blown-up shots of the tent cities which sprang up on the way to the former Spanish Sahara; close-ups of strained but beatific faces; hands by the hundreds holding up a sea of Korans; banners on the move, waving aloft; the reality of survival and the glory of the experience – if not the cause behind it all per se. I didn't tire of these images, which brought together the dubious grand design and the passion of individual commitment in such a stark way. No amount of well-aimed criticism of the Green March, as a political manoeuvre, could detract from the almost messianic enthusiasm of the three hundred and fifty thousand participants. The desert war against the POLISARIO and the Saharan separatist tribes may well have weakened the national economy and led to the ten per cent per annum inflation, but it had ensured the army's loyalty to the throne and bolstered nationalist sentiments – as well as claiming an area rich in phosphates. The real losers were the twenty thousand Saharan nomads who rejected Moroccan claims to sovereignty and made the trek to Tindouf, Algeria, where they now starved in POLISARIO-run refugee camps, dispossessed, their land settled by Moroccans lured to the area by the promise of high wages.

Malcolm Forbes' study looked as though it had just been dusted for a photo-session. Three upholstered late-nineteenth-century red and gold velvet chairs, a large desk and a coffee table which held, aptly enough, copies of *Forbes Magazine*, were illuminated by a selection of manly lamps which hinted that the master was often hard at work in the wee small hours. Large sculptures asserted themselves in alcoves and I sensed the single-minded designer's hand at work behind every aggressively butch 'statement'. In contrast, the beautiful garden had been permitted to cater to the eye and not the myth, and its gently sloping terraces, lawns and flowerbeds reflected inspired, loving maintenance. The soil had been recently turned over, raked and readied for spring bulbs; every plant had been staked and nurtured, trimmed to perfect proportions. Palms, geraniums and birds of paradise blazed around odd pieces of modern and classical sculpture, framed French windows and encircled the pool which Forbes, in a burst of generosity, apparently allowed his staff to use at the end of the working day. I found myself listening out for the tinkling of glasses on trays, the buzz of conversation, relaxed laughter; waited to be invited to sit down and join in.

Coming out of this somewhat desolate if crowded monument to a troubled life, I was almost flattened by a brand new white Toyota Supra with Ketama number plates and a young driver. An expensive car by British standards, the Supra appeared to have found a special place in the hearts of the drug barons of the Rif and was a blatant advertisement for the profits to be found in 'business'. Nissan Patrols and the occasional Porsche also regularly descended from the highlands, but the Supra reigned supreme in November 1990. The Rif, with its barren, rocky soil and its history of dissidence and separatism, is the centre of the Moroccan drug industry. Yet while it is legal to cultivate hemp, and kif smoking is open and apparently tolerated by the authorities, the profits and risks of illegal trafficking are both huge. This government, like its predecessors, has neglected the Rif and the eastern mountains remain off limits to travellers and officials from Rabat alike. Separated from central and southern Morocco by a geographical and cultural divide, historically the Rif has always resisted interference, integration and pacification. In the recent past, when the Treaty of Fez established the Spanish Protectorate in the north, the region's response to the arrival of foreign troops was predictable. The Islamic Republic of the Rif was immediately declared by Abdel Krim, a self-professed descendant of the Prophet. The revolt against the new overseers continued, for Abdel Krim and the Beni Ouriaghel tribesmen of the eastern Rif gradually drove the Spanish back and then launched an attack on French Morocco, fighting to within fifteen miles of the gates of Fez. It was not until 1926, when Marshal Petain led a joint Franco-Spanish force into the region, that some semblance of civil order was restored and Abdel Krim himself was captured and exiled to the remote island of Réunion. The Riffian resistance was thus both effective and populist, reinforcing the inhabitants' sense of alienation from a throne which they had opposed with tribal uprisings and armies fronted by pretenders since the time of the Almohads – irrespective of the dynasty in power. The Alaouites have fared no better, for when Mohammed V came to the throne at Independence in 1956, the Rif held itself apart from the general euphoria and celebrations. Hassan II has avoided visiting the area since the 1968 attempt on his life and his new palace at Tetouan promises to stand empty once it is finished, for it is here that the food riots of 1984 first blazed into open confrontation with the state apparatus.

The poverty of the Rif's heavily eroded soil is reflected on market days when Tangier is flooded with Riffian women, bedecked in their extraordinary straw hats, festooned with colourful pom-poms or thick black strands of wool which straddle the body of the hat and link the brim to the crown. Their bright red and black striped blankets tucked around their waists, towels draped over shoulders, they squat on cardboard squares, lining the medina alleys or in the covered market below the garish mosque of Sidi Bouabid. One may display four eggs lying in a tin can full of straw; another a few bundles of mint or half a dozen freshly dug turnips; while still others guard small heaps of pomegranates, a thrush, or a turkey, its feathers spread wide like the skirt of an expensive black ballgown. The soil is thus visibly poor, so it is not surprising that cannabis remains the preferred crop in the mountains, a situation which seems doomed to persist unless light industry or the tourist trade mop up a percentage of the unemployed workforce.

Of all the monuments to be found in Tangier, my personal favourite is the elegant Syrian mosque, just outside the new town by the bus station on Avenue Mohammed V. It cuts the skyline with its graceful, thin profile and highlights the gaudiness of the mosaics splattered on the minaret of the mosque of Sidi Boubid and the clumsy lack of proportion of the huge new Kuwaiti mosque. Aziz told us that, some years ago, a Kuwaiti minister was flying over Tangier and noticed that the spire of the old French cathedral was visible from the air, dwarfing all signs of Islam and dominating the town. He donated money to redress this state of affairs, money which the Moroccan government accepted – and promptly spent on constructing a new jail. Five years later, the Kuwaiti mosque started to ascend heavenwards, a giant and expensive waste of resources, according to many, its two vast, cumbersome wings spreading to right and left of the minaret. Aziz was not impressed by the Kuwaiti mosque, arguing that God's house should be open twenty-four hours a day, not merely at prayer times, and should serve as a sanctuary and meeting place, somewhere believers could gather to eat, sleep, talk, cook and even learn a trade. These days, the mosque was peripheral since it was often inaccessible, and women, in particular, tended to visit the nearby shrine of Tangier's patron saint, Sidi Bou Araquiza, or the tomb of Sidi Ahmed Boujiani (the man who always said the opposite of what he meant) in the medina if they felt troubled and in need of solace. Indeed, the candle seller outside Sidi Bou Araquiza's shrine asked me and Sheila if we too were seeking husbands and gestured that we were welcome to join the slow, steady stream of ladies making their way up the path with their votive offerings. Aziz disapproved noisily, telling the stout, smiling woman that it was contrary to the teachings of Islam to ask for intercession with Allah, and that the only reason so many women came here was because holy men wanted to get shot of them and their romantic problems and imaginings. The candle seller turned her back on us impatiently and Aziz dragged us to take a look at the new town.

A chic, unexceptional area redeemed by its proximity to the sea, Tangier's new town is full of bazaars geared towards the well-heeled tourist trade, wonderful crumbling-balconied Spanish mansions, and excavations for villas and blocks of flats. The smart apartments off Avenue Mohammed V are favoured by drug dealers who can afford upwards of fifty thousand pounds to maintain a pied à terre in town and need the security of a uniformed doorman, enjoy the arriviste touch of a marble entrance and hallway. Along the November-empty Avenue des FAR, grand old-fashioned hotels lined up to loom across the bay, beach clubs slumbered, waiting for the summer explosion and car hire companies dusted off their prices and brochures. Concrete benches, gravel paths and herring-bone patterned brick rectangles divided neatly planted terraced municipal gardens. Tangiers is smartening up its act, introducing conference halls, schools and colleges for foreign students; all the trappings of Western planning, Western blandness. At the same time it is turning its back on the glorious extravagances of the past, follies like the abandoned Spanish theatre with its lurid pink, blue and green painted mouldings, faded Arab cafés where old men smoke kif, chomp on peanuts and watch westerns with Spanish sub-titles beneath faded Moroccan Tourist Office posters. And yet the new concrete veneer is nothing more than a smoke-screen which hides continuity, for it is impossible to believe that anarchic, pig-headed Tangiers will ever allow itself to be effaced by municipal architects.

18 November is a national holiday, a celebration of Moroccan independence or, as the editorials put it, 'the perfect symbiosis

between the Alaouite throne and the Moroccan people'. Admittedly, Independence Day does not seem to be celebrated with great enthusiasm, unlike Mouloud (the Prophet's birthday) or Aid es Seghir (which marks the end of Ramadan, the month of abstinence from all smoking, eating, drink and sexual intercourse from dawn to dusk). We spotted a few drummers down by the railway station and watched a gang of men erect huge posters of the king wearing dark glasses and army fatigues by the Café de France. Green March Day, on 6 November, is another product of newspaper rather than popular excitement and both holidays seem marked by the most peculiar mishmash of charitable and public works: poetry readings, parades, the opening of a new bank branch, the distribution of rice and powdered milk, the laying of foundation stones for retirement homes and new factories. That year, however, conspiracy was in the air and added a flash of interest to the various local and national addresses scheduled to follow the king's speech once one hundred and thirty needy infants had been circumcised and handed food and new clothes en masse, races run and exhibitions declared open.

The scandal of France's Channel Two's transmission of a documentary criticising the current king and his government was still hot news and everyone from columnists to academics, expatriate businessmen to rural communes seemed to be competing to find the choicest words of condemnation, the most convincing tone of outrage. The inter-media fight was particularly savage, and Channel Two's directors were being accused either of being controlled and manipulated by the Zionists ('the enemies of the Moroccan state') or of being the puppets of an occult group determined to destroy national unity and the sacred values of Islam. Over half a million telegrams protesting the defamatory nature of the programme had been sent to poor Francois Mitterrand, whose wife had further exacerbated a tense situation by asking, of all things, to visit the western Sahara. Madame Mitterrand's interest in the welfare of the Saharan tribes challenged the Moroccan government head-on, since it suggested that the Saharaoui might be less than thrilled to have been incorporated into the Moroccan State. Channel Two was forced off the air by the Moroccan authorities and the beleaguered French postal service continued to be flooded with telegrams. I wondered if this whole campaign hadn't inadvertently scored something of an own goal, for by all accounts the programme, seen by a minority, said nothing which the Moroccans didn't already know themselves. Now, with the anti-French campaign dominating the newspapers and tele-vision, everyone was aware that the king had been found wanting by outside opinion-makers. Of course, as head of the faithful and descendant of the Prophet, Hassan II was sensitive to the point of paranoia when it came to personal criticism, and the combination of censorship and the threat of imprisonment ensured that any which was voiced, was implicit or couched in economic or social terms. Open discussion of the king's record was, in short, forbidden – and dangerous.

The Union Generale des Travailleurs du Maroc, the trade union wing of Istiqlal, a major opposition party, chose this moment to call for a general strike to safeguard workers' rights and protest against cuts in hours and the ongoing rise in the price of basic foodstuffs. On 20 November 1990 they issued a communiqué which called on all regional, professional and cultural organisations to join in the planned national stoppage and halt the rise in the cost of living which was devastating the poor at a time when the government was showing its class bias and according the rich economic privileges – as well as privatis-ing businesses created from 'the sweat of the working class'. The government was attacked for not fulfilling its duties to the masses, for its indifference to the degeneration of health, housing, transport and education levels, and its enthusiasm in restricting public and trade union rights. Istiqlal thus called for better social conditions, a higher minimum wage, a guaranteed right to work, unemployment benefits, pensions and an end to the system of wage deductions for services which were no longer acceptable. For once, the call to action came as a surprise, since it ended with 'Long live the working classes' – and not the king. Istiqlal's appealingly blunt statement of what needed to be done excited me, a sentiment not shared by the majority of the Moroccans I quizzed on the communiqué, since none of them believed the strike would occur. 'Old slogans,' they muttered. 'We've heard it all before.' I bet Aziz five pounds against a T-shirt of his home town that the strike would take place, and succeed – if not in its reforming, social aims, then at least in galvanising the people into protest. There was something in the air which anticipated change, the breaking of bonds, patience running out, muscles flexing. Istiqlal's message was nothing new, but it raised the prospect of united action and stated, eloquently, what people felt to be true of their daily lives, their struggle to survive.

The days rolled by slowly. Sheila and Aziz circled each other on a merry-go-round of highs and lows. He was now loath to accept his daily fee, returned it to us in the shape of bags of almonds, gifts of food and coffees in our favourite rooftop café overlooking the Grand Socco where I played gooseberry as they discussed their pasts – the woman Aziz was hoping to marry who turned out to have another fiancé in Chaouen; Sheila's need for independence. When spectator status became too irksome, I spent time with Abdelatif, a Berber carpet seller, watched him make obscene profits by playing the incompetent fool, read his star-studded visitors' book or just walked, losing myself in the skyline, with its minarets and crosses, domes and mosaics, as a watery sun crawled out from behind low, black clouds.

One afternoon I glimpsed a funeral procession, the mourners

driving to the cemetery in a hired coach, the shrouded corpse on its blanket-covered stretcher preceding family and friends in an ambulance. Apparently, the business of dying was expensive, for a plot of land, burial fees and transport hire can add up to a crippling sum, but neighbours do rally round to comfort and cook for the bereaved, who observe forty days of mourning. Another grey morning yielded minor dramas: a pickpocket caught in the act; a woman soundly beating her husband with a slipper to the encouraging yells of a swiftly gathering crowd. Time gradually became meaningless, for there was little to do. On the entertainment level, cars with loud-hailers cruised the streets drumming up enthusiasm for the imminent arrival of one Malek. No one seemed interested in Malek's blend of poetry and music, but a large queue was ever present outside the cinema which was proudly advertising an Indian film whose heroine had the unfortunate tendency to turn into a serpent whenever night fell, and was too embarrassed and frightened to reveal her secret to her fiancé. Madness. Aziz assured me that it had a happy ending and seemed perfectly willing to go and see the wretched thing a fourth time. I declined the kind offer.

Just as Sheila and I had resolved privately to make a move south, confident that we had now exhausted Tangier's possibilities, the town showed us another profile entirely, destroying our equanimity, and adding a sour taste to the trip in the process. Sunday morning started quietly enough, with a stroll through the medina and kasbah, to look at houses which were currently up for sale at an average price of ten thousand pounds, daydreaming about putting in fitted bathrooms, knocking through walls and restoring cracked tiled floors to their original russet, gold and black glory. As we turned into a wide street, a group of policemen, walking three abreast, brushed past and casually hooked Aziz by the arm. Sheila and I walked on, pretending that we did not know him, certain that he would come panting up the hill at any moment, his face creased in a grin, apologising profusely. He did not come. A young boy who sold individual cigarettes – and was thus liable to a fine of four hundred dirhams and four to eight months in jail for showing initiative – told us that he had been taken to the commissariat for questioning and offered to accompany us there, if we wanted to get involved. The 'if' was superfluous, insulting. Of course we were going. After all, this must be some kind of simple misunderstanding. By the time we walked into the commissariat we had persuaded ourselves that the police owed us an apology for taking us so far out of our way, ruining our plans, and we strolled in, fulminating, yet quite prepared to be gracious for the sake of a quiet life.

Two men were standing by the open doorway, heard us out and then waved us into a small room with half-tiled white walls, a couple of old wooden desks, a corner sink and a large electric typewriter. A door in the far wall was slightly ajar and through it we glimpsed a long corridor with steel-barred cells off to the right. We sat down, uninvited, on the narrow wooden bench which ran the length of the right-hand wall, waiting. Minutes passed and an old man in a black turtleneck jumper and grey jacket walked in, asked us to explain our business. I told him that Aziz was our friend, not a hustler, and that it was our fault that he was there (and where the hell *was* there, I wondered) because we had failed to clear up the misunderstanding and intervene on his behalf in the medina. Black jumper smirked, asked me how we first came to know Aziz. He listened, then admired my Allah medallion and asked for our passports. This did not seem a promising development, but we duly handed them over and waited again, our confidence ebbing away rapidly.

A grey-uniformed policeman sauntered in and sat down behind the typewriter. 'So,' he started off, 'this man is your friend. What is his name? His full name?' We were stumped. It was looking bad. 'Where does he live?' he continued.

PART TWO

'The medina,' Sheila answered quickly.

'What can you tell me about him?' This was problematic.

'His brother works in the Canary Isles, his mother is in her sixties and his father is dead.'

It sounded lame to my ears.

'Where did you meet him?' the questioning continued. 'When?' 'How?' I hoped that by sticking to the truth on all but the issue of Aziz's pay, we would end up giving the same answers as him, controlled my voice and kept on repeating the story: our meeting outside the Palais Mendoub, our subsequent walks and sightseeing trips. I lied, kept emphasising that this had never been a business arrangement, that no money had ever changed hands. A younger man in dark glasses had entered and half-perched on a desk. He was obviously well aware of our presence, but militantly refused to glance in our direction or acknowledge us. I felt nonplussed, tried to work out why he was posing, lost track of the questions. Sheila was trembling as she shook my shoulder and passed me a cigarette, a look of panicked enquiry in her eyes. I shrugged and raised my eyebrows. God only knew what was up ...

Suddenly, there was a scuffle at the doorway and three men in their twenties were pushed through, forced to half-sit, half-fall, with their backs to the wall by the sink. They were laughing and gesticulating, yelling out to the smooth-cheeked interrogator by our desk, half-rising from their crouched positions. Our boy slowly uncurled from the chair. A crack and then another crack split the air. Sheila and I did a double-take. Was that a slap echoing? Surely not, not in front of tourists, not so openly and brazenly. I risked a quick glance at Sheila who seemed shell-shocked and was inhaling her cigarette in deep, nervous draughts. A scream from the corner removed all ambiguity, was cut off by a low grunting and moaning. The man closest to us was holding his stomach. Blood was pouring from his nose. There was blood on the tiles behind his head. His friend leaned across and cradled the injured man in his lap, but was shoved aside and fell. As the two men righted and disentangled themselves, the interrogator aimed a booted kick at their faces, then another jab. The whimpering died down.

Obviously, I was stunned by the violence, but what struck me most clearly at that moment was the contempt which these uniformed men had for the law, their certainty that they were beyond the reach of complaints, censure or reprisals. There was a tacky sexual element to the scenario they were staging, a strutting arrogance which said: 'Look how powerful and therefore how attractive I am.' I started to wonder if we were in some way responsible for the other men's pain; if they would have been touched in the absence of a female audience. If I was right, then Sheila and I could not afford to be seen to be reacting. I lit another cigarette, removed my sunglasses, as if bored by their little play, and sat up straighter. The interrogator was walking around, stretching his legs and looking at nothing, casually flicking our passports against his thigh. I asked him why we were being subjected to this delay; he ignored the question, continued in his perambulations. The minutes dragged past. It was hot in this airless, medium-sized room, and our dialogue had degenerated into a war of wills. A yellow form was suddenly placed before me and I was handed a pen. The policeman noticed my quivering fingers and was obviously pleased, smiled slightly and lay a flat, warm palm over mine to hold it still. I tried to fill in the personal details on the form but couldn't concentrate, certainly couldn't remember the colour of my eyebrows. 'Grey,' Sheila hissed in my ear. Grey? Outraged, I turned to argue the toss but lost interest as the next section, nose type, caught my attention. I lay down the pen and confessed that I really didn't know which box to tick. Tears were close now. The policeman ticked 'straight', at random, and read through what I had written. He was obviously enjoying himself now and pleased to see that we were both worried and diminished by the run-in.

PART TWO

Suddenly, he rose to his full height and put out his hand. I shook it automatically, while Sheila had the presence of mind to scoop up our passports and tuck them away in her jacket pocket. We shook hands for long seconds, eyes locked. A final mocking jerk and he turned away, saying, 'Welcome to Tangier,' satisfied. Well brought up to the bitter end, we rode the sarcasm, replied, 'Thank you,' and walked out onto the street and round the corner, still not convinced that it was finally over.

Somewhere along the line we'd totally forgotten about Aziz as, safely back at the Chellah, we resolved to get out of Tangier for a few days. Minutes later, we flagged down a taxi and sped down to the station, a change of underwear, tights and clothes rammed into a Duty Free carrier bag, and were consequently shocked to find him already there, waiting. Aziz was shaken – but more to the point, he was moved that we'd bothered to intervene. Apparently, the police were flummoxed when we materialised out of nowhere and, at first, believed that we'd come to lay charges against him. When it transpired that we were just meddling on principle, they decided that there was no telling what we might do and that the best way to handle the situation was to put on a show of strength and thereby warn us not to meddle, in short to drop the topic. As soon as we left, they released Aziz with a warning, glad to wash their hands of all three of us.

The day was in shreds and, with the relief of knowing that Aziz was free, the hysteria erupted, the compulsive talking and picking over of details. We were in need of rest, but decided on alcohol, and set out to explore what remained of Tangier's once notorious, risqué night club circuit.

In its heyday, Tangier was renowned for its bars and brothels, its spectacular floorshows, the cheap hotels which could be rented by the half hour and the excesses which were available in every shape or form, narcotic and sexual. Nowadays, everything which was larger than life and flamboyant about the town has diminished, so it should not have surprised us to discover that sordid tension had replaced naked need and the quest for pleasure in this quarter, too. We arranged to meet in a two-storey Moroccan café, an all-male preserve, a fact which persuaded the elderly manager to urge Sheila and me to mount the winding marble staircase covered in litter, post-haste. Sitting on wooden chairs with thin metal legs, we sucked on olives or tiny squares of lamb skewered on toothpicks, watching the crowd below indulge in bottles of Flag, a weak, watery beer, as gales of laughter and shouted greetings rose all round, to compete with the strong smell of garlic wafting from a tiny kitchen tucked behind the bar. The lino floor was covered in cigarette butts and strips of old newspaper, and all hope of conversation was swamped by the volume of the jukebox, the tide of voices bobbing and reverberating all around. A young boy brought us a battered blue metal ashtray and the daily newspaper (the Arabic version), winked and retreated, his endearing gesture of respect for our sex as welcome as it was unexpected. As we chewed our way through metal saucers-full of tidbits and gulped back orange juice, some of the strain of the afternoon began to recede and we relaxed, made eye contact with friendly faces, shook off the images of bleeding heads, blood-spattered tiles.

Aziz's materialisation caused Sheila to moan in what seemed like pain. 'What is it?' I enquired, concerned.

'Just look at him,' she shook her head resignedly. 'Look, he's dressed up for me.'

And so he had. The brilliantined curls seemed glossier and tighter than ever; the fake Levi's were gone, replaced by off-white cotton trousers topped with a fake leather jacket. Ominously, two long-stemmed pink roses were clutched, stems-upward, in his hand as he waved towards the balcony. Sheila narrowed her eyes menacingly to stifle any quip I might be incubating, and tripped cautiously down the stairs to a round of hearty applause from the drinkers below.

The Ambassador, our first pit stop, would have been a strange choice of setting for a truly romantic date, and I noticed that Aziz was a trifle embarrassed to lead us through its doors. A rectangular room with a bar by the main door, it featured shelves laden with copper jugs, stuffed birds, plates, fish tanks and arrangements of dried flowers. Among all this finery we spied a large contingent of call girls, who all seemed to have watched the same American movies in their youth. The women were a parody of their own calling: one strutted, hands on hips, in stilettos and a black dress slit to the thigh; another leaned seductively against the bar counter in a Lana Turner-style angora jumper, nibbling a man's earlobe, while focussing her attention somewhere else entirely well over his shoulder. We were greeted by an attractive, lean man in a stiff white shirt and black trousers, who indicated a free table at the far end of the room. This corner housed rifles, collections of pots, clocks and nego-tiating couples, the women with dyed blonde hair which was showing three inches of black roots, the men Gestapo types with their jug ears, bull necks and maroon leather jackets. I gazed at the foursome in wonder, marvelling at how men need to delude themselves while undertaking sexual transactions, amazed to see how they, and virtually every other man in the room, were buying artificial roses, silk flowers on plastic poles and tiny bunches of jasmine for their new lady-loves. The main door flapped open regularly as peanut, cake and shell bracelet vendors walked in, carrying trays, and did the rounds of the tables. The men seemed obliged to demonstrate affluence and generosity, to add romance to their encounters by buying trinkets and edible gifts. The girls, who received a hundred or two hundred dirhams, alcohol and the price of the room, played their parts too, licking necks, smiling up demurely, as if 'in love', linking arms and whispering sweet nothings.

Aziz was gloomy and censorious – this was not the setting he had dreamed of for his beloved Sheila; he couldn't understand why we were here. He told us that many of the city's working women were bringing up children on their own, some were widowed or divorced, and a minority could not marry since they were responsible for old, dependent female relatives. He knew that quite a few of the women were wealthy in their own right and had accumulated gold jewellery and property by plying their trade. And yet they did pay a price for this material success, I mused, watching my nearest neighbour suffering her companion's clumsy embraces, tears pricking her eyes as he yanked her head back by the hair and smacked her playfully on the cheek. She smacked him back equally playfully, misjudging his mood, and had her face rammed, hard, into the table-top. Only a smudge of mascara revealed her pain and anger as she raised her head, smiled, took his hand and started sucking on his fingers. Whatever tension had momentarily erupted between them seemed to have been dispelled, for they rose soon afterwards, and made their way over to the till, to pay. I glanced at the woman's black leather boots, black tights, her sixteen stone poured into a Lycra dress with net trim, her smeared lipstick, the peanut husks attached to her mouth by dabs of dried saliva. And still I worried for her. An hour later she was back – thankfully in one piece – and took up her post on a bar stool again, prepared to keep on working the now crowded room until two or three in the morning. I was depressed and sobered by the risks she took every night.

On to the Koutoubia, a low, black-ceilinged underground club with a parquet floor, red lights and a green spotlight illuminating a perfectly ghastly six-piece Egyptian band, complete with over-large amplifiers and a ballad singer with the lungs of a professional deep sea diver. The place was empty, except for a cleaner sleeping on one of the padded benches by the entrance to the ladies' toilet. The cacophony was unimaginable, the ultra-

PART TWO

violet lights seemed eerie and, to top it all, we were charged three hundred per cent over the odds for fruit juice to suffer the aural assault. Samantha Fox's breasts cried out for attention on the walls, and the final straw came when an electric violin was activated, creating a wall of pain. We fled.

Prostitutes and castrators of melody. What else could Tangier offer? Well, Scott's, the town's most famous gay bar, presented a bleak vision of lonely old age. Its small, red-painted square room had a DJ's booth and a tiny bar, a strobe turning lazily above the dance floor. George McRae was belting out 'Rock Me, Baby' to what looked like a large heap of clothes dumped in a singularly dark corner. In fact, this subsequently turned out to be a young couple covered by a leather jacket and raincoat, for every ten minutes or so a slab of midriff or a face emerged, only to disappear immediately in a writhing mass. A man in his early fifties wearing black horn-rimmed glasses was sitting at the bar, watching an eighteen-year-old boy opposite. The boy was clean cut, demure and angelic in his light blue V-necked cardigan, his white shirt as tasty as listeria-bearing cheese. Sex, the heartbreak of and the possibility of scoring, was heavy in the air, but there were no takers and by midnight the place was empty and desolate. I found Scott's a singularly sad spot and only the framed picture of our own Elizabeth II and the king, walking along, heads bowed, lifted my mood, for the angle of the shot and the smile on their faces gave me the impression that they were sneaking away, holding hands, to dance till they dropped. Scott's was dead, too, then – another myth hit the dust.

Just when it looked as if Tangier had gone to sleep, quietly and without fuss, we stumbled across a professional drunkards' bar, the Alhambra, which apparently enjoyed a poor reputation and did not seem accustomed to Western visitors. The décor was odd: cartoons garlanded in tinsel of every shade and hue hung, framed, on the walls. Many of them seemed to be portraying George Best – this couldn't be right. The plates of nibbles we were offered were of the three-star hotel variety, a large selection of nuts, meats, tiny grilled fish, even a sloppy but appetising mixture of herbs and tomatoes. The prostitutes who worked the nearby Africa Hotel were having a beer-break and offered us cigarettes, squeezing up to make space at the table. Trade was apparently bad. I made conversation of sorts with a young Spanish-speaking girl with a weak smile and numerous thin pink scars under her eyes. She leaned intimately on my shoulder, told me that I looked tired and should go to bed, and stared blankly out into the night. Ten minutes later, she was gone, wandering down the street clutching her packet of Marlboros and a blue leather bag. She turned and gave me a tiny wave, fingers flapping before she disappeared around a corner.

Seconds later, just as I was sinking back onto my chair, a young man in a red and blue tracksuit exploded from around the same corner, tearing and pumping along as if his very life depended on his muscle-power. Two distinctly less gazelle-like men followed, visibly labouring under the strain of running, policemen in pursuit of a drug seller. The dealer would get away, this time, and anyway the three hundred dirhams he earned a week would easily cover the cost of bribing his way to freedom the next time the heavy hand of the law fell on his shoulder. The human cost of the north's drug trade was visible on every street corner at this time of night. Six- and seven-year-old boys reeled around outside the late-night tobacconists, scraps of glue-soaked rag held to their faces; older boys with the heavy, fixed eyes of kif smokers begged for money, grabbing at our arms as we emerged from the Alhambra. A young child lay, half-upright, in a doorway, unable to raise himself fully and mutely held out a thin palm, asking for a dirham. Many of these children are runaways, some have been thrown out by new step-parents and told to fend for themselves, still others are simply unsupervised and will end up making their way back home in the early hours. We gave nothing, then changed our

PART TWO

minds and bought chocolate, cigarettes, apples and bread, handing them over. The children were puzzled, put out by the gifts, would doubtlessly try to sell them back for drug money – but it was all we were prepared to do. My sympathies lay elsewhere: with the girl with leprosy who wrote to *L'Opinion Des Jeunes*, asking for pen pals, reassurance, worrying what will happen to her face; with the legless man opposite the El Minzah Hotel trying to lever himself out of the gutter; the mother whose newborn son died when the cord was cut with rusty scissors by an indifferent nurse.

Aziz and Sheila had walked on ahead and were gazing intently into each other's eyes by the Chellah entrance when I meandered in. Some watershed appeared to have been reached, but, upstairs, Sheila's slamming of make-up remover and shampoo bottles suggested that this was not the time for intimate confessions and questions. She sat at the window, chain-smoking and gazing at the swimming pool below, occasionally flicking an errant strand of hair back from a set face, glaring abstractedly at me when I switched on the travel jug, knocked into a chair. I leafed through a train timetable, adding preparation time for hair washing, breakfast and waiting in the ticket-buying queue, and set the alarm clock for 7:00 a.m. We obviously needed a change of scenery for a few days, for the combination of witnessing self-inflicted and doled-out abuse and violence had left us less than enamoured of Tangier. I tried to sleep. Sheila continued to glower and look out of the window, occasionally fishing out lumps of duck paté from a tin on the table. Two Mates condoms sat on her thumb and middle finger to protect them against the grease. Freud would have taken out his notebook, but I dared not and simply turned over and stifled a peal of laughter with my pillow.

◆ *Chapter Nine* ◆

Sheila must have spent a tortuous albeit highly fattening night, for we missed the early Asilah train due to her play-possum pose at 7:00, 7:15 and 7:30 a.m. and ended up tramping down to the gare routière and negotiating places in a grand taxi. Tangier was shrugging off its misty wrap and warming up as we took the coast road south, wedged close together, the windows rolled up hard, as usual, against the merest suggestion of breathable air. Patches of ochre, green and brown, rolling hills and a calm, glistening sea dotted with the odd struggling wind surfer flew past as I drowsed, lulled into a semi-comotose state by the lack of oxygen, waves of body heat and the rocking motion of the white Mercedes.

The small town of Asilah enjoys something of a showpiece status these days and has been dubbed the artists' colony of Morocco. Every August, the town plays host to an Arts Festival which attracts painters and musicians to its immaculate streets. Many murals adorn the walls of the medina, chronicling passing trends and prominent visitors alike: a trompe l'oeil of a house, embossed sculptures, wild, extravagant abstracts all wrestle, shriekingly, with the Toytown-neatness, the almost cruel whiteness of the environment. The contrast with Tangier, a mere twenty-eight miles away, is almost shocking – from the backstreet stews to the self-satisfied home of 'Culture'.

Disentangling ourselves from the limbs of others and

ungluing ourselves from the sticky leather seats. Sheila and I practically tumbled out into the main square, just outside the signposted medina. Mustapha, a mechanic from El Jadida, whose left shoulder, torso and thigh I now knew intimately, by virtue of having pressed and bumped against him for forty-five minutes, bought us a Fanta at a roadside café. Mustapha was a man at home with himself and his environment, perfectly happy with his work, his lifestyle and his prospects. His parents had left him a house on the coast, he earned a decent wage servicing heavy goods vehicles and hoped to start his own business in a few years' time. As we sipped warm Fanta in the sun, he peered furtively to right and left as if looking out for someone. Whenever I followed his darting glances, I came up with nothing interesting and simply succeeded in appearing shifty myself. Exasperated by the pantomime, I eventually asked him why he seemed so tense. Mustapha was embarrassed, laughed it off, then explained that he must leave us for he had been 'fined' fifty dirhams by the police over the summer when they noticed him sharing a café table with three Italian girls.

They gave me a choice. I could give them the money and go, or they would arrest me for being a "false guide". So I paid. Today I haven't got much money on me, so I can't afford to get into that kind of trouble.'

We assured Mustapha that we understood his position and were not offended. He left, relieved, cheerful once more, waving his newspaper in farewell. Sheila and I exchanged glances of enquiry – paranoia or fact? Overall, we tended to believe the worst.

Asilah was beautiful in a manicured, twee fashion. We made our way past an ancient cemetery which was being turned into a park, and along a wide, paved road. The pavements themselves were as super-clean as the scrubbed battlements of the medina, which sits by the seashore. A new port was under construction and red and blue fishing boats were drawn up on the beach, members of the small fleet which still works out of Asilah. The Atlantic surf was strong that day, thumping into giant, smooth boulders and saturating the group of children fishing off the break-water. Looking down into the water, we spotted silver bodies aplenty darting to and fro; they'd get a good haul today. Retracing our steps to the medina gate, we stood still, admiring the good taste on display. Gone were the rickety metal tables and spine-cracking wooden chairs of every Moroccan street; in their place stood tables covered in checked cotton tablecloths, ceramic ashtrays squatting alongside discreet vases of long-stemmed flowers. Tree-lined streets stretched off into the distance and walls groaned under the weight of bright purple and red flowering creepers. Inside the medina, the paving stones were scored with loose symbols of waves and fishes, maritime life, and tiny green, blue and white houses with neat knockers and painted entranceways stood sentinel across swept, litter-free alleys. The walls all around were so white in the sun that they seemed to be made of royal icing and I was tempted to check, to break off a chunk, like Gretel, and chew on it. The sun was bright as we passed slowly down the shimmering, heated streets and out along the ramparts onto a terrace by the town's abbatoir.

A small group of teenagers was beating tambourines with muscled well-practised fingers, the tips flying from the centre to the rim, the palms stroking then slamming into the frames. We stretched out and listened as a canary-yellow, T-shirted lad playing a five-stringed instrument joined in. Below us, balanced on the rocks, small children were scrubbing skins clean of fat, dunking the abattoir's produce in the crashing waves before laying it to dry higher up the slope, near a napping man curled up on a low wall. Nourredine detached himself from the musicians and offered us tiny hand cymbals to accompany the beat. We fixed the thin, round discs to thumbs and middle fingers, and clicked along happily. Nourredine was twenty-six and studying EFL at the American college in Tangier. He reminded me of Bill Wyman, both physically and in his phlegmatic style of speech, his relaxed good humour. He spoke with a strong American accent, and hoped to go to UCLA to study physics, inshallah. Born in Asilah, he made enough money over the summer months, when up to three hundred thousand visitors invade these streets, to supplement his income and pay tuition fees. Talking of the tourist trade, Nourredine pointed out a recently finished conference centre in the middle distance, flags flying, to underline his town's prosperity.

Asilah's fortunes have always depended on outsiders. Under the Romans, this strategically important port suffered the deportation to Spain of all its citizens and resettlement by Spanish immigrants. In the fifteenth century, the Portuguese seized and held Asilah and it wasn't until 1691 and the reign of Moulay Ishmael that medersas and mosques replaced Christian churches, and Riffian migrants settled in large numbers. The flamboyant bandit and hostage taker, Raisuni, head of the Djeballah tribes, moved to Asilah in 1906 and declared himself a descendant of the Prophet and future sultan, building his palace, The House of Tears, from whose windows captives walked the plank straight into the embrace of the Atlantic below. Nowadays, Raisuni's palace is shut in the winter months, but we paid an old man ten dirhams for a quick tour and walked into a huge, fantastically vulgar room with stairs leading to a balconied first floor and couch-lined reception rooms off to all sides.

Black and yellow scatter cushions screamed out their presence, fighting with metres of intricate stucco-work, multi-coloured, shoulder-high wall tiles with curved edges like snakes' coils, and garish floor tiles, to hold the visitors' attention. Pictures of the royal family sat, propped up, at one end of the room, dominating it completely. The designer here had been without a doubt, a crazed and colour-blind megalomaniac and I wondered how on earth the annual artists' meetings, workshops and exhibitions could find this riotous background conducive to defining taste, style and oral and aural excellence. Cracked glass panels in the roof let in shafts of sunlight and showed up the spotlights suspended uneasily a few feet below. Nourredine was proud of the palace and insisted on showing us the suicides' windows and the rocks below. We looked. And shivered. It seemed such a long way down.

Asilah was slumbering in the afternoon heat. A belly dancer in a purple, diaphanous garment zipped past, sitting up pertly in the front seat of a Jeep, doubtlessly heading for rehearsals at the Hotel Atlas, which puts on a fantasia for tourists every Sunday. We noticed a curious mural on a wall, an eye, and Noureddine explained that this was the famous Eye of Asilah, which brings the town's inhabitants luck and refracts evil, preventing curses from touching anyone within its walls. I admired it automatically, while disliking the flat, one-dimensional effect intensely, and looked around, only to catch sight of a most peculiar, even damning image: a donkey pulling a cart, a sling swinging under his tail to catch the falling excrement. Oh poor Asilah. It did take itself seriously. No leaking, ebullient tiled fountains with barefoot children splashing in line; no disorganised grill cafés, no bellowing fruit traders. Neat shops and neat schools service new, neat houses – most of which are bought by the Spanish, according to Nourredine. Outside the medina walls, a large paved street shaded by eucalyptus trees sheltered an impromptu selection of goods spread on clean blankets: table lighters at one hundred and fifty dirhams, umbrellas, shoes and bottles of lemon shampoo large enough to do every townsperson's head, twice over, even a collection of reasonable watercolours sitting on easels. As the blankets died away, the produce market took over and we walked into a sea of bright pompommed Riffian hats and chattering Spanish. The women sat under impromptu tents made of long poles covered in lengths of material, displaying rubber plants in old cans, baby banana trees in cut-off metal containers and red peppers arranged in

star-shaped clusters. Heaps of tiny potatoes and jars of sour milk
sat next to purple coleus cuttings; olives rubbed shoulders with
pink geraniums in earthenware planters. We bought apples,
helped a woman whose load of firewood seemed about to slide
off the cart she was attempting to flatten, watched the animated
but organised business of commerce flowing past. There was a
distinct Andalucian feel to Asilah and this was obviously siesta
time.

Eight grand taxis slumbered in the square just below the
round medina towers as we retraced our steps. Nourredine
pointed out one crumbling tower and told us that the
Portuguese wanted to build it high enough to glimpse their own
home shores from its peak. They had obviously over-reached
themselves, but at least they did not destroy the port when they
left, as the Spanish did, and the ramparts they built stand to this
day, girding this model, if aberrant, Moroccan town. Asilah has a
grace and prime donna attitude which renders it amusingly artificial and yet welcoming. Its very existence proves, if proof were
needed, that Morocco defies generalisation on every level and
that the north is a world apart. We resolved to see more.

Chaouen or Tetouan? Both, in their own fashion, emphasise
different sides of the Rif. Chaouen, a town immortalised on
numerous tourist postcards and posters, and a magnet for all
Western tour group buses, is said to be one of the most attractive and memorable spots in the north. In Berber, the name
means 'gaze on the mountain horns', for the town is rammed
into the twin peaks of the mountainside, its white- and blue-
painted housing spilling down steep paths, its tiled red roofs
setting off the successful marriage of Moorish and Andalucian
architecture. Relaxed, groomed and picturesque – a Moroccan
Sidi Bou Said – it was shut off from the wider world and hence
the European traveller until well into this century. Indeed, up

until 1920, only four Christians are known to have penetrated its walls and survived to tell the tale.

Chaouen was established as a mountain hideout in 1471 by Ali ibn Rachid and effectively shut itself away both from the hostile Djeballah tribesmen (against whom it was originally fortified), and the rhythms of world history. A xenophobic atmosphere prevailed, along with a passionate devotion to Islam and a concomitant anti-infidel sentiment. When the Spanish entered Chaouen in 1920, they were flabbergasted to find that medieval Castilian was still widely spoken and to hear odd voices calling out 'Viva Isabella' and demanding the liberation of Christendom from the heathen yoke. Unfortunately, over thirty millimetres of rain had fallen in the Rif in the last twenty-four hours, visibility was poor and the journey fairly pointless. It was pouring bleakly as we slithered and tumbled down to the CTM depot, resigned to seeing the nearer destination, Tetouan, instead.

The mere idea of Tetouan gave us pause, for every traveller we encountered started off by recounting nightmare moments in Tetouan as a prelude to sagas of minor rip-offs, which more often than not also took place in the Rif. Still, perhaps it might be different in the winter, Sheila and I consoled ourselves. We had dressed smartly for this leg of the trip to avoid the drug-scoring hippy look, aiming for a cross between West End secretary and feeble-minded pauper – and as our numbers were ticked off by a black-suited CTM official and we drew out I prepared to put prejudice aside and enjoy the town. Prejudice be damned. All the calumnies are true for, unpredictably enough, Tetouan was actually worse than its critics had warned us and, even now, miles and months away, I look back on our expedition with horror.

At first, all went well. We adjusted our navy blue curtains, unveiled our glasses of milky coffee smuggled from the bus station bar, and rubbed dry crinkling hair, ready to gaze in awe at the Rif. The closely packed pines lining steeply winding roads cascaded gallons of tears, lashed by savage gusts of wind. Old metal signs announcing the fact that 'Fire destroys forests' spoke of searing summer heat and, in spite of the stormy skies, the occasional wickerwork or ceramic seller squatted by the side of the road amongst the clumps of gorse or astride the thick roots (visible signs of soil erosion) poking out onto the tarmac. Mixed herds of sheep, cows and goats braved the rain, supervised by young boys, their heads covered by large squares of plastic. The surrounding evergreens and heather framed what must surely have been their village, a kilometre or so down the valley. The Rif boasts a venerable and enduring history of feuds, and single houses (which traditionally had their own pillboxes) rather than groups of dwellings appeared to be the norm, strung like neck-laces across the countryside, rather than clustered together ksar-fashion, for mutual protection. It's everyone for himself in the land of dissent.

And it's everyone for himself or herself, too, in Tetouan. As we drove through the suburbs I realised my fantasies had been totally inaccurate, for Tetouan was a bigger, far more developed town than I had imagined. Motorway-style road signs, large apartment blocks and show rooms full of giant, gleaming tractors all emphasised the existence of a large population and heavy traffic. No quaint village here. The town's setting is dramatic – dark green and navy hills blending into each other – and the streets were jammed for we had hit town on market day. Diesel fumes poured from our exhaust as the bus drew into the station and parked, downstairs. A rush of noise, shoving, sharp tweaking of shoulder straps and we were expelled at street level, to take a first, cautious look around. Someone offered us a rundown of return times to Tangier. How did he know where we had come from, whence we were bound and when? I shrugged him off with a perfunctory thank you, and tried to follow Sheila into the hellish furore of the teeming streets, leers, *hola*s and smiles, smiles raining down all the while. We had no idea where we were, and moved vaguely north and away, following the nearest group of women carrying shopping bags, but soon lost them in the throng, and ended up circling back to the same street, going round in ever smaller circles, half angry, half panicked. Sheila spotted a café, the first we had seen in Tetouan, and we made to enter, but the owner barred the door and turned us back with a dismissive side-swipe of the hand. No sanctuary there. We turned right and then right again and every bend brought with it a new hanger-on who asked us where we were from, offered mandarins or a trip to the cinema, commented on bra-cup sizes and what he'd like to do to us, slowly.

I was losing track of where we were heading and when the central market reappeared yet again, I wanted to scream with frustration. Sheila tried to talk to a traffic policeman, but he was too busy to do more than wave, and every side street looked identical, lined with birds in cages, produce sellers, women squatting on open sacks, rubbish, foraging cats and carts spilling over with bananas. Suddenly we spotted two beacons of light: a place name, Place de l'Oussa, and a café. We dived in and ordered tea, hesitated to uncurl our defensively arranged limbs until two tiny china cups had touched our pursed lips. The ludicrousness of the situation surfaced and, with it, a change of plan.

Since Tetouan was so menacing, we would simply have to join in the fray and to hell with femininity and good manners. The square was surrounded by tall Spanish buildings which looked like iced cakes with their elaborately curling white balconies, friezes and cornices. Statues sat amidst ornate iron-work railings; an ornamental fountain spluttered erratically. Encouraged by the fact that the buildings had not reacted to our arrival, for such was the level of my current paranoia, we first snuck quick glances and then boldly looked onto the square.

PART TWO

Winking faces and horn-rimmed glasses moved past – the thug and the student – along with dozens of children wearing the same type of Wellingtons, which we later saw for sale in the souks. Tetouan is a large university town, but most of the campus is located away from the town centre and, walking through the streets, I was more aware of its recent history than its contemporary life and status.

Established as a pirates' hideout in 1305, it first enflamed Spanish fury in 1339, and the vengeful Christians enslaved and slaughtered the population in retaliation for the Tetouanis' raids against their shipping. Successive waves of sixteenth-century Moorish expulsions from Spain contributed to a rise in the town's population, and a complementary rise in the activities of the corsairs based there. Spain eventually seized and temporarily held Tetouan in 1860, and when the Rif fell to the Spanish upon the establishment of the Spanish Protectorate, Tetouan was chosen to be its political and administrative capital. The corsairs live on, in the guise of today's drug dealers, the piracy certainly continues and, if the craftsmen of the medina are any indication, the Andalusian decorative tradition too is alive and well in 1991.

Rebuffing a disagreeable, goat-featured student with ginger hair and a tatty beard, we reached the Bab er Rouah and darted through into the medina. Water and mud were flowing everywhere, and the fish sellers were gutting their catch from nearby Martil straight into the flood. The shopfronts seemed to be peeling and rusty; and whitewashed dark tunnels led off the main drag through numerous small arches. We were not tempted by the plastic tea strainers and umbrellas on display on Rue Terrafin, but walked on to Souk el Hots, with its ceramics and terracotta ware, then on again through a passage festooned with colanders, tea-trays and saucepans, all of which were suspended in the air by string, turning gently. A wheelbarrow heaped with spices had met a messy end; voices raised in indignation floated above the ever shuffling crowd. Shopkeepers were shutting up for Friday prayers as, drenched and speckled with mud, we pushed through a large gate and emerged into a watery, fresh landscape, free of the medina's odours. It was almost too quiet to be true, but we looked around and immediately saw why – this road was flanked with cemeteries. Moslem graves and the graves of the Sephardic Jewish community stretched out on both sides, separated by a road lined with crumbling walls. The Moslem area was overgrown. A woman sat by a grave, weeping in large gulps, while two Koranic chanters prayed over her dead; green-topped koubbas broke up the sad regularity of simple tiled tombs, all facing east, to Mecca.

It is sobering to dwell for a moment on the millions of Moslem faithful all over the globe, naked within their simple white shrouds, clothed in their faith and all waiting for the Day of Judgment. I shook myself and rejected apocalyptic sentimentality as quite unhelpful in the circumstances. Sheila was leaning against a wall, trying to find out, more or less, where we had blundered to this time, the smudged ink of her map removing a daunting percentage of place names as she mopped at it wildly with a tissue. An ass trotted, then galloped by, skittering sideways and dropping dozens of plastic bottles as it bucked and tore down the road, pursued by a furious middle-aged woman in a crocus-purple headscarf embroidered with black and yellow threads, her velvet, backless slippers effectively preventing her from giving the beast a good run for its money. Sheila and I felt like using up the energy born of our tension so we whooped off, undecorously no doubt, down the track in hot pursuit, and grabbed for his halter when he paused to munch on what looked like a mixture of couch grass and nettles. After handing back the unrepentant runaway, who barely flinched as his owner set about him with a wooden switch, we followed the rapidly thinning crowd to a hillside dominated by a decayed Spanish mansion. Many of the windows were partially boarded up, but scraps of dirty net curtain showed that at least one wing remained open and habitable, presumably by a caretaker. We stole closer and gazed in. Even in its death throes, with collapsed ceilings heaped on the floors, and exposed roof beams visible through the last areas of plaster which had defied gravity, the house remained magnificent in a haughty, aloof fashion. Elaborate ceiling roses and the odd run of cornice-work reflected meticulous, loving craftsmanship, while wide wooden fireplaces with carved sides and generous mantlepieces made a mockery of our own yuppies' pride in their mean, Victorian 'original features'.

A cough and a scuffling sound nearby warned us that we were not alone. Sheila and I unglued ourselves from our perches and turned round. The hillside was alive with bodies. Groups of teenagers were sprawled among the boulders and the sandy debris, smoking kif and, as far as I could tell, enjoying the view of Tetouan which had suddenly materialised below us, as if by magic. I could not fathom how we could have managed to leave town altogether without even noticing, or why we were so far away from the medina. Two boys in lurid shellsuits ambled over and rattled off their prices: two dirhams fifty centimes for a large, thick joint; ten dirhams for a lump half the size of my thumb. For free they threw in the information that kif kills five thousand brain cells per smoke and stood there expectantly, waiting for our response.

'We don't smoke kif,' Sheila explained cautiously, waiting to be knifed, denounced and beaten, every nightmare scenario she had ever read flashing through her mind in a matter of seconds.

A grunt of bored assent and the two shellsuits apparently lost interest in business entirely and sat down in the dirt by our feet instead. We all stared at Tetouan for stretched seconds. Mohammed spoke fairly good English and, apropos of nothing, started to talk, to talk of the endless, boring days which stretched out before him before he died; the long periods of waiting punctuated by casual labour; the emptiness in his heart.

I looked at him, an attractive boy in his early twenties, all dressed up and nowhere to go personified. Mohammed was still two steps removed from the café crowd, however, since he was carving out an image for himself, aiming for self-importance and originality; hence, he was refusing to lie back and drown in the sea of resigned unemployed. Today he was wearing yellow pants and, under the matching jacket, a tie-dyed top sporting a misprint in large letters: AMERICAN PSYHICAL EDUCATION. His Walkman doubtlessly hailed from Ceuta, his Frank Zappa tapes were good quality Moroccan bootlegs. I liked him for all the wrong reasons: because he reminded me of my brother, because he was a Libra and because he giggled like a bashful five-year-old. On the basis of this objective character assessment, I found myself asking him and his reticent friend, Yussuf, a surly carpenter with a stump instead of a little finger on his left hand, to guide us back to town. The boys were keen to have a purpose and swung Sheila to her feet as if she were a doll and told me to follow as we picked our way down a rubbish strewn slope, sliding and bumping into each other as footholds melted away into nothing, setting off avalanches of vegetable matter and aluminium cans in the process. Mohammed was obviously stoned and started to exhibit unnerving mood changes. Every time he laughed, we had to laugh too, but immediately, for if the cue was mistimed, more likely than not he would forget that he had cracked a joke or offered up a witticism and demand, roughly, why we were mocking him, what was so funny? As the drug lifted him up, up and away, he calmed and became solicitous, holding out his hand to support us over thin ledges, smiling encouragement and asking us about pop music. As the kif wore off, he started to look round to check if anyone was listening and talked of spies. It was wearying to constantly have to gauge his state of mind as he glowered and giggled, bounced and prowled in turn down into the valley.

By the time we reached the Ceuta motorway Mohammed

was becoming increasingly aggressive. We sat in a large café and watched the steady stream of cars heading east while he muttered about the union meetings which took place in town, the workers' organisations with muscle and Spanish links. Suddenly, he flared up, seizing me by the shoulders and whispering 'You know, Morocco has forgotten Tetouan, so Tetouan will forget Morocco.' Saying this, Mohammed was only repeating what all Riffians believe; that the land of dissent has been shunted off into a siding and left to fend for itself. Rabat was happy to persecute farmers and contraband dealers for trying to make a living; happier still to take its cut and percolate it down through the system of corruption. But as for investing in the north, well, where was the industry, where were the prospects of employment? Where, indeed? Was it therefore not inevitable that the siren call of Spain, Spanish goods and the tantalisingly close and visible mainland itself should continue to seduce Riffians into turning their eyes north, rejecting the otherness of imperial cities they had rebelled against over the centuries, a Saharan legacy which meant nothing to them?

Eventually, we returned to Place Hassan II, an inaptly named square, given the fact that the king has no apparent intention of settling here or even visiting this turbulent corner of his kingdom. Four minarets and huge floodlights sit at the corners of the tiled approach to the new palace, which is still being worked on inside and was designed by Italians. Mohammed looked blankly at the towering building and rhetorically asked which streets would have to be demolished to provide access to the forecourt. I wanted to take a photograph, but noticed a few curious glances and hastily stashed the camera.

Inside the Café Sidi el Maruni, the air was thick with hashish fumes and the entire back row of clientele seemed to have collapsed over their stumpy wooden pipes. The rich smell of urine blended with the fug, and kif sellers glided quietly from table to table, making deals. The flaking ceiling and cracked wall tiles were set off by a filthy floor covered in cigarette butts and old LOTTO papers. Everyone was facing a fading, flickering television set tuned in to one of the seven Spanish stations which can be picked up in the area. From what I could make out, they were watching a soap opera about identical twins, sex and betrayal. Looking at the hard-eyed, vacant faces, the slumped bodies draped over tables or sitting on bar stools whose red plastic covers had exploded many moons ago, I suspected that they would all watch the testcard with equal attention. All around us, fingers deftly and automatically rolled thick, cigar-like joints. In the past I had seen stoned people, stoned rooms and even stoned halls, but this was surely the first time I had come across an entire stoned town.

It was time to leave. The grand taxi stand on Avenue de Moulay Abbas took on an appealing aspect as we thanked Mohammed and Yussuf for their company and time and handed over a wad of notes – for coffee. Volatile to the bitter end, Mohammed thrust the money away, then changed his mind and palmed it. He asked for our addresses, then dismissed the idea by saying that he knew we would not write. Finally he swivelled on a heel and just faded away into the crowd. Released from the contrived rituals of a protracted farewell, Sheila and I dived into a grand taxi, handed over thirty dirhams and attacked a packet of Opal Fruits to restore saliva to our dried out mouths.

Tangier seemed like heaven when we spotted the elegant Syrian mosque. The city had never looked so good with its shimmering bay and its pastel and white houses. Of course, the sea provided an illusion of freedom a fingertip away on the horizon. In contrast, Tetouan seemed hemmed in by mountains, trapped by unemployment and a bitterness exacerbated by the temporary escape offered by smoking cannabis. Martil was just slightly too far away to provide an outlet. Come the revolution, as we used to say back in the hopeful '70s, I'd certainly put money on Tetouan's being in the forefront of the struggle once again – irrespective of the cause or the foe.

The small fishing village of Larache promised quite a different slice of the north, since it was said to be something of a mongrel, a cross between Tangier and Tetouan, and yet remained a backwater rather than a destination. Taking the train to Ksar el Kebir, we were swept into the first-class carriage by a noisy Italian contingent who appeared to be staggering under a pyramid of Tupperware boxes and hampers, and were thus condemned to sharing a compartment. As we slowly drew out of Tangier station, past goods trains hauling ballast, long wooden planks and petrol, the plastic boxes were opened. Plates, napkins and steel cutlery emerged, to be followed by dollops of cole-slaw, cubes of chicken, melon balls and red wine. It was too early in the day for feasting and I felt oppressed by their delight, the smells. Unfortunately, all the other compartments had been taken over, either by people who had drawn the curtains the better to feign deep, undisturbable sleep, or locked tight by the guard for his own use. I decided to walk up and down the corridor in feeble protest at the state of play all around us and people-watch, calculating that this might shame place-hoggers into an act of generosity. One particular Moroccan couple who had commandeered six blue seats seemed fair game, and Sheila and I planted our backs against the gently rocking corridor windows and stared fixedly in.

The girl was in her mid-twenties, at least six feet tall with a model's build and a made-up face reflecting the ancestral arrogance of the born-rich Moroccan. From her manicured hands, which were leafing through a current copy of *Vogue*, to her low-heeled black ballerina shoes, her appearance screamed: well-groomed. A black linen three-quarter-sleeved top with a scalloped hem embroidered with red flowers set off a thick gold chain, and gold and ruby earrings framed a wistful, patrician face. Her chignon was flawless, her high-waisted linen trousers immaculate in cut and condition. I doubted whether she would offer us the time of day, let alone a seat, even if we collapsed in a heap at her feet. Her companion was reading *Le Figaro*, as befitted a salt and pepper haired man in his early fifties. His crumpled smoking jacket with rolled up sleeves revealed a white silk T-shirt and an abstract medallion which appeared to me to depict copulating horses. Surely not. From time to time the girl drew his attention to the winter fur collection she was perusing, whereupon they both simultaneously removed then replaced matte-black sunglasses to take in details, comment sotto voce, massage each other's temples to relieve the strain of it all, the demanding call of high fashion. Sheila and I turned our backs on this intimidating display of high chic, and squatted on our heels, resigned to puffing on distinctly plebeian but cheap Casa Sport cigarettes all the way to Ksar el Kebir.

Ksar el Kebir, home of contraband and site of the sixteenth-century Battle of the Three Kings which placed the great Saadian sultan, Ahmed el Mansour, on the throne, is today a tacky market town, full of kebab stalls and grands taxis. As we picked our way through the throng outside the station, jostling with the best of them, young boys pressed forward with attractive tea towels, men's handkerchiefs and gold-plated bracelets. A couple of young women were hosing down their legs and feet in the gutter, their calves covered in angry, raw sores, and an older woman in a black flowered shawl tried to interest us in her horde – a pile of British ten pence pieces wrapped tightly in a scrap of pink lace – failing which she offered pomegranates from her hand cart. The din was unbearable and the lack of a breeze held grey clouds of charcoal smoke and a thin layer of grease suspended, immobile, around us like a halo. Glancing into the teeming bus station with its long, pushing queues, the notion of fighting our way to the ticket windows palled and we gladly retreated from the enthusiastic greetings. *por favor*s and *que pasa*s and handed over seven dirhams for a place in a grand taxi to Larache.

Sheila was silent today, still chewing over Aziz's marriage proposal with a heart full of despair. She could not bring him to understand the impossibility of combining clashing lives and personalities on some notional altar named love, and suspected that his possessiveness and reproaches were about to turn into accusations of betrayal and promiscuity. This was one game she was destined to lose, however she played it, and Sheila hoped that two days' absence might magically change Aziz back into a cheerful, fatalistic and gossipy companion, rather than the rumbling volcano of discontent he currently resembled closely. At least they had avoided two potentially fatal steps: having sex and meeting Mother.

Our first impressions of Larache were unanimous: it was a Spanish relic. The town slept under its flaking blue and white paint, a spent, pineapple-shaped fountain rusted opposite the bus station and the strong smell of fried fish lingered on every street corner as we walked up a short, cobbled road flanked with general stores, restaurants and dry cleaners, to the heart of Larache, Plaza d'Espagne, which is now grudgingly called Place de la Liberation by the locals. Nothing much seemingly happened in Larache and what little does happen must surely happen right there, we reasoned, in this café-lined square, proclaiming innumerable fish menus from twenty-five dirhams up. Since the possibilities of entertaining ourselves seemed limited, we decided to stay on the square itself so that we missed nothing, and so dragged our bags into the shabby reception area of the formerly palatial and magnificent Hotel Espagne.

This large echoing building with its wide corridors and tall ceilings had grand iron balconies large enough to picnic upon, solid heavy doors, a parquet floored, empty ballroom I associated with diplomatic receptions and chandelier-lit soirées. Times had obviously changed, for the hotel seemed virtually empty as the obsequious receptionist led us to our suite: two interconnecting rooms full of dung-brown and orange-doored filing cabinets now masquerading as bedside tables. The electrics seemed tailor-made for suicides, fraying material-covered flexes and cracked plugs; and the four armchairs matched neither one another nor the small sofa which leaned drunkenly under a faded poster of España. The bathroom was large, I'd give it that, but anarchic with its fatally tarnished mirror, broken toilet and plug-less bath. We asked about the water, whether hot water was available – were informed that it was indeed, twenty-four hours a day – asked again, just to make sure there was no room for ambiguity or later disclaimers. 'No, no,' the receptionist assured us. 'It is always hot.'

It wasn't. Ten minutes later I was sitting on a ladder in the loft area, looking at a large immersion tank. The receptionist was balanced two rungs above me and we both gloomily surveyed the red thermostat light.

'Well, I don't know,' he muttered, throwing his arms wide and pantomiming well-practised gestures of deceit and despair. 'This heater works for rooms one, two and three,' he explained, 'so the people next door must have just used up all the hot water.'

I asked myself whether anyone short of a wallowing hippo could possibly use three hundred gallons of water in the space of five minutes, and clambered down and then round the corner to room two. The occupant had obviously been called back from a far better place and protested vigorously that he hadn't opened so much as a bidet tap that afternoon and, more to the point, he was trying to sleep. A door slammed and the receptionist and I returned to the immersion heater tank which would now take upwards of five hours to achieve a lukewarm state, amidst much shrugging and commiserating on the part of the assembled staff. I resigned myself to a long wait, and returned to our room to give a limp-looking, deflated Sheila the bad news. Her new semi-permanent scowl embedded itself a few millimetres further into her skin as we snatched up our bags and clipped down the vast staircase to explore the town.

Standing stock-still in the middle of Place de la Liberation, we were presented with two choices: going left, and thus out towards the sea, or right, through a rather pretty arch into the medina with its galleries and locked-up shops. The medina could be crossed, twice, in under five minutes, for neither the bright lilac trousers with contrasting black knee patches, nor the expensive, bruised fruit made us want to pull out our purses and indulge in shopping. A fourteen-year-old had been watching us pick up and assess peaches from the sole barrow with passable wares, and came over to inform us that we needed his assistance and that the fruit seller did not speak French. A heated and quite pointless argument now erupted as he wrestled the four good peaches we had unearthed away from us, turning them into a bruised and liquid pulp, and then flung them back onto the barrow. The fruit seller calmly served someone else as I exploded, telling him that we had a right to buy what we liked when we liked and how we liked, thank you, without interference. Sheila rummaged resignedly for new peaches as a small crowd of women gathered round, only to waddle off again when they realised that this was not serious business: no accusations of selling shoddy goods or theft. Strung out, sticky from the heat, our fingers fused together with peach juice, we gave the coast a whirl, recrossing the square to stroll down a sparkling clean paved esplanade with regular if under-planted flowerbeds and concrete benches. Out at sea, children were swimming, buoyed up by car tyres, or splashing waist deep and throwing rocks into the violently heaving surf. A small, deserted fairground with miniature airplanes stood waiting for summer, and even the gulls were moderate in their demands for food.

A lone figure sat on the sea wall, disentangling a rod and line. Hassan, twenty-eight, was a fisherman and had a postcard stashed in his denim jacket signed 'Heinrich, Munich'. The card had obviously been dissected, displayed and admired numerous times, judging by the grey, tatty corners, the smudged ink, but we duly translated Heinrich's mundane greetings out loud once again and Hassan beamed with satisfaction. Over the next two days we saw him pulling out this evidence of foreign friends at various café tables in town, invariably using it as a magnet to reassure foreign female visitors that he was neither harmful nor dangerous – for look, he had a Western friend. Sheila and I felt both depressed and moved by this gambit, and resolved to help him along by waving and smiling enthusiastically each time we saw him holding court. And why not?

As evening fell, so the Spanish spirit of Larache was affirmed by the *paseo*. The trees which ring Place de la Liberation were revealed to harbour long strings of multi-coloured fairy lights which blazed out above the buggy-pushing women and their proud husbands, the groups of men and courting couples who walked, slowly, round the square. By 7:00 p.m. every café seat was taken, every restaurant table full. Cars honked, oil, garlic, fish and tomatoes fried briskly and saucers and spoons clinked on the hot night air as animated figures circled, stopped to eat, only to stroll on again. For a moment it was easy to forget the wide, flat backstreets, the decay and crumbling masonry which the critical rays of the sun had revealed. Suddenly, Larache was almost magical in the same way as Christmas windows and aerial night views of the Houses of Parliament. Sheila and I talked food (we lusted for Marmite, mature cheddar, mushrooms and vegetable curry) as we spread processed cheese squares on baguettes and tried to summon up enthusiasm for still more oranges and almonds. The hotel management had attempted to compensate for the enduring lack of hot water by carrying two brown armchairs onto the ballroom balcony, thereby giving us without a doubt the best seats in the house.

We were waiting for Abdul, promotions manager for the ONCFM (Moroccan railways), to join us. An impeccably mannered, portly and well-educated man, Abdul was closely involved with the Transatlantique hotel chain, luxury behemoths whose portals I had never darkened in my travel clothes, and was visiting Asilah to purchase a tracked-down and long since coveted book at an antiquarian's in town. Originally from Fez, a city he considered to be both dirty and the victim of unchecked urban sprawl, he now based himself in the most elegant residential street in Rabat (of course), and seemed to spend much of his life attending planning meetings or checking hotel standards. God only knew what he would make of the Hotel Espagne.

A timid knock at the balcony's French doors revealed the receptionist, with the message that a gentleman was downstairs. And there he stood, besuited, welcoming and in command. Over the next hour, we drank fresh orange juice as Abdul recounted the ONCFM's plans to open a chain of two and three-star hotels and the recent drive to ensure Marrakesh's official guides were wearing well kept, traditional clothes; explained why the numbers of tourists were rising and receipts falling, and discussed the successful packaging of trips to the wedding moussem in Imilchil, a remote High Atlas hamlet. Over the summer I had noticed numerous advertisements in the newspapers highlighting upcoming moussems, without having realised the extent to which the Moroccan Tourist Board had taken over and exploited this particular event.

Legend has it that the lakes Tislet and Isli were formed from the tears shed by two separated lovers and, as a result, the Aid Hdidou tribe decided to allow their children a free choice of marriage partners. Traditionally, therefore, the Berber young would come and gather at Imilchil on one designated day of the year (mid-September), and notaries would draw up marriage contracts on the spot while parents reprovisioned and visited the sanctuary of Sidi Hmad Oulmghani. Nowadays, not only do numerous local hotels organise three-day trips to coincide with this engagement ceremony, putting their clients up in 'authentic Berber tents', but foreign travel firms have also got in on the act, and throw in trips to the Plateaux des Lacs as part of an organised autumn package deal. Accordingly, the first day of the moussem is now given over to a 'folk evening' on the banks of the Isli, the second reserved for the 'spontaneous engagements', and thus dedicated to the wielders of video cameras, while the final day heralds mass organised trips to regional sites of interest. And thus dies a singularly moving local tradition.

Abdul sipped his drink and reflected that, in the Islamic world, only Iran, Turkey and the Sudan had managed to perfect representations of the human body. He further criticised the new mosque at Casablanca as obviously beyond Morocco's means, as well as the general standards of craftsmanship for good measure. This obviously sparked off thoughts of his new acquisition, as he lovingly stroked his bundle. He asked if we'd noticed how any foreign article on Morocco, however obscure its origins, received massive coverage in situ. The government subscribed to an excellent press cutting service, he quipped, and his job would be much simpler if he planted ONCFM news items in Canadian travel magazines or bicycling monthlies, since he would get ten times the coverage, gratis. Abdul was quite right, of course, for the authorities draw on grateful letters from visitors, paragraphs in *Marie Claire*, even motoring and catering magazines for anything remotely flattering, and then proceed to trumpet the outsiders' complimentary views and quote them as proof of how well the system is functioning. Insecurity writ large, of course. Negative sentiments and reports by international bodies are attacked mercilessly by the press and dismissed out of hand. The Maghrebi Arab Press slogan 'information is sacred; commentary is free', is showing its age these days, and is evidently no longer an accurate picture of the role of the written word in contemporary Moroccan society. But this was all contentious, indiscreet stuff and I kept my thoughts to myself, rather than present Abdul with a dilemma: a choice between caution and candor. Nine o'clock struck and I watched him limp off back to his car, back to Asilah, the ritual unwrapping of the bundle he had been guarding, and the true collector's passionate gloating which he had kept in check all evening. Sheila and I had no such bundles, no passion and no hot water, either, awaiting us in our filing cabinet-infested 'suite', yet we also heeded Larache's call to retire and even managed to read for ten minutes by the light of our standing lamps before they plunged us into darkness with a miraculously coordinated explosion of old bulbs.

At 6:00 a.m., raucous young males were noisily stirring coffee under our balcony. The bedclothes seemed damp, and men with hosepipes were out spraying pavements and walls, adding further unwelcome moisture to the already saturated air. It was, however, a cloudless day and time to move away from the centre of town to investigate Larache's raison d'être, its relationship with the sea. During the summer, Larache is a popular holiday resort and small red and blue boats link the town with its beach, crossing the estuary every few minutes, laden down with passengers. The boat we took at the wharf gave no hint of Larache's venerable tradition of constructing vessels for the Bou Regreg corsairs and was instead an old and battered thing of no beauty and finesse. Cautiously balancing on the bench which divided the craft, we lowered ourselves onto the narrow ledge which ran all the way round the sides of the boat, and handed over the fare, one dirham up front. The fisherman who jumped on nonchalantly had calloused feet, a rippling torso and a wind-scored face. He was obviously no blushing violet and shoved bobbing rival vessels out of our path with his oars before settling on the prow, propping one foot against the bench and slamming both wrists out, hard, then together, only to bring them back to his shoulder and push them taut once again. The oars looked old and heavy and were fixed to the boat with frayed orange cord. As we pulled away from the wharf we drifted through increasingly large puddles of diesel oil, its glorious (if polluting) purple and pink metallic sheen reflecting back our dancing faces and odd flashes of sunlight. A large grey sewer pipe was pumping waste straight into the water, and the stench of gutted fish enhanced the visible filth.

It was pleasantly cool out on the water, and the ten-minute crossing must be a blessing at the height of summer when temperatures hover well above thirty degrees centigrade for weeks at a time. The beach itself was small, sheltered and unspectacular. November is not the month for swimming or sunbathing, of course, so there was a distinctly forlorn mood to the spot. Down by the waterline a couple of young boys were swiping wildly at a tennis ball with cracked wooden paddles and a teenaged goddess was half-reading a book and warming her face, an obscenely high cut old gold swimsuit partially concealed by the large beach towel she had draped across her shoulders. One of Larache's many 'mumblers' wandered past, his fly undone, apparently desperately looking for something, since his eyes were glued to the ground. He addressed the sand, waved an arm and paced on. An obviously predetermined number of yards later, he turned and started retracing his steps. The goddess looked at him doubtfully, drew her towel closer and returned to her paperback. Sheila and I were thirsty, but all the wooden café shutters were up and a lone nut seller, holding a basket of crushed ice and cans, seemed to be our only hope of refreshment. We purchased two bottles and looked in vain for a clean patch of sand. The ground was littered with sea weed, melon rinds, cans and whole, unblemished red peppers; further down in the shallows, dozens of burst tomatoes bobbed gaily among curling wisps of onion peel. We could have opened a fruit and vegetable shop on the salvage alone. The incoming tide was further limiting our possibilities of rest by reducing the available sitting area before our very eyes, washing away thin ranks of seagull footsteps and even making a presumptuous grab for the ends of the goddess's towel. There was nothing to keep us there.

We sprinted back to the jetty's stone steps and just made the departing blue boat. Seconds later, I wished we hadn't bothered to run, as a foreign thigh squashed closer to my beskirted knee and a hand collapsed on my shoulder. The old man who owned the offending limbs asked for a cigarette. We feigned incomprehension, shaking our heads slowly. The thigh pressed more insistently. I eyed up the opposite shore and tried to work out whether I could possibly swim across, if pushed. No, it was certainly further than twenty-five metres. Nothing for it but to endure the mauling. As we alighted back at the wharf, I stepped on my 'friend's' babouche and received a smirk for my pains. This was certainly not the level of excitement I had hoped for in Larache, but bid fair to be the highlight of the day, judging by the sleepy streets all around. Cats were eating discarded croissant tails under café tables and another 'mumbler' had taken root on the pavement and was chastising either a set of plastic straws or a discarded lump of creme caramel. And, yes, his flies were also undone. He was treated with affable patience by the waiters, who seemed to echo their Costa brethren in their black trousers, shiny shoes and starched white shirts.

. The Spanish influence permeated every level of life in Larache: carrier bags were printed with Spanish logos, thanking us for shopping X; *hola* resounded in greeting; and there seemed to be an overabundance of restaurants selling lengths of battered squid and octopus. People frequently say that Larache has never been integrated into Morocco and remains a border town whose inhabitants reflect ancient uncertainties as well as present day alienation. Surely the contemplative, solitary nature of fishing and working at sea must contribute to the town's peculiar air of transition: neither old nor new, Moroccan nor Spanish, it straddles eras and cultures unhappily.

Our last image of Larache was a joyful one. A sudden clashing of cymbals and beating of drums signalled the appearance of four men carrying large red and green ceremonial banners, followed by a tall white horse bearing a beaming, waving four-year-old boy. The child was dressed in a white gown with gold braid, a green cap perched on his head, and seemed to be delighted by all the fuss, the crowd of dancing women beating tambourines as they twirled in time to their celebration chorus. The boy had just been circumcised and was laughing as he was bounced away on his steed for the traditional meal, having first been paraded around the Place de la Liberation for all to share in his triumph. We waved from where we were standing on the steps of the local Catholic church, all the discrepancies between architectural heritage and local custom neatly and glaringly summed up in this little scene.

Back in Tangier, eight hundred and sixty kilograms of hashish had been discovered in boxes of tomato purée destined for Holland, a minor setback for the drug barons; and, it was still raining. Reading the evening paper, I noted that equal weight had been accorded the increase in poaching (which had been noted along with the decline in the standard of living) and plans to create more ice-making factories in Safi to cater for the needs of the growing fleet. Only one factory was still functioning and the article urged the government to intervene, help, nationalise and create more jobs. Dwarfing both paragraphs, however, and by a substantial margin, was a half-page spread extolling 'the most prestigious architectural marvel in the world ... a unique sacred monument which inspires pride in its beauty and grandeur' – an appeal for more money to be spent on Casablanca's Mosque Hassan II. It didn't take a fortune teller to know where any available funds would be channelled. Saddened, I cast my mind back to a conversation with Aziz, when he had argued that Western powers had financed Salman Rushdie in his writing of *The Satanic Verses* in order to check whether Islam was still vigilant, a power to contend with in the modern world. Judged by this mosque project, Islam, Moroccan State style, was more concerned with the trappings of temporal splendour than with the law of God, more interested in two-hundred-foot-tall minarets than with dispensing the vitamin A supplements new mothers needed to ensure that their children would have the sight with which to see these minarets.

PART THREE
(January–February 1991)

THE GULF CRISIS

Cast
Alexis: my nine-year-old son.

◆ *Chapter Ten* ◆

It was 15 January 1991 and I was standing at Heathrow Airport, bags at my feet, listening to the fire alarms clanging. Security was tight with the Gulf deadline a matter of ten hours away and I was unable to fight off waves of unease and panic. Over the previous two days, Britain had been hit by a tide of jingoism and hysteria, and numerous friends had been ringing me, attempting to dissuade me from my upcoming trip, offering to telex escape money, to repatriate me at their own expense should I be stranded in North Africa, attacked by lynch mobs or worse. An evening spent watching the various television programmes on the build-up of the military hardware in the region and the projected destruction had finally cracked my composure. The Foreign Office travel bureau was trying to dissuade Britons from visiting Tunisia while conceding that Morocco was less fraught, but travel officials were counselling cancellation or postpone-ment and a mass exodus of package tourists was already underway from Sousse and Port-el-Kantaoui. I was booked to fly from London to Tunis via Casablanca of all ironies, and doomed to spend three days in the capital come what may, to meet a group of Moroccans who had left their native land after the abortive food and wage strikes of early December 1990, to hear how they had fared in the neighbouring Arab states.

Tunis was dark as our half-empty plane finally taxied in and the traditionally placid Tunisian Customs men tipped everything out of my bags and subjected me to a thorough and slow personal search. There was a sombre mood in the air. It was as if we were all waiting for history to catch up with propaganda. The normally jolly Place d'Independence, slap bang in the middle of town, Tunis's equivalent of Marble Arch, was surrounded by tanks and patrolled by groups of armed soldiers. Large navy vans full of back-up troops were parked off to the side of Avenue Bourguiba and the taxi driver told me that all the schools and universities had shut for the day, and lessons had been suspended indefinitely in the name of public order. I shivered and glanced around cautiously. Café owners were shutting up early, brushing down the pavements, pulling over heavy iron shutters, methodically carrying in their stacks of metal chairs. Outside the French Embassy, a dark green tank turret turned slowly, right and left, right and left, and passersby were being asked to show their identity cards, empty their pockets, their bags and briefcases. It was infernally quiet and only 7:00 p.m. I had booked into an old French hotel in the medina, its grand exterior as ponderous and eternal as the best Bordeaux can offer, but inside the public restaurant was full of fist-banging and agitated comment – which died down as I walked in, an unwelcome curiosity.

An old man looked up from his seat at the bar and baldly stated, 'Vive Saddam Hussein'. Predictably enough other heads turned to see what I'd say, how I'd react.

'Vive Saddam Hussein,' I repeated, as calmly and matter-of-factly as possible.

'Down with Bush,' he added.

Oh Lord, what a nightmare. 'Down with Bush,' I managed to croak out.

Satisfied, the heads turned away, back to the TV screen which was showing a never-ending stream of pictures of American pilots loading bombs in the Gulf, smiling broadly, and lurid graphics describing the effects of future air raids on Baghdad in blue, red and white. The commentary appeared to be in Italian, as far as I could make out from the doorway, and the obscenely confident grins of the American pilots set my teeth on edge. I distributed cigarettes at Reception, just in case of literally anything, and found myself cringing when the desk demanded my passport, embarrassed to be both on the wrong side and in the wrong place at the wrong time. Of course, the notion of bad timing was not the sole reason for my discomfort. It is impossible to spend any period of time in a foreign country without being willing to see the people's point of view, and the Maghrebi argument for linking the Palestinian problem to the issue of the annexation of Kuwait was a convincing one.

Taken at its most simple, it argued that the Allied forces have felt no commitment to respecting sovereignty or upholding international law unless their own interests have been under threat. Thus, when Israel annexed the West Bank and Gaza, few voices were raised in protest and the UN Security Council resolutions which had been passed on the Palestinian question had never been implemented either. The West had nothing to win and everything to lose in criticising Israeli aggression. In addition, most Arabs would argue that Kuwait deserved annexation. Countries whose average annual GNP reaches four hundred pounds, with upwards of sixty per cent unemployment and a rising birth rate, find it difficult to drum up sympathy for the Emirates, with their casino-obsessed princelings, American-educated elites, Western lifestyles, gross consumer-good consumption and lack of Pan-Arab sentiment. Saddam Hussein was seen as God's messenger, the man who was drawing the line and putting an end to the abuse of 'common' Arab resources. The wealth of the Gulf, so the argument went, should be used for the good of the Arab peoples and not the indulgence of a corrupt and pampered minority who had fallen from God's path and were thus no longer protected by His grace. Kuwait had finally got its come-uppance, and good riddance.

PART THREE

The arrival of Allied troops in Saudi Arabia was seen as a blasphemous act, further proof that the Saudi guardians of the holy places, Mecca and Medina, were more interested in protecting their oil wealth and the profits they gained from organised pilgrimages than respecting Islam and its spirit. Mecca and Medina symbolise the inheritance of all Moslems, and are not mere geographical points on a map, to be owned, exploited or fought over. The Saudi stand on the invasion of Kuwait found no champions in the streets of Oran or Alger, Fez or Sfax, and many of the most bitter articles found in the press were directed at the Saudi ruling family.

Morocco had contributed one thousand three hundred men to the international force; Tunisia and Algeria none. The Moroccan troops were in the Gulf in the name of international law, according to the king, who added that both his and the Moroccan people's hearts were with their Iraqi brothers. This addendum did not satisfy the man in the streets. In Tunis, Ben Ali was trotting out peace initiatives and mobilising blood donor units. Algerians were openly pressing their government to organise recruitment centres for volunteers to join the Iraqi forces, and demonstrating vigorously to support their demands in the streets of towns and villages alike. It seemed clear that both the Moroccan and Tunisian governments were exploiting the crisis to repress all forms of opposition, under the guise of maintaining calm and order on the streets, and would not allow popular, that is pro-Iraqi, sentiment to erupt into defiance of the powers that be, or turn into food riots or demonstrations against domestic policies. And, of course, the morning of the 17 January demonstrated that real life does imitate fiction. Staggering out into Avenue Bourguiba, awakened by klaxons and chants beneath my balconied window, I grabbed *La Presse* and *Le Temps* and looked for hard news – statistics, assessments, targets, casualties – only to find pages of remonstration and official statements.

THE GULF CRISIS

Over the following month, I was constantly stymied in my desire to understand the state of the conflict, precisely who was where and, to put it baldly, who was winning. The Moroccan press told me nothing and, apart from denouncing Allied aggression and printing innumerable accounts of the king's peace initiatives, the ambassadors he was dispatching, it contented itself with exhorting solidarity with its Iraqi Arab brothers. The occasional short paragraph describing the bombing raids on Israel at least let me know that Israel was involved, but how and to what degree? Where were the Allied troops in all this, and how was naval and air power being deployed? No answers, no place names, no numbers, just a tirade against the West's desire to destroy Iraq, culturally, socially and economically, a never-ending soul-searching and breast-beating on the state of the fragmented Arab world.

Having inadvertently parked my bags in a highly guarded spot behind the French Embassy I found myself loath to circulate in the streets, since this involved so many checks and intense scrutiny on the part of the military, just to get out of the area. A trip to the suburbs of Carthage and Sidi Bou Said to get away from town merely underscored the tension in the air, since the PLO assassinations, five days earlier, were being laid at the door of the Americans and/or the Israelis, and armed men with walkie-talkies were silhouetted above the Antonine Baths, at every crossroads, and patrolling the streets in Renault saloons and on motorbikes. Whenever my walking pace slowed, whistles encouraged me to keep moving, and even squatting down on the pavement to tighten a boot-lace, I was hailed, reprimanded and encouraged to get up. This forced march around a succession of overgrown Christian .chapels, Roman villas, oil presses and crumbling granite columns seemed endless and it was a relief to finally board the efficient light railway which services the area and return to less isolated streets.

PART THREE

Needless to say, in two days the war had already precipitated a mass exodus of holiday makers and tour group operators, and only the odd German couple strolled these usually cluttered, attractively-presented 'sights'. Hotels in popular Hammamet and Sousse alike were under police guard, but no amount of visible protection could seemingly halt the tourist retreat, a fact the Tunisian press bemoaned daily, well aware that a decline in figures spelt economic ruin in a country which lives well off its international reputation for miles of pristine white beaches and low prices. I sympathised with those fleeing, for two days of heavy-handed national security manoeuvres had reduced my ability to circulate confidently. Groups of pro-Iraqi demonstrators, numbering a few thousand, duly turned up in the centre of town at 2:00 p.m., were permitted to walk down the main roads and then firmly dispersed, only to reassemble in the morning. Their opinions and vocal support of the Iraqi war machine seemed pointless when one considered Ben Ali's navy-canvas-topped troop carriers, the silent armed men, the government's decision to stay out of the fray on everything but the diplomatic level, the manned crossroads, the frog-like tanks squatting all over town.

Media coverage grew apace. Italian television covered the Gulf crisis round the clock and the local cafés, sporting photographs of a grizzled Yasser Arafat, cages of finches, plastic flowers and enormous twenty-six inch sets, allowed passersby to crowd in and watch the screens, gratis. *The Sun* also materialised at the foreign newspaper kiosk, its 'Sodding Saddam' headline repeated in neat rows where it was pegged to long pieces of string. Walking past, I shrank away in embarrassment when the display caught my eye, but realised that the Tunisians didn't understand the message. Inside, a tactless blast of patriotic blindness complete with bosomy American female soldiers was complemented by a picture of a target, with Saddam Hussein's image superimposed over the board. Needless to say, to score a bullseye you had to plug him through the heart. Surely inflammatory material should be prevented from reaching sensitive spots in the world? I pegged it back gingerly and felt ashamed to have handled the pages. My rendezvous beckoned at the Africa Hotel coffee shop.

The Africa Hotel is to Tunis what the Thorn Tree is to Nairobi and Raffles is to Singapore – the meeting place of choice for travellers, expats and anyone willing to exchange information or wheel and deal alike. This morning, the cool tiled lounge seemed as animated as ever as I ordered an overpriced espresso and sat down with Nasser and Khalid. In the six weeks since we'd last met in Tangier, the boys had finally secured their Moroccan passports and crossed over via Oujda into Algeria, in search of work, a fresh start, somewhere where they could feel 'like men'. Obliged to change one thousand dinars at the official rate at the border, they had spent a fortnight sleeping rough and trading in hard currency on the black market at Alger, before being arrested by a plainclothes policeman masquerading as a client. Their profits were confiscated down to the last dinar and they were told to make themselves scarce for a few months. Left destitute, they eked out a living smuggling people across the Tunisia/Algeria border at night, toyed with the notion of arranged marriages in order to acquire residence status (too expensive at three thousand dinars and they suspected the women would hold them to their marital obligations), and contacted the POLISARIO. Listening to their tale, the bitterness with which they described how they'd realised their longed-for Moroccan passports entitled them to nothing but endless wandering east, through similarly repressed and impoverished lands, I felt powerless, angry, incapable of finding soothing words. This was hardly the time for talk of trips to England. I was also struck by the wonder in their voices as they described how polite the Algerian authorities had been, how little coercion they'd encountered, in spite of the fact they'd obviously been breaking the law. And yet I could see two cigarette burns on Nasser's knuckles, fresh ones and obviously not self-inflicted. Seeing my gaze of enquiry, he shrugged.

'Oh those were the Moroccans at Oujda. They wanted to search the collar of my jacket and, when I asked why, they pulled the cigarette I was smoking out of my mouth and stubbed it out for me.' He smiled tiredly, adding, 'You know how it is, at the commissariat.'

Casting my mind back·to Tangier, I nodded. Yes, I knew how it was – easily, almost naturally done, a routine incident of no importance whatsoever to the painmonger.

'And then what happened?' I asked, all the joy of the encounter draining out of me suddenly, as I realised that this trip, the big gamble, the saved for, planned for new beginning, had obviously failed. Well, apparently things had gone smoothly. A problem-free twenty-four-hour crossing into Tunisia· by bus, border guards who failed to confiscate beloved cassettes or money, days of meandering through Tunis, only to reach the conclusion that there was no work to be had, culminated in a taxi ride to Tripoli. Libya is, of course renowned for the comparatively high standard of living enjoyed by its citizens, its wide roads, free education and health care and the almost palpable influence of the Guide of the Revolution of First September, Colonel Gaddafi. Nasser and Khalid had been offered employment at two hundred dinars a month as waiters, but given the fact that as 'guestworkers' they would have to spend six dinars a night on hostel lodgings, this was hardly sufficient to live on and certainly precluded saving any money. They had disliked the Libyan treatment of the immigrant labourers, in particular the large Egyptian contingent, and quickly tired of arbitary document checks – for every Libyan citizen has the right to examine a foreigner's papers at will. The water was apparently desalinated and undrinkable, the food repetitive and the pace of life slow – a deserted California with shades of the theatre of the absurd thrown in for good measure. Nevertheless, as the words flowed, I noticed an animation in their faces, a grudging affection for citizens who refuse to handle the new Libyan dinar note because the Great Guide's portrait has been printed on it, who gawp at women openly, stopping their cars in the middle of a main road to watch buttocks, who seem to thrive on inactivity, rice and chicken and live for their annual trip abroad.

'And there are so many homosexuals around that we could have lived like kings,' interjected Nasser, mixing sexual and popular cliché in a spate of stories which all ended up with streetwise Maghrebi boys being fêted by gay, dumb Libyans who ended by paying for hotel rooms, food and clothes and receiving nothing in return.

They told me a joke about the very hotel in which we were sitting: 'One day a visiting Libyan comes to Tunis and stands gazing up at the Africa Hotel admiring its height. A Tunisian walks over and tells him that it is forbidden to stare at hotel buildings unless you've paid a fee. 'And what is the fee?' asks the Libyan, reaching for his wallet.

'Ten dinars for each floor you've looked at,' answers the Tunisian.

'Well, in that case I owe you forty dinars,' the Libyan admits and passes over the notes. The two men then part. The Tunisian is well contented as he recounts the tale to his friends. The Libyan too is laughing as he strolls away, muttering: 'The fool. He doesn't know he's been had. I actually looked at seven storeys!'

The conversation moved on to one Abou Khalid, who was, it transpired, Tripoli's own live-in PLO recruiter, who worked out of a private house with three offices downstairs, processing the dispossessed, the young, the politically motivated and the hungry with the help of his Sudanese assistant. A cautious, white-haired, handsome man who had no personal history and worked under an alias, Abou Khalid supplied hopeful freedom fighters with papers, flights to Amman and transfers on to Lebanon, where they underwent a six-month training course before being sent out on active service. Estimates of his true age varied from late thirties to early fifties, but both Nasser and Khalid agreed that he was a bulky, intimidating man of great persuasive charms and well-known to the Libyan authorities.

They had met with him three times at various hotels in the city after contacting him by phone and on each occasion found themselves driving to the airport to see off another Lebanon-bound contingent. The men who survived their first six-month contract were purportedly free to leave thereafter and given a return or single flight plus the necessary papers to disappear – as well as a reasonable pay packet. Abou Khalid himself had a wry attitude to the war, warning Nasser and Khalid to keep clear of Abou Nidal – 'a real maniac, that one' and telling them that they'd be bound 'for hell' if they signed up. As I was trying to digest this James Bond-like twist in the conversation, Nasser added that he was not convinced by the free flight worldwide assurances at the end of six months, but that they had not yet decided whether or not to join up.

'Where else can we go now? No one wants Moroccans in Europe. We can't get the visas or ever cross the sea. We've gone as far east as we can, and travelling south to Africa is fraught with currency exchange regulations, visas and the same old crap we're trying to get away from in the Maghreb. What options do we have?'

The idea of dying for someone else's cause because of a lack of better options appalled me. Abou Khalid: the procurer; the soft-voiced seducer; the man who sends the seekers for freedom to oblivion; another unappeasable maw thrown up by human society with its gods of war. We sat gloomily over our empty white china cups, snapping matches while a soft rain trickled down the windowpanes, watching the nightly levée of thousands of twittering birds which rose at an unspoken signal from the trees which line Avenue Bourguiba and darkened the sky, making conversation impossible. No one had anything left to say and I couldn't summon up a single suggestion – just a handful of dinars, which they accepted sombrely.

'Algeria was the best, though.' Nasser broke the silence.

'And it's going to profit from this war, you know.' Khalid agreed. 'Perhaps we should try again. At least we're popular there. At least we have some rights.'

Perhaps. I bade the boys goodnight and promised to contact their families in Tangier, to keep in contact via a local shop owner, to pass on a few intentionally cheerful messages: they're eating well, sleeping well, look healthy, etc. Their situation seemed hopeless, for Tunisia is not a cheap country to live in and as soon as the dinars were gone they'd be faced with Hobson's choice: Abou Khalid or a shamefaced return home. Outside, I stumbled over a lump of garbage, discovered that I was trampling a sleeping man and cried out wildly. My helplessness and passivity irritated me: every problem I encountered was too big to tackle or to eliminate, whether it be on the personal or general level. I couldn't do anyone any good and simply being in Tunis and tank-spotting didn't justify watching my son Alexis being trailed by machine guns when he broke into a run. It was time to leave, to see whether the Kingdom of Morocco would yield new perspectives, new facets of its rich, frustrating self at a time of international crisis.

The bureau de change creature at Casablanca airport refused to cash travellers' cheques, rudely and arbitrarily, when I landed at 10:00 p.m. Since one is forbidden to import dirhams into the country, I was thus stranded at Mohammed V airport, twenty miles away from town, clutching four hundred and fifty pounds but lacking the one pound forty we needed for the airport bus. Glancing at the small group of fellow travellers who hadn't yet flagged down a grand taxi. I assessed the friendlier faces for a touch and reluctantly plumped for my Algerian co-passenger, a tractor salesman from Tlemcen whose blond good looks, rugged face and interminable meandering chatter about his wonderful homeland had all intruded into my space for the past four hours. I was glad to bid him farewell, but there was nothing for it now but to backtrack and beg. Within a matter of minutes he had taken charge, packed Alexis and the bags onto the coach, bought tickets for the three of us, given me a potted history of Casablanca and his experiences therein over the last decade and taken on the role of protector. Firmly propelled back into the airport lounge for a coffee, which I was told I needed, I leaned against the snack bar counter and watched the waiter pointedly ignore us – the Westerner and the wealthy Algerian. We were evidently not welcome in Morocco, though the airport posters would have had us believe otherwise. I giggled and told Bensâad how good it felt to be foreigners – together. Bensâad was less amused by the boycott and chewed his mildly-lemon gum viciously.

'Fundamentally,' he snapped, 'I hate these people and this country.' A thump on the counter forced the elderly, lizard-eyed waiter to slide two espressos in our direction. Bensâad was becoming excited and his sharp, attractive features relaxed into a natural ferocity – slitted eyes, thin lipped mouth, slightly wrinkled forehead. He reminded me of a stalking tomcat and an incident of some type seemed on the cards.

'Come on,' I urged him. 'Leave it. Let it be.'

Making an obvious effort, he placed his partially-ready fists into his brown leather jacket pockets and dug out a ten-dirham note. 'No tip,' he instructed the waiter, prodding me in the back. As we reached the now revving bus, a middle-aged man sidled towards us, demanding payment for having loaded the bags, only to be thrust aside so hard that he bounced off the glass automatic airport doors. Embarrassed, I averted my eyes and crept on.

'The Moroccans would do anything for a dirham,' Bensâad attacked as I plonked myself down resignedly next to him. For the next twenty minutes, as the well-lit motorway sped past, I listened to the classic Algerian criticism of Moroccans, the cowardice of the Moroccan cowed, the heroic popular overthrow of the French in Algeria. I yawned and nodded, nodded again each time he seized my arm. Oh when would this day end? And end it did, in an unclassified hovel near what appeared to be Casa's main meat market, judging by the offal I shoved my bags through to reach the door. Bensâad paid for our, separate, rooms and handed an extra five dirhams over to assure me a spot in the communal shower next morning. I thanked him prettily, and barred the door with two chairs, half a broken bidet perched across them, a metal dustbin and the box of Algerian dates he gave me. Huddled in my leather jacket, watching Alexis finally sleep, I gazed, fascinated, at the pyramid, waiting for the final straw, the intrusion which, thankfully, never came.

Having suspected Bensâad of designs on my body and been proven wrong, I was totally, painfully embarrassed to see him lurking outside reception at eight the following morning, and could barely stumble out a 'salaam aleikum' without blushing. Egocentricity and arrogance prevented him from noticing, of course, as he set about organising me for the rest of the day and, a trip to the bank, two wedges of madeira cake and a taxi ride later, I had boarded the Kenitra-bound train and escaped his crushingly generous and overbearing personality. Boxes of large dates and postcards of Tlemcen (usually of the main hotel at night) have been arriving in London regularly ever since.

Built in 1913, Kenitra was formerly called Port Lyautey, in memory of General Lyautey, the French architect of modern Morocco, the governor who designed the new towns to complement the old medinas rather than destroy the hearts of the imperial cities, and who showed a rare sensitivity for the country's architectural, cultural and social heritage. His European, grid-style street design, wide boulevards and town planning policies have their downside, of course, since they demarcate past and future and mothball the colonial era, but it is difficult to fault the man's intentions even if the concrete uniformity which has resulted moves no hearts. These days, Kenitra is known for three things: its bars, its prostitutes and its thieves, all of which, popular gossip has it, exist in profusion. The town is small, home to thirty-five thousand, and has a raffish air, with the elegant pink municipal buildings on the main square and the Hotel Safir dwarfing a curious selection of fast food joints, discos and boozers, which all cluster around the main grand taxi terminus. The railway station was being refurbished as I gingerly picked my way across the low gravel-set tracks, to fall straight into the arms of Fateeha, a twenty-six-year-old university student who had generously agreed to put us up for three days, sight unseen.

The home to which she led me was a simple three-storey affair down an unpaved street. Young boys were listlessly turning over the appallingly bright thick orange mud with picks. Unemployed youths, they worked for the municipality, which gave them twenty-five kilos of flour, fifty dirhams and one and a half litres of oil a fortnight. Most barely stuck it out to the first pay-day, since the work epitomised everything one conjures up when thinking of a dead-end job. A month later, when I passed through, no progress had been made and the street was the same gloppy, repellent mess of upturned, cracked grey paving stones, string lines and rich filth churned to a stew of mud and domestic debris. On the corner a man was perched on a flattened cardboard box which supported a treadle sewing machine and an empty carton of Winstons containing various coloured reels of cotton. Children bounced a fast-deflating, thin-rubber pink ball with black spots against a wall and the warm spicy smell of numerous lunches hovered on the air. I was hungry and relieved to be shielded from the crowd. Poor areas tend to get their priorities right and the daily struggle for survival occupies a central place in people's minds. The war would not matter here; I was safe.

Upstairs, a selection of relatives sat on banquettes surrounding a glass table bearing bowls of peanuts, almonds, olives and the unmistakable Sim orange bottle. I slipped off my mutilated sandals and did the greeting rounds before we all plunged, wrists flapping, into the eighteen-inch enamel white plate bearing a mountain of couscous, coloured with what looked like scrag-end, carrots and potatoes. The food was good, the scrutiny well-meaning, the conversation loud and animated and, as I leaned back against the wall sipping my glass of mint tea with its bobbing pine nut kernels I felt a long, long way from the Gulf, from the Allies, even from the Casablanca I'd left one and a half hours ago. There is a rhythm to this type of extended family life which soothes the senses, blots out notions of time and, over the next four days, I felt both cossetted and surprisingly enough even useful, as I took up my role as a woman and helped with domestic demands. On that first afternoon, however, I grasped that I was expected to join in the weekly hammam (steam-bath) session and duly agreed to unearth the necessary cleaning unguents and find a spare change of clothes.

Armed with a blue pail full of black, sap-like soap reminiscent of treacle, yellow bars of pre-wash conditioner and a selection of shallow round plastic dishes as large as cat bowls, Fateeha led half a dozen chattering women and children and myself down past the potato and parsley sellers into a low building. Inside, I adjusted my eyes to the gloom and saw that we were in a half-tiled room lined with wooden benches, with pigeon holes which ran at eye level all around the walls. This open-plan room was cool and crowded with partially clad and naked women cleaning their teeth in the mirror fragments embedded in columns. Babies sprawled face-down and wriggling on their laps or were tied to their backs. Teenagers were throwing on jeans and older women were struggling to either disrobe or dress; I wasn't sure which. The din was deafening, but before I could take in the scene, I was gently thrust towards a bench and told to strip. Knickers on or off? I glanced to right and left. My age group seemed to be predominantly a knickers-on crowd. Oh, hell, they'd soak through and I hadn't brought a spare pair. I vascillated for a moment and then stuck to the original, modest impulse.

My companions were ready and we gingerly picked our way past the counter-hand, handing across our wrapped bundles and three and a half dirhams, paddling in one quarter inch of warm, dirty, athlete's-foot-harbouring water. Just inside the first warm room, Fateeha indicated that I should pick up two solid looking buckets and follow her to a stone sink full of boiling water replenished by a cold tap. So this is why there'd been so much wood piled up outside. The two tiny windows in the ceiling scarcely let in enough light to make out shapes, let alone bodies, and I noticed that one intrepid soul had actually brought in her own candles, which were burning fiercely by a distant wall. Cautiously slithering past the drainage hole, I lugged my buckets over to rejoin the rest of the gang as we all waited for a spare patch of floor. To my horror, I discovered that my theoretically waterproof mascara was by now melting into my eyes, along with the bitingly-acid royal blue kohl, laughingly dubbed hypo-allergenic, I'd used to line my lids that morning. As the greasy film dripped into my watering irises, I remembered a Berber woman recommending boiling butter inserted drop by drop under the eyelids to remove unhealthy white patches on the eye, and shuddered. This was surely caustic enough to burn out the whole pupil, let alone selected areas. No time for self-pity now. Blue plastic mats emerged from the bottomless pail and there we were, finally seated on a hot tiled floor, ready for the scouring hand-gloves and the treacle treatment. Amina, Fateeha's sister, decided to lead me through the various stages of self-purification, all of which consisted of manic scrubbing of skin and crevices with neat abrasive gloves, rinsing with copious amounts of warm, cool and hot water and yet another cycle of concentrated rubbing. The room began to snap back into focus once the last dollops of mascara seared through my brain, and just as I blinked curiously at the host of breasts, Caesarean scars, babies tucked under arms and nymphettes surrounding me, my knickers left their waistline anchorage.

'Wash down there,' commanded Amina, and wash down there I did. The second room into which we repaired some twenty minutes later was torturously hot and I suspected that some of the bodies flattened to the floor in crucifixion positions had passed out rather than taken a break. We'd reached the mutual back-scrubbing and hair washing stage by now and I felt and looked like a boiled pig, my eyes smudged slits from all the steam, my legs bending with fatigue as I staggered up for still more water. A final pummelling and apparently we were done. Back in the changing room, I shivered under a towel and gloomily surveyed myself in a mirror. The blotchy, beetroot-hued face shone, the eyes wept, but by God the body was clean! Amina and Fateeha retrieved their bundles, stuck the pail under the bench and proceeded to dress up in layers: bra and knickers, T-shirt, velour dressing gown and jogging pants, caftan with two headscarves, one tied flat to the head with ears, the other under the chin. Pots of weak mint tea began to circulate as I dwelt on the curtain of veiled decency they all now wore, the stark contrast of sexual, lively Hammam flesh and bundled-up, sexless anonymity. It was hard to associate the energetic ladies of the tortuous scouring pads with the demure, padded pillars of cotton they now all resembled.

I repaired what damage I could and listened to Amina recounting her recent and secret tubal ligation operation and the conflict she was having at home with her husband over her desire to finish her degree and work rather than further enlarge the family. Apparently, grandmother, the hearty if not hale eighty-nine-year-old woman with whom they lived, was a traditional thinker and could not fathom why any woman should wish to leave the home or consider it appropriate to circulate alone, without her husband to protect her. Since Amina's husband shared this view to some degree, he rarely backed up his wife at critical moments and felt that time would bring the child he longed for though she had tied her tubes against conceiving. Amina believed that he would come round to her point of view and allow her to work only when he was certain that she was sterile – hence the deception. The crowd of listening women were sympathetic and clucked in the right places, but their overall lack of reaction suggested that this was a hammam-tale they had all heard before. Since Amina appeared to be something of a gynaecology specialist, and my period was due the next day, I asked her where I could buy some tampons. She had heard the word but knew nothing about the product itself and responded by thrusting a gigantic clean sanitary pad at me, as a present.

'No,' I stammered, 'no. They're slightly smaller.' I indicated my little finger for guidance and Amina laughed good-naturedly, assuming that I was teasing her.

'It's all right, take it.' she whispered. 'I've got loads at home.'

I stuffed the offending lump into my bag, tied on a headscarf and off we went. This hammam visit had taken four hours.

The rest of the day was spent preparing the evening meal. We sat up on the flat roof, under a string washing line, squatting on our heels, and cleaned ten-inch radishes, huge new potatoes, carrots and onions, throwing the rinds into a corner, arranging the rest on enamel plates. The sun was dipping but still comfortably stroking our bodies as the last vegetable was peeled and washed in the kitchenette's granite sink. From time to time the doorbell rang and a cloaked figure came in and, without being introduced, handed over some money and left with a paper-wrapped bundle. I couldn't control my curiosity and asked what was being sold and why the secretiveness. Pastis, bought as contraband in Ksar-el-Kbir.

'Sometimes we deal in mortadella and Mars bars too, but that comes down from Ceuta,' Fateeha answered. Ceuta and Melilla, the Spanish duty-free towns of the Rif, are the first stopping place for contraband in Morocco. I'd frequently read of medina street traders being fined for dealing in illegally imported electrical goods. But Mars bars and mortadella? The mind boggled.

I was content here with this hospitable, affectionate group of women. Downstairs, a cousin who was improbably named the Cannibal, since he ate whatever moved and had been seen hiding bread on the WC roof and cooking surreptitiously at night, was watching Egyptian movies intermingled with Gulf news on television, along with Abdullah, the head of the household. The younger girls had just returned from school and were sweeping floors and mopping the maroon tiles with rags, running errands for their mother and yelling down to friends through an open window. A sister's child popped in and sat down quietly; a neighbour poked her head around the door and asked if anyone had any penicillin salve – her child's leg was badly swollen and thick with pus. The improbable collection of vegetables we prepared was turned into salad, rice was boiled with cheese and milk and Fateeha ran, singing to herself, up the stairs, four flat loaves covered with a small yellow cotton cloth balanced on her head. Mother started to boil yet another pot of mint tea as a prelude to the meal and I scaled a narrow wooden ladder to distribute scraps to the forty rabbits on next door's flat roof. Looking down across a patchwork of drying blankets, washed clothes, TV aerials, roosters and herb gardens, I saw military vehicles positioned by the nearby post office. Schools were shut today because a national emergency had been declared, so everything and everyone was under martial law. Military tribunals would be convened to hear cases now that crimes were crimes against the Moroccan state and not simple law breaking.

The shadow of last December's urban rioting lingered in the streets and the numerous lorries full of soldiers, doing nothing but waiting, reminded everyone that the people had lost that debate and remained cowed. Living conditions varied here. They do throughout the whole country, where it is still common to see bidonvilles with their stand pipes, and corrugated iron shacks, roofs weighted down with rocks, nestling next to Alsatian-guarded villas with iron gates, tiled window boxes, façades and entryways with pretty private gardens. The same fifty metres houses the chic woman in her sports car and the woman kneeling in the mud, washboard to hand; the designer-clothed child and nanny and the barefoot urchin chasing an escaped chicken or bringing home the family cow and goat which have been tethered out on scrubland to graze all day.

Fateeha's home was forty-two metres square and there were nine of us sleeping there tonight. The main room was lined with padded banquettes and pillows in one corner, a large heap of tightly rolled blankets and sheets wedged behind a table. We were entitled to one blanket apiece and I resolved to take the fawn, scratchy one with the black lines because I knew that no one in their right mind would choose it over the nylon ones. A token of appreciation and penitence alike. A sharp cry of 'Aji' from upstairs signalled trouble. A local cat had stolen two long pieces of tripe from the washing line, where it had been drying for flavour, and disappeared with its bounty. Good. Now that was gone I'd finally be able to reach the WC door without feeling it brush against my neck and shoulders. I carried glasses down the narrow concrete stairs for dinner and yet again admired the way one tiny gas ring, a minute oven for bread and a sink could be coaxed into producing so much food. The women ate with their hands and mopped up with bread, silent; the men talked about the potato seller who was obliged to give vegetables to the police, the fire chief, if he was not to lose his patch, how ill the man's pregnant wife looked, the ten to fifteen-year sentences the rioters and demonstrators of Fez were receiving from the courts. I listened, quietly and drowsed. 'Kuhl!' – came a sharp reminder that guests can only signal appreciation by gorging. I 'kuhled' and smiled languidly. The hammam had worn me out completely. Abdullah took me to one side while the plastic-topped table was being wiped down and cleared for the coffee.

'You, Sylvia, must always remember one thing here in Morocco. You have seen nothing, heard nothing, know nothing and agree with everything anyone in uniform has to say. If they say you're Belgian, then be Belgian. If they tell you your country is wonderful, then so it is. If they hate it, you hate it too. Remember that.' A pat on the shoulder and he returned to watching royal pronouncements on the Gulf and I was ready for bed.

Abdelatif, the scourge of Amina's life, materialised the following morning, bearing a large volume on psychology – 'the science of the future' – as he called it pompously, which he had borrowed from his school library and was photocopying, fifty pages at a time. A weak man with an earnest attitude and complacent demeanour, he was obviously incapable of holding his own on the domestic front and would not leave the nest, either, since abandoning his mother was a shameful act which didn't bear considering. Adjusting his gold-rimmed glasses (the type favoured by French businessman), he quizzed me earnestly on our schooling system and shamefacedly puffed on a strong Marquise, his one self-professed weakness, waiting to be caught in flagrante. The schools here were due to reopen on 28 January, and he was at a loose end. My duties beckoned, however, for I could hear the rattling of plates and glasses upstairs. The daily round of meal preparations was underway.

Breakfast was a simple affair of weak, sugary coffee with slices of buttered french sticks, and then caftans were donned for the market round. Fateeha steered me through the side streets, past the rubbish cart parked at the crossroads into which dozens of women were emptying the metal cans they kept on the roof. Swarms of flies lifted into the air in surprise and then landed again. It was warm but many of the women were wearing winter clothes: footless, knitted long johns in predominantly pastel colours, woollen jumpers and calf-length skirts, along with the requisite headscarves. Balancing carefully on broken paving slabs, I watched an unsmiling Fateeha take on her shopping mode: first she looked, then she prodded; finally she nodded and suspiciously watched both weighing and packing procedures, her left hand on her hip. We picked up avocados and milk, two fish, a 1-dirham sachet of Nescafé and, at my insistence, a large bar of almond chocolate. A whole bar of chocolate cost the equivalent of eight loaves of bread; hence it was usually sold by the square. The children also bought tiny, dark fish-shaped pieces, handfuls of sugar-coated green gum and individual paper-wrapped chews. Bounty, Twix, Kit-Kat and Mars had all appeared in the grocery stores here but were expensive at five dirhams and frequently grey, old and tired under the wrappers.

Fateeha was bemused by my interest in what, to her, appeared a commonplace, boring round of tasks. Like most Moroccans, she was totally unimpressed by vegetarianism and could not quite bite the bullet and swallow the shame of not greeting a visitor with a table weighed down with meat. All important celebrations culminate in the slaughter of a sheep or cow in Islamic societies, and I felt that I had slightly cheated the family with my dietary peculiarities. Any sense of incipient guilt was brushed aside when I noticed the horse flesh seller, his shelves holding plaster and china figurines of prancing stallions, portraits of galloping mares, his counter a mess of bloody hunks. No, vegetarianism is a good thing, in spite of the fact that everyone I know who has travelled these regions ends up living on omelettes and the odd dish of couscous. Tagines are theoretically made of vegetables only, but all too frequently one finds cartilage, a slab of spinal column or connective tissue nestling among the raisins and tomatoes.

Back at the house, I slipped off my shoes, washed my hands at the communal sink and set a pan of water on the boil, to rinse my hair. Aziz, a relative, of course, but I had no idea how or to whom, was setting off to sit his written driving test paper; the practical test was that afternoon. Nadia was busy whacking dust out of blankets and I noticed with a pang of sadness that every discarded object I had put in the ashtray had been retrieved and laid out on the dining-room table; receipts, a long-dead biro top, torn black tights and a hairless powder brush. In a house where everyone's possessions could fit into two suitcases, nothing was valueless. I watched the neighbour's sausage dog wriggle and spit with excitement amongst the corrugated iron scraps that littered their terrace, and was instructed in the intricacies of dressing up candles and bars of Camay soap with pins and ribbons. After fastening it in flat ribbon one runs a knife down different coloured pieces of ribbon to make them curl and then cuts off irregular lengths to stick onto a handle made of reinforced cardboard. The bar of soap disappears beneath the mass of pins and a decorative basket emerges. I ask how I can get to the soap without making my fingers bleed. Howls of incredulous laughter.

'It's only supposed to look pretty. You can't use it – ever,' Fateeha explained. And indeed it did look pretty, but I was subsequently pleased to discover that it also had its defensive uses, for whenever uniformed bullies rummaged through my bags, they inevitably ended up sucking on their fingers immediately afterwards. It's hard to quake before a man with his thumb in his mouth.

◆ *Chapter Eleven* ◆

The bus to Marrakesh was half-empty as I wedged my bottle of Sidi Harazam into the gap between the seats in front and slipped a coffee glass containing half an inch of water next to my headrest, to act as an ashtray for the eight-hour trip to come. It was hot and stuffy and I glanced around to check if any fool had bought oranges or tangerines along. I find it impossible to stomach the combination of black tobacco and citrus fruits. Yes, lo and behold, I could see at least two thin plastic bags with the dread fruits inside. Taking leave of the family was more upsetting than I'd imagined it would be on the basis of a brief stay. I now knew why my sandals and Indian mirror bag had disappeared for an afternoon. The former had been seized so that the right-sized sequinned slippers could be ordered; the latter, Bombay's own, had finally been sewn together with thread, not simply Indian good intentions. Promising to return in three weeks, I fled the house and onto the bus, suddenly dismayed by the miles ahead, the possibility of encountering awkward if not positively dangerous situations. After all, five Europeans (all men, I reassured myself) had already been murdered as infidels. Ah well, if it was going to happen, I'd close my eyes, laugh, and hope they stabbed hard and true. There was no point in worrying, and my headscarf, Allah medallion and little Alexis' presence might just cause them to hesitate long enough to allow me to run. Regret and fear are bad travelling companions.

The five hard-boiled eggs I'd bought were too hot to handle as yet, but as the bus finally gathered speed, having crawled along, picking up men, women, children, mattresses and a huge chest of drawers to boot, my companions lunged for food and I felt ravenously hungry. The sweet dry smell of marijuana filled my nostrils. A youngish man was hunkering down behind today's copy of *L'Opinion*, puffing on a badly made joint. I'm too old to care about drugs, other people's bad habits, but I did feel irked that he couldn't roll his own correctly and itched to lean across and re-do the travesty. Next door, a black couple cradled a white plastic radio cassette player on their laps. The woman smiled across and offered me a slab of nut and honey bar. She was young and obviously excited by the trip as she fingered her filigree Hand of Fatima earrings and sipped a strawberry-flavoured Yogo drink. Her severe husband rebuffed the wallet and tin bracelet sellers, intent on reading his instruction booklet. I sighed as we stopped for yet another deceptively small group of travellers. They'd probably got six goats and a double bed hidden in a nearby ditch. No, it was sacks of uncombed wool instead.

While we waited for the tarpaulin to be taken off the rooftop luggage rack and the orange peelers set to work, a young man leapt on and distributed small printed slips extolling the many virtues of his acne cream. Blackheads, whiteheads, scarring, clogged pores – his tube could remove the lot. Lugging a small suitcase in one hand, he stopped expectantly before each passenger, waiting for an order, or the return of the publicity material. I handed over the slip, thinking back to the boy who had come to that café in Kenitra last night and passed out similar slips of information, these concerning his father, missing now for eight years, his own lack of work, the brothers and sisters he had to feed. Virtually everyone gave the grieving son 1 dirham, wrapping it in the photocopied letter, which they returned. Acne did not inspire the same empathy.

When the movies crackled on, I was bemused by the theatrical swooning and, needless to say, Egyptian-made nonsense which filled the air. Blood was shed, women fluttered around and screamed, and a bridegroom was put to the sword. The plot seemed simple, but no one could hear the dialogue because my black neighbour had switched on his cassette player and the bus-boy was still keen on drumming up trade and persisted in yelling out our destination from the back window every few seconds: 'Marrakesh, Marrakesh.' Since we were driving down a road full of bed-heads, metal goods and garden furniture, it seemed a pointless exercise. A baby vomited copiously and his father asked me for some water. The acrid smell mixed with the odours of lamb kebabs, peeled eggs and poultry. My torn window curtain did little to impede the sun's efforts to blind us all, and I retreated under my Walkman and into the strains of the Gypsy Kings. Peering round from time to time, I watched as pull-down seats were installed in the corridors and noticed that there was a new set of characters on the now violently bouncing video screen: the Libyan struggle for independence circa 1911, or so the sub-title suggested.

Outside, the ecological disasters which signal Third World indifference to the environment caught my eye: large uncovered dumps, kilometres of scattered cans and mattresses, factory chimneys belching out pollution, streams blocked with débris. Women knelt by the roadside in groups, chatting, their dark scarves and bright clothes a flurry of gaiety against the well-cultivated, sombre rural background of herds returning home, waving children and patient horses silhouetted on the horizon. The men went in for individualism and lounged alone against telegraph poles or sat at distant café tables, surveying their world. The driver had stopped pretending to be interested in when he arrived, for we couldn't be doing over thirty kilometres per hour and, by the time our bus ground to a halt in Beni Guerir, an hour out of Marrakesh, I was half-dead and glassy-eyed. Hooded, bobbing heads stretched; smiles were exchanged. We all felt as though we had known one another forever, as if we were friends.

Ben Guerir is said to be a town of the future and boasts numerous skeletons of villas in the making, a wonderful children's playground complete with giant dinosaurs and large metal birds, and a horde of kebab-sellers and shoeshine boys. The temperature was dropping rapidly now and the sun was a blood-red ball beneath a heavy cloud formation, hanging under the snow-capped High Atlas peaks. I felt great affection for Marrakesh as we skirted the palmery and I caught a glimpse of the familiar pink walls, the simple grandeur of the Koutoubia. But Marrakesh was but a pit stop this time round and, after sleeping a dreamless sleep, eight hours later I was clutching yet another bag of provisions, marzipan pine cones and pears, complete with leaves and stems, orange and strawberry tarts and the usual hunk of Edam. The road and the bus seemed my only reality now, and even though it was a new vehicle, a new set of passengers, my bruised spine soon assumed the most comfortable angle in the seat and I prepared for the next leg, crossing the Tiz-n-Tichka pass to Ouarzazate, gateway to the Deep South, Land of the Thousand Kasbahs.

My neighbour, Hassan, and I started to talk after I'd set his jacket on fire and singed my own hair. We brushed ourselves off and quietly exchanged views on our respective societies and described our own lives. Hassan had just returned from Libya and was still reeling from the shock of seeing an exhibition of nature's wonders – three-headed goats and creatures half-dog, half sheep – in Tripoli. A pious man, he peppered his conversation with 'Inshallahs', annoying when they referred to matters such as the next coffee stop, rather than the larger designs of destiny. Life can't be so arbitrary that it's tempting fate to intervene merely by mentioning say, the desire to see a new film. He told me that when he wanted to ring France from Libya, he was requested to fill in a form with the phone number he needed, the name of the person he intended to speak to, their address and his own details before the operator would try the number – and even then she proceeded to listen in and cut off the conversation when she considered it had gone on for long enough. Now he was back in Morocco, seeking that elusive quarry – work. I remarked on how attractive Settat appeared.

'It's where the Minister of the Interior comes from, so what do you expect,' he smiled. 'You see, the king is a good man at heart. It's the ministers who change everything. God bless him, he tries his best but what can he do?'

I recalled listening to a group of Moroccans talking about the wastage at the Palace of Rabat, Hassan's rages, and his ability to shoot men down in cold blood. The reality was less important than others' perceptions and, as long as people believed in the myth, both pro and anti, they would hit the streets to protest his indifference to their poverty. In a country where public telephones are few and far between, the media is censored and everyone fears his neighbour works for the Deuxième Bureau, information all too often consists of snatches of rumour and the gossip of the medina and the café.

If I had a head for heights, I might well have found the three-hour Tiz'n'Tichka crossing to Ouarzazate a splendid, thrilling ride, rather than a nerve-racking ordeal. A zig-zagging series of blind twists and corners which claims entire busloads of tourists and locals at regular intervals, it is astonishingly picturesque in an aggressive, startling way. Aleppo pines cling to crumbling rock-faces; streams frozen into long crevices glint as they reflect the sunlight. It was winter and the deciduous trees had long since been stripped of their foliage, their emaciated grey witches'

fingers clawing and scratching at the air. The high peaks swelled a deep maroon, which gradually ran into too many variations of green and brown to count or credit.

As we climbed unsteadily upwards, I was surprised to spot flat, grazing areas reminiscent of the Alps. Dry riverbeds were the norm now, but recent floods had thrown down huge boulders here and there, as far as the eye could see. Berber villages clung to the beige landscape, flowed back into its beige crags. Peering through the sun's glare I wondered how people could possibly spend their lives here, how they survived November to January.

A large, old Berber woman who spoke Tachelhait and could therefore communicate only with the bus boy, waved us down. Planting herself in the aisle she stuffed a recently decapitated bull's head, complete with hair, facial expressions and richly pink and still oozing neck, beneath Alexis's seat. We both winced and put away our food, drawing up our knees.

We were in Berber territory now, for Ouarzazate means 'place where there is no noise' in the local dialect, and the white-turbanned farmers started to prepare for their stops, rearranging large sacks and two-handled plastic shopping bags, rapping at the handrail to signal their desire to stagger off towards unseen homes hidden amongst the rocks. The radio was blaring as our precipitous ascent ironed out into a gentle downward roll. The old man sitting behind me increased his efforts to both stroke and surreptitiously pull out hunks of my hair, pinning me to the seat in a war of wills as I wriggled my neck to right and left, determined to get away without a confrontation. In the end, the score was even: I escaped, but he did achieve a minor victory and left my scalp tingling.

We reached the summit and emerged for a half-hour rest. Everyone was relieved that the roads had been free of rockfalls. The mineral stands, with their chunks of amethyst, sand roses and fossils, were unmanned today: a dog sprawled on a patch of dust and a rooster with a broken leg dragged through a shallow ditch, pecking at his own shadow. I drank mint tea, slowly, and watched the bird's frantic stabs at the dirt, wondering what was happening in the Gulf. That morning I heard that my flight home had been arbitrarily cancelled by RAM and no substitute date was available yet. I might never leave – a disquietingly pleasing idea here, half-drowsing in the crisp, sunny purity of a mountain peak.

With a tired treble-honk of the horn, our leader signalled that we were off, and diesel fumes emphasised the message. As we climbed down towards the dirty plain which signalled the final approach to Ouarzazate, low lying pisé houses appeared by the roadside, surrounding tiny mosques. The town was being promoted as 'the tourist desination of the Moroccan south, take-off point for the dunes of Merzouga, the Tafilalet oases and the Dades and Todra gorges.' It was anticipated that it would eventually possess over ten thousand beds and UNESCO and the government were drawing up a masterplan which would restore numerous collapsing, ruined or abandoned kasbahs on the 'kasbah/ksour' route, and thus further increase Ouarzazate's strategic importance.

All this seemed a pipe-dream as we rolled into what must be the dullest place on God's large earth. I remember hearing someone yell 'See Ouarzazate and die' at the Marrakesh bus station. I'd interpreted the phrase incorrectly: seeing Ouarzazate was akin to dying, not the culmination of a life's ambitions. Three giant hotels and, of all things, a Club Med monstrosity loomed over what appeared to be part building site, part gravel pit. The streets were empty. Opposite the Belair Hotel, the arcade of trendy, expensive boutiques selling pottery, jewellery, kaftans and soft, multi-coloured handbags, had been freshly refurbished to resemble a kasbah, of course (for everything in Ouarzazate looks like a kasbah), but was shut. Dozens of low pink, beige and taupe houses sat on the edges of town, some partially completed. others protected from the wind by scaffolding. Three-storey, self-catering apartment blocks and groups of villas stood, deserted and quiet, down unpaved roads. I was appalled by this desolate dump and tried to remember something positive about the town. Ah, yes, the film studios which had produced epics such as *Jesus of Nazareth* and *Lawrence of Arabia* in the chi-chi village of Ait Benhaddou nearby. They were shut. Well, what about the nearby kasbah Tiffoultoute, another of the Glaoui's fortresses, a partially commercialised but nevertheless purportedly magnificent place to eat? It was shut as well, because there were no tourists. I considered this and agreed that yes, there were no tourists bar myself and Alexis in town, and reminded myself that all the hotels were quite empty, their windows unlit, their car parks unused. It felt strange to be wandering down Boulevard Mohammed V, the street of streets in this one-horse town, and meeting no one. Perhaps an epidemic had wiped out the population. Nonsense. I saw a queue (two people) down by the main post office, feeding what I subsequently learned was a machine which ate and did not process money, and one young man by the CTM depot. Two soldiers stood near the hotel-school entrance, listening to the Niger-Morocco football match on a small radio. I asked the score. It was one-nil and they were not impressed.

I considered where to park my bags and decided on a tiny, empty hotel next to a supermarket. Once inside the box which passed for a room, I stroked a family of cats who entered from the courtyard, noted their fleas, and resigned myself to a new batch of bites. Who was going to notice here, anyway? The Gypsy Kings no longer raised my mood and there seemed little point in walking the twenty minutes it took to go up and down the main drag. I thought back to earlier trips to Morocco, standing in Agadir bus station and being enchanted by the musical promise of the name Ouarzazate, the way in which I stashed it aside, another magical destination. And here I was. I slept.

By late afternoon, a magnificent splash of red, black and orange signalled a soul-wrenching southern sunset in the making, and I emerged from under a blanket of orange and white cats and decided to try to find something to appreciate. Walking past two garages down the empty but well-tarred road, I populated Ouarzazate in my imagination, filled the apartment blocks with tourists hanging out towels and swigging red wine, visualised the dwarf palm trees in their solid prime, finished off the decorative touches, inserting white window grilles and elaborate crenellations, even, why not, hanging plants in the pink and taupe shells of half-started villas.

The purple, ice-topped hills on the horizon changed hues with the disappearing light, and splashes of red and gold tore through the thin clouds which hovered over their peaks. The lone traffic policeman and I watched the road. Nothing. The war had destroyed Ouarzazate, gutted its potential. Only Chez Dimitri, a restaurant owned by a larger-than-life former foreign legionnaire, which first opened here in 1928 and boasted having the town's first telephone and bar, was welcoming passing trade. A legend in its own right, Chez Dimitri is an obligatory stop and I sat down at a beautifully laid square, sturdy table, hung my bag on an upright hardwood chair and waited. A cheerful man wearing a red fez with a black tassle, black trousers and white shirt came over, adjusted the table-cloth and set out a bowl of olives, passing across the menu du jour in its stiff maroon-plastic cover. The bar was supporting a sleeping figure, leaning half on its polished surface, half on the espresso machine. No one had been in that night, judging from the lack of kitchen activity, the cleanliness of the black and white tiled floor, the absence of half-eaten bread in the baskets. The waiter and I talked sotto voce. Yes, the war had emptied the town. No, they wouldn't be opening for breakfast if this went on, but they would still prepare an evening meal in case anyone came on the afternoon bus from Marrakesh. And yes, it was a tragedy for the world.

PART THREE

I ordered asparagus soup, cheese pancakes and orange tarts, all of which would have been perfectly at home in a top-notch Mayfair restaurant, and fiddled with my napkin. A man walked in and handed me a pink pamphlet written in Arabic. Tomorrow, 28 January, had been declared a general strike in support of the Iraqi martyrs. People were being asked to stay at home and send in their day's wages for the orphans of Iraq, to fast from sunrise to sunset to protest the allied destruction of a brother Arab state. I wondered at the logic of it all – an already undernourished people fasting – but realised that it was probably one of the few, safe ways in which the Moroccan population could give vent to its sentiments without crossing the line into confrontation.

In the morning, everything was shut, bar the post office, one café by the bus station and a scattering of small hole-in-the-wall shops. Grey metal shutters remained closed at the supermarket and cats took over the streets. We had four hours to kill before the bus left for Tinerhir and decided to visit the kasbah where Thami el Glaoui (1879–1956), pragmatist, Lord of the Atlas and sub-Sahara, and traitor to the cause of independence, once surveyed his dancing girls, exiled his women relatives into the custody of eunuchs and dreamed of extending his power. Like most nineteenth-century pisé buildings, Kasbah Taourirt is showing signs of age now, and though portions of the fortress are still inhabited by descendants of the Glaoui's slaves and servants, it seems to be undergoing slow but thorough reno- vation. A regional campaign funded by UNESCO and the Canadian and Moroccan governments is underway to restore the kasbahs of the Atlas and Anti-Atlas and seven hundred thousand dollars has already been earmarked for this part of the world.

A bulky, battlemented mass which overwhelms the village

that squats in the shadow of its thick walls, the kasbah housed fourteen hundred inhabitants as late as 1949, and is one of the much-vaunted 'sights' on the southern tourist trail. Today, a solitary, bored young boy squatted on a low wall just inside the arched main entrance and waved me through without a ticket. The sunny courtyard within housed a large German cannon, a gift from Sultan Moulay Hassan, which was capable of ensuring that the Glaoui's dominance over the area came from Mao's 'barrel of a gun'. No construction of mud and palm could withstand this fire-power. Climbing upstairs, I passed numerous empty rooms: some tightly grilled windows, others allowing in the world. An attractively tiled reception room with plaster bosses decorated in Arabic calligraphy boasted a stone seat upon which the Glaoui sat when he held court. Some of the tiles had been hacked out barbarically to make room for single sockets, and the cracked whitewashed walls and gently collapsing palm-beamed ceilings all reflected piecemeal renovations vying with years of neglect. The kasbah was an oppressive, gloomy building with its prison and slave quarters, the lingering screams of the castrated rippling on the air across the years. I was glad to leave. By the kasbah's back walls, women in bright red skirts squatted above the riverbed. A young boy was trying to stone a puppy. Watching him methodically bowling rocks overarm at the screaming dog, as if he were playing a leisurely game of bowls on a Sunday afternoon, I automatically squatted down and picked up a rock myself, prepared to enter the fray. A tiny child dashed out from behind a scrubby hedge and picked up the screaming scrap of fur, and tore over to a group of girls who crowded round the injured animal. The screams continued, then died. I placed my rock in my pocket and took a last, lingering look at Ouarzazate. This was a place to commit suicide, but oh, what a memorable, almost redeeming, sky.

Looking back on Ouarzazate a week later, I cursed myself for not having appreciated its silence. For, virtually from the

PART THREE

moment I moved on, life suddenly became one uninterrupted nightmare of military harassment and paranoid responses. The war had entered my world.

◆ *Chapter Twelve* ◆

At first, as I settled into the rocking rhythm of the latest ancient diesel vehicle, I resigned myself to yet another day of scenery-gazing. The landscape appeared highly unpromising in terms of entertainment-value, tinged with admittedly glowing but nevertheless distant and unchanging hills and mountains. Odd saltpans and a barren rocky plain spread out for miles to right and left. Giant orange boulders stood balanced on hill tops, apparently ready to fall at any instant and crush passing life-forms below, but the meagre tufts of greenery seemed incapable of supporting anything but the hardiest handful of goats. In the distance, I made out groups of fortified villages waiting for the cool of the evening to tempt their inhabitants out from behind their pisé walls.

Occasionally, we'd pass a flat-roofed house by the roadside – sticks leaning together in teepees, drying washing, completely veiled women wearing haiks squatting with bowls between their knees, a dog barking – but these were few and far between. I gazed patiently at the unravelling landscape of ksour architecture and began to notice details. Many of the buildings had elaborate iron grille windows, the coloured wooden shutters behind adding a touch of variety to the beige and pink walls. Some were decorated with thick slashes, others almost frail and Gothic in their towers. And everywhere, palms upon palms: individual trees, groups, scatterings and thick palmeries – the proverbial manna of the desert stretching its neck towards the heavens, providing food, building materials, wealth, shelter, fuel and a means of survival. It is hardly surprising that the palm has a special place in Islamic mythology, that it is protected by law, harvested at religiously determined times, that its groves shelter marabouts and ascetics and that Jesus is said to have been born beneath a date palm.

I was idly trying to sketch a number of different pisé decorations when the bus shrieked to a halt. The back door opened and a member of the Sûreté Nationale hopped up onto the bottom step, peered in and gestured with his thumb that I should get out. Standing in the road, my passport spread out on a large, low rock before him, I went through my hotel stops to date, my itinerary and my personal details. All were noted in a navy-covered book and then the questioning began: Why have you been to Morocco eleven times? What is the purpose of this trip? Where is your husband and are you a journalist? I feigned stupidity. I also stuttered something about enjoying travel. He looked unimpressed but was distracted by the arrival of a Frenchman who had been fished off another bus and was complaining bitterly about having to answer questions he had answered only two days ago. Hearing this, my interlocutor got up and prepared for an 'interesting confrontation' with a Western upstart who had no respect for authority.

The Frenchman sidled over, threw glances to the right and left and plumped for an ingratiating mode of address, after all. Visibly nervous, he began to ask about the Mauretanian border, Algerian currency regulations, how the war was going. He was told to be quiet in a long, drawn-out hiss and his passport was held at arm's length, only to be dropped into the sand a few yards away. International relations were poor today. I was cold and need a pee. Moving from leg to leg, I eventually had to ask permission to relieve my bladder. The man was horrified. 'No. Absolutely not,' he answered. 'Get back on the bus immediately.' I needed no second invitation and legged it.

The silent passengers, who had been waiting for the journey to resume, relaxed as the engine purred and jumped. One man spat into the aisle, his face expressionless; another muttered '*les salauds*' and smiled encouragingly back at me. I was shaking with cold and anger. But what of the Frenchman? Peering back, I saw him standing by the rock, motionless, presumably answering the questions he had answered before yet again, paying for the Allies' alliance in his own small way.

Although I tried to force the incident to the back of my mind, something I recognised on the officials' faces had left me doubting the wisdom of choosing this southern trail to Erfoud, passing so close to the contentious Morocco/Algeria border, travelling through military/administrative towns. The herds of baby camels and goats which sprang out on the landscape signalled the approach of Tinerhir, and I resolved to try to ring London and get some hard news as to what was happening in the Gulf, to assess my potential popularity rating in the days ahead. Given the fact that Algerian radio was hogging the airwaves – and the Algerians have an abidingly anti-Western bias, on every level – it seemed likely that the natives would not be thrilled to see a member of the murderous-imperialist-neo-colonialist-Zionist coalition on their streets. I smoked and watched the road, worrying about whether it was wise to carry incriminating notes around in my bag, whether my camera would antagonise the police and persuade them they had finally caught the journalists they seem so keen on finding, and ejecting.

Tinerhir, with its twelve-kilometre long palmery, one of the finest in Morocco, ruined kasbah and small population, seemed like a welcoming, friendly town as I sat down in the main square and looked around. The local farmers, wrapped in deep orange burnouses, light blue turbans with indigo ends and the odd brown djellabah, were finishing their day. Trucks loaded with bales of hay purred on the edge of the main square and elaborate chess sets balanced on white café tables, waiting for their champions to finish earning their daily bread. The public garden was locked tight against visitors, a Moroccan custom I cannot comprehend, but the edges of the square hummed with activity, as grands taxis filled up and pulled away, throwing up clouds of dust. Sheep were propelled past obstacles, their back legs gripped like handlebars, and veiled women sauntered along, firmly holding both their baskets and children's hands. It was hot and still and clouds of smoke billowed up from the communal oven, to float on the air. The tick-tock of metal striking metal reminded me that Tinerhir was home to a host of metal workers and has long been a thriving Berber town rather than a tourist resort. Watching greetings being exchanged all around me, as Leonard Cohen's 'Dance me to the end of Love', of all obscure tracks, belted out from a side street, I was ridiculously, totally charmed by the completeness of the scene and impulsively decided to book into the nearest hotel for five days.

Since Tinerhir boasted only three downmarket eateries and shut up shop at 8:00 p.m. or so, it was perhaps inevitable that I should meet the only other Europeans in town, Tracey and Dave, that same evening across a stained blue and white checked tablecloth. Unlike so many young 'travellers' who boast of hardship and pride themselves on having stayed in remote and obscure spots, contemptuously dismissing anything which has been heard of, admired or acknowledged as worthwhile in the past, Tracey and Dave epitomised the best of British liberalism, open-mindedness and the laid-back approach.They, too, were in Tinerhir in order to see the famous Todra Gorge, a stunning natural rift which, at its most spectacular, is merely thirty feet wide with cliffs rising to nine hundred feet on either side. Digging into the speciality of the house, vegetable tagine, we swapped gossip. Apparently, the police had informed the hoteliers in the gorge that Westerners must not be allowed to stay in the area after nightfall, for fear that snipers might once again decide to pick off tourists, just as they once assassinated members of the Foreign Legion from those same cliffs.

Tracey had been in touch with the embassy in Rabat and advised to avoid large crowds, to keep a low profile and to steer clear of Fez, a tempestuous city at the best of times, whose anti-government riots in December 1990 hit TV screens the world over. I remembered seeing the image of Bab Boujeloud in the newspapers at the time surrounded by troop carriers and tanks, the body count in dispute and ranging from three to three hundred. The Fassi have always played a vocal role in determining the course of Moroccan history: the forts surrounding the city were built by the Saadians to control the local population. In the fifteenth century, the citizens revolted regularly against the Merenids. In 1465, Sultan Abdul Haqq was executed in order to make way for a short-lived Fassi republic. In this century, the signing of the Treaty of Fez, by which Sultan Moulay Hafid consented to the creation of the French Protectorate (30 March 1912), also brought the mobs out in protest and some ninety Europeans were killed before the French army restored order by occupying the town. Avoiding Fez thus seemed like sound advice; but the Todra, potentially dangerous or not, was just too close and too compelling to be missed.

Nine o'clock in the morning saw us perched in a small grotto, pigeons swarming overhead, marvelling. Having seen so many photographs of the gorge, I felt prepared for, and almost blasé about, its impact, but still couldn't quite take in the grandeur of the rockface which emerged before us as we rounded the final twist in the fourteen-kilometre road up from town. Images of mythology, secret worlds and Jules Verne all merged as we gazed up at the vastness of it all. Palm trees stood rooted in the riverbed, its clear, swift-flowing water threatening to sweep away footholds and sandals alike as we followed the curve of the gorge around past its narrowest point and into an open expanse of gravel-bed streams and gleaming, scrubby cliffs.

Climbing up some fifty yards, we could see a patchwork of terraced herb, mint and vegetable gardens; a procession of women laden so heavily with logs and palm fronds that their heads seemed to be touching the ground. Basket-swinging mules picked their way through the nearby fields and a group of giggling young girls covered their mouths with their veils when they saw us and ran inside a low pink house. Minutes later, a small boy came racing across and placed a selection of camels and birds woven out of palm leaves at the base of our perch. Immobile and lulled by the hot sun, into squinting at nothing in particular, we watched one shadowed, gloomy slab of rock turn from black to orange; a single-file caravan of mules bearing palm fronds disappeared into the distance; V-shaped formations of birds took flight with a heavy flapping of wings.

The blend of nature at its most powerful and simple human endeavours taking place all around roused the romantic in me and I muttered about harmony and sharing the earth, sentiments which my companions smiled at benignly and then struck down, reminding me that there was a war on and bombs were planted here in the 1950s. As the afternoon dropped its shadows onto the streams and the prickly pears, the crags took on a menace which raised suspicions that panthers and trigger-happy Berbers might well be nestling, half a mile up, preparing to sharpen fangs and cock triggers. The usual shuttlecock stream of grand taxi traffic to and from the gorge was non-existent and we were faced with a three-hour walk back down the winding road to the plain. The rocks seemed to lean inward now, as their mass was sliced into odd threatening shapes by the light of the sinking sun, and we started to march down quiet streets, past errant cockerels, skipping children and numerous dark huts, doors partly ajar, which housed feeding asses.

Nothing passed us on the road for what seemed like an hour, but just as the chill hit the air and I was smoking my last Marquise and gloomily working out an ETA, footsore and shivering, a large Bedford van chugged down the mountainside and stopped. The side door was torn open and we stepped up into a bastardised vehicle full of white-veiled women with black-hennaed hands, babies and bags of washing. Two free-standing, short vinyl benches had yet to be filled in this bizarre people-carrier, with its hardboard partition separating driver and passengers covered in strips of maroon wallpaper with pink roses. Wet cardboard and mismatched vinyl squares covered the floor and inadequate red curtains hung on a small length of string by the back windows. All the way down the mountain, we stopped to pick up Berber women, old and young, who chattered animatedly and peered at my face and jewellery with as much interest as I peered at theirs. In this part of the world, the hennaed patterns applied to hands and feet were predominantly black, not orange, and less elaborate and meticulous than any I had seen in the Anti-Atlas. One woman appeared to have simply plunged her arms to the wrist in the stuff, another to have dipped the ends of fingers and thumbs, a third to have smeared dots on her knuckles. I admired the heavy silver rings on an older woman's hand. The younger the woman, the lighter and more delicate the bangles and earrings she wore, for it takes strong muscles and years of practice to lug around much of traditional Berber silverwork, particularly the earrings, which are guaranteed to disfigure a feeble Western lobe in an afternoon. I snuck a glance at the astonishing layers of clothes peeking out from beneath their white haiks, and stifled a giggle: two net petticoats were clearly visible, along with a pink flanelette shirt festooned with roses and a black caftan embellished with what looked like lime-green telephones. Lace skirts, cotton overshirts, cardigans and jumpers struggled for visual supremacy with bright men's argyle ankle socks and embroidered and sequinned slippers. A true embarrassment of riches. I noted the two men in the bus had averted their eyes and were looking straight at the maroon wallpaper in order not to gaze at the Berber ladies. I had no such shame and grinned when a toddler was plonked in my lap, for security, as we bumped down the road. My hand was seized unceremoniously by an older woman with flushed red cheeks and magnificent false teeth, rings surveyed, bracelets rolled between thumbs and assessed for weight and decoration, nail-varnished toes examined with interest. We both laughed at our mutual incredulity at each other's appearance and, as I descended at Tinerhir, she patted my face, whether with affection or out of a sense of sympathy, I could not tell.

Back in Tinerhir, life was continuing at its usual pace: a semi-standstill with lurches of action. The hotel owner had taken down his trophy, a lizard, for my perusal and waved me over to look at it in the light. This nondescript, brown reptile with sharp pointed teeth can grow to the length of a Renault 4 and gives off an odour which intimidates and repels snakes. I dutifully smelled it. Nothing. 'No, no,' the man explained. 'Only snakes can pick it up.' We admired it and I stroked the length of its dry back. This was taking intimacy too far, apparently, for the trophy was whisked away back on to the reception wall. Two men from Casablanca were discussing the war, the pointlessness of power, but before I could be drawn in, my mind turned to the Café-Restaurant Central's tagines.

The owner possessed a two-ring gas cooker upon which he heated couscous and tagines, knocked out plain omelettes, and had promised to try to fry chips for four. I could not see how he was going to manage this sleight of hand, but ambled in anyway, at the prearranged time. Activity seemed to be minimal behind the counter, but some forty-five minutes later, water and Florida orange had emerged, and baskets of wonderful flat bread studded with grains were brought to the table to accompany the meal. I admired the café owner for making the effort to open his doors, for optimistically laying place-settings for sixteen diners who would not come, and for the touches of décor he had tried to incorporate into the tiny square blue box, with its lemon border, which was his domain. Two faded photographs of the gorge and a sad, wrinkled birthday card were stuck on the wall, an old calendar hung, ragged, by the upright fridge, and miscellaneously chosen dried and faded plastic flowers perched on various ledges and surfaces, stuck in bottles and tall glass vases.

The inhabitants of Tinerhir were welcoming and, after a few days, our faces became known, and nods of greeting accompanied our bitter hot coffees each morning. The palmery was a goldmine of meandering walls encompassing slices, glimpses of the Ait-Attas' age-old way of life. Each time I wandered through, I discovered new rhythms, new occupations underway. Entering a palmery, what a visitor first notices are the irrigation channels, the main ones made of poured concrete; the minor arteries, divided by red earth walls which are just wide enough to walk on; and separating rectangles of animal fodder, mint and wheat shoots. Spring begins officially on 15 March, but bright green shoots were already pushing through and I was mortified when I lost my balance, to avoid a couple of young men carrying armfuls of books, and trod, hard, on a patch of hard-won fertility. The women of the Ait-Atta use the riverbank for all-purpose washing, hanging their clothes amongst the olive and eucalyptus trees, and when they are not stripping or binding palm stems, they congregate there, with their metal pails. The ksar which they inhabit sits behind a heavy plain door, a huge hinged affair, which used to be pulled fast at night. Inside, many of the houses are visibly crumbling to nothing, their shells tethering the odd braying ass or used to store wheat. Straw is laid on the dark, muddy, winding alleyways and it is a shock to emerge, blinking, into the sunlight of the newer town with its cafés and nail sellers, general food stalls, meat and fruit market – a mere twenty feet away up a steepish road.

As dusk fell, human activity sped up apace. Down in the palmery, the surrounding hills turned purple, then lilac and black while individuals positively sprinted back to town across the mud walls, the field workers gathered up their possessions, and young girls brought out the plastic water bottles and fetched bread from the communal ovens. It seems that life is kinder to the Berbers than to the Arabs of the plains; their standard of living is higher. The former argue that this is because they work harder. The Arabs blame the differences on social structure. According to them, Berbers live in groups with other families and protect the community while, historically, Arabs have tended to limit settlements to the immediate extended family, and barred outsiders, thereby weakening their stock and cutting down on their options at most levels.

Having so recently sampled once again legendary Arab hospitality and been moved by its limitless spontaneity, I was pleased to be asked to tea by Nasser, a thirty-four-year-old cook who, in better days, worked for overland travel companies, preparing meals for their clients up at the Todra campsites. A small man who favoured navy blue clothes, Nasser did not speak very frequently in European company, merely padded along, watching, a silent assessor, occasionally breaking away to shake hands with a friend or pick up a child and toss it up into the air. Tracey and Dave were fond of him, but I had reserved judgment and was waiting for him to declare himself a friend (unpaid) or a guide (paid). The ambiguity of his stance unsettled me and this unexpected invitation promised to clarify matters once and for all. Tea took place in a carpet shop which belonged to a 'brother', but nothing was unfurled or described in glowing investment terms as we sat on low wooden stools, around a metal tray on legs. Three cups later, I mentioned Alexis's desire to go round the palmery on a mule and Nasser readily offered to help me hire one for a few hours, adding that he would accompany us to a local family in the ksar who frequently hired out animals in the late afternoon once they had no further work for them.

The family turned out to be three men in their twenties who were nestling in a large pine bed, smoking thick joints of grass. The bed was covered with an attractive royal blue kilim and another brown striped one hung on a wooden pole, simulating curtains. I paused on the threshold, taking in the scene, wondering why we were there. Nasser nudged me forward. 'The ass is coming now. Let's just sit and wait for five minutes.' No introductions were made, for everyone was listening to Gulf news on the small portable radio. Gingerly squatting down on a broken wooden armchair, I smiled and waited. A large collection of Livres de Poche sat by the radio. Zola, Cendrars, Sartre. Somewhere nearby I could hear dishes clattering, the bleating of lambs; a timelessness, a sense of ennui hung in the room. As the minutes ticked by, my impatient boredom gave way to resignation. Perhaps there was no mule. I asked to go to the toilet and was ushered into the women's room – which was WC-free and covered in kilims and runners from the High Atlas. Radically crossed wires, here. Nasser turned on spotlights which revealed niches in the walls covered in jewellery, boxes and short daggers. The exhibits were tastefully arranged and well displayed, but where was the toilet? I reiterated 'women's room' in a crude fashion and Nasser laughed. 'Oh, I thought you wanted to see the weaving.'

Like hell he did. He invited me, mock-seriously, to stay for six months to learn traditional Berber skills with his family; I could make burnouses like the elegant soft black woollen one he draped over my shoulders. I declined with a frozen smile, amazed at his nerve, my own stupidity. Two rug showrooms in one day verged on the insistent, and where on earth was the donkey? The burnous draped comfortably over my back, slipped softly across my body. What a wonderful garment. Dave had bought a cotton version in Marrakesh for one hundred and forty dirhams but this pliant, reassuring and theatrical expanse of wool was a different animal, a warm cloak with a life of its own. The temptation to twirl and swirl, to play with its drapes and edges was overwhelming and, much cheered, I pointedly asked to borrow it for the palmery. Nasser seemed to admit defeat and within minutes the cobbles resounded with hooves and we were out of the ksar and watching feeble flashes from the sinking sun lighting up crumbling pisé buildings and outlining solitary dark palms in classic Hollywood fashion.

I snapped photographs happily, listening to Nasser talking with half an ear. He believed life in Morocco had seen many positive improvements in recent years and that the rise in the standard of living hung in the balance now. War in the Gulf would foment an upsurge of Pan-Arabism, and social unrest and the State might well respond with repression and cut off the new dialogue with the people. I murmured soothingly, focussing, instead, on the hay piled high on large flat wagons, hay which had been bleached gold by the sun, the sacks of olives and dates being dragged up to the ksar gates, the children playing ball games with a can. This was a blessed place, and I was disinclined to leave, but Tracey and Dave had booked seats out the next day and there was comfort if not safety in numbers. Latest reports said that the Allies had mounted twenty-two thousand air strikes against Baghdad, and the two-day-old newspapers which reached Tinerhir spoke of mounting anti-Western feeling throughout the Maghreb, as well as incidents of violence. If we were going to make it to the politically sensitive town of Merzouga, with its fabled sand dunes, then we could not afford to wait any longer. Even in peace-time, entry to Merzouga necessitates signing a visitors' book. If the war intensified, we might well be turned away.

I churned these thoughts round, pondering the best route. Rural communities tend to be conservative and to see war merely as a disruption of natural rhythms and trade. On the other hand, small villages in the south do not welcome strangers at the best of times and the Gulf Crisis might well exacerbate their hostility and suspicions regarding our designs and presence. Algerian radio still appeared to be whipping up anti-British feeling on a round-the-clock basis, and Nasser warned me to be prepared for heavy, constant military scrutiny anywhere east of there. It was odd to be entertaining such thoughts in such a blissful setting. Tinerhir was far-removed from my London life, but equally far-removed from Casa and Rabat. The other travellers I expected to meet had fled and we four were now the sole representatives of the West in an area which the tourist trade had been in danger of swamping and changing.

This sense of isolation injected further spookiness into an already exhausting journey. I felt marooned on the wrong side of the fence, a visible incarnation of a currently hated society whose culture was judged in terms of the Gulf War, *Robocop* and widespread sexual decadence. Tracey and I had dug out headscarves, and I now wore a long skirt over jeans and buttoned my sweatshirt to the neck. This was hardly high fashion, but perhaps it helped for, apart from one dribble of spittle, and a 'Vive Saddam' launched from God knows whom by the grand taxi stand, hostility here had been nil. Perhaps this was because the townsfolk did not share the frustrations of the urban poor and were content with their mini-universe? Since my field of vision had been shrinking to where to eat, what time the sun would set and the availability of hot water, the idea of moving to a smaller community seemed a good one, on balance. Yes, it was decided. Alexis and I were leaving. Accounts needed to be settled, foremost amongst which was twenty dirhams for the mule.

The Banque Populaire on the main square dealt with VISA transactions and I slumped, pleasantly toasted from the walk, over the wooden counter, watching their unsuccessful attempts to ring through to Casa to get authorisation for a withdrawal of fifteen hundred dirhams. I was worried by what they were going to say and, knowing my account was embarrassingly full of pounds, could not at first work out why. It was probably because Casa now struck me as a powerful, distant, higher authority, and thus capable of making totally arbitrary and final decisions. After forty minutes, I had talked myself into a negative corner coloured by foreboding, so when the elegant, cheerful teller handed me a slip for fifteen hundred dirhams I was astonished and raced back to the Todga to use the telephone and make enquiries regarding my annulled flight of 6 February. It was still cancelled, but a bus would, I heard, take me to Er-Rachida at lunchtime the following day.

Tracey and Dave were sitting outside the Gazelle d'Or doing precisely nothing as 8:00 p.m. struck and Tinerhir went to bed. It was not surprising that, as in much of the south, the town was full of older men and babies as the younger men had emigrated north or abroad, to work. I hoped the razzamatazz of Tangier or Marrakesh, with their lights, bars, cinemas and nightclubs, would compensate them for the loss of the stillness and contentment they had left behind here. We swapped bus times – no one had received the same information on any morning or evening departure – but there was a reassuring consensus that, yes, at 1:00 p.m., a bus would come for Er-Rachida. And we would be on it.

The first document check came within an hour of leaving town. Two hours and two passport checks later, I was standing, hands on dirty bonnet, by a Sûreté Nationale van, once again encountering disbelief over my lack of profession (she's obviously a journalist) and twenty-two entry and exit stamps. A soldier stomped across the scrub to relieve himself, but did so facing me, defiantly pissing on convention, Western women and the orange rocks in one yellow stream. I was disturbed by this upping of the ante, but tried to remain impassive. Two earnest-faced Japanese girls in square, black-rimmed plastic glasses stood nearby, and a young soldier beckoned me over. He was obviously having difficulties filling in their forms, since the girls spoke no French and were just smiling benignly at him in a fashion guaranteed to unhinge even a Mother Theresa, let alone a bored official. 'Why do they write like primitives?' he asked me. I took this as a rhetorical question and remained silent, waiting. 'Go on. Ask them,' he insisted, obviously itching to slap their faces.

I rephrased the question entirely and passed on their answer: 'They spent many years perfecting their writing at school.'

Dissatisfied, and aware that he was losing the struggle for supremacy, his status, the soldier fired two more questions: 'What are their fathers' names, eh? Karate or tae kwondo? Don't they have opticians in Tokyo? Just look at those slitty eyes.'

I asked the girls for their fathers' names, ignored the second part of his statement, and continued to wait, voluntarily bending over the bonnet again, before I was invited to resume the stance. Someone had been watching too many American thrillers here, for the mood was both ugly and theatrical. But not as ugly as Er-Rachida, the military garrison town constructed by the French at the turn of the century, which we eventually reached that evening. Driving in past an enormous red-walled barracks with guards posted at each gate, I was horrified and mesmerised by the state of alertness in the air. Brown and green army heli-copters swooped in rough, low circles above the main street, and troop carriers were parked on every corner, at every crossroads. Something was happening somewhere and, given the fact that the Algerian border was a mere six hours away, the large military contingent on the streets made sense: this was probably a poor choice of stop-over. Just how poor took a while to sink in.

Over the months I had encountered many reactions, ranging from indifference, politeness and curiosity to kindness on arriving in a new spot, but nothing had prepared me for the smack of crude antagonism and open dislike we all felt directed at us here, dragging our bags away from the bus station towards a nearby café. The waiter was in no hurry to serve us and I scanned the Milton Keynes-style municipal buildings, the low concrete planters, the modern 1960s street lights and public walkways, with dismay. Eyes were diverted, a passerby spat, an older man came over and whispered in Tracey's ear. She jumped back with a mixture of disbelief and fury and started to shout at his departing back in broken French: 'You are a filthy man. That is not good.'

'What's going on?' Dave asked.

'He was describing the size of his penis and what he was going to do to me,' Tracy glowered.

I was amazed by the difference travelling one hundred and twenty miles east could make and wondered how we were going to find a place to sleep, given this anti-Western climate of opinion. In better days, Er-Rachida was the convenient stopover for travellers to Erfoud and the four large cafés by the arched exit from town which can seat dozens would have been packed every night, the hotels equally full. Now, even the patisserie on the main road stood empty, the restaurants were dead, and the shopkeepers seemed likely to pull down their shutters rather than serve us. We milled around uneasily and looked through our selection of guide-books, all of which recommended the same walk-up, concrete box just off Avenue Moulay Ali Cherif. The two Japanese girls had evidently run out of money or bought the same guide-book since they were waiting in reception when we arrived, along with Heather and yet another Dave, further last frontiersmen from Glasgow. So now we were eight.

The evening had crept up and we settled downstairs in the restaurant eager for news. Heather and Dave had just come from Paradise Beach (Taghazoute), north of Agadir, and regaled us with stories of the Germans they had met who were travelling, complete with campervan, motor boat and trailer, and a small tractor for hauling the latter down to the beach. At Christmas, the German families stuck miniature trees complete with fairy lights on their fake-snow-sprayed windows and balanced an inflatable Santa on the dashboard, to boot. Their poodles were regularly clipped on the table which sat between them, laid to the last wine glass, on the sand, surrounded by the wagon-train style formation of motorised hardware they favoured. We all shook our heads in wonder. Heather and Dave had also noticed the anti-Western bias in Algerian news dispatches on the local radio, and the parochial xenophobia of Er-Rachida. They had just been to the municipal market to buy watery red apples, fresh pears and oranges, and received their change straight from the heart. It was slammed down on the counter, whereupon the storekeeper turned his back on them, as if polluted by the transaction. What was happening here, we wondered. Unfortunately, none of us had seen an up-to-date newspaper, not that this would have clarified matters necessarily, so we had no idea if Israel had entered the war, which might have explained the military frenzy here, or if the oil fields were burning, the Allies scuppered. Perhaps Saddam Hussein had been assassinated? We theorised uncertainly and, as the theories multiplied, so did our sense of anxiety.

Alexis came in from the porch, where he had been kicking around a ball, normally a sure-fire gambit for attracting company. A young boy had taken his ball; another pushed him and made the now universal sign of contempt (upraised middle finger) which he asked me to explain.

'I don't know, darling,' I reassured him. 'Perhaps it's some sort of game.'

PART THREE

What a game! This was not the Morocco I knew and loved, the country which had drawn me back to its shores over and over again across the years. Instead, we sensed a militantly pro-Iraqi state whose soldiers happened to be with the Allied forces for the sake of the continuity of World Bank loans. My impression that traditional hospitality had been cast aside was reinforced as we gazed up from our lukewarm omelettes and cauliflower – all the restaurant offered – and found that a cordon sanitaire seemed to have sprung up out of the air around our table. All the Berbers were clustered around the counter at the far end of the room and no one wanted our money or came over to clear plates, offer coffee. I strolled up to the manager and, before I could ask for the bill, he laid it down by my hand and walked off. Defeated by this attitude of condemnation, we threw a heap of bills on the table and sat there. Tracey and Dave decided on a night bus to Meknès. They'd had enough and would head straight on to Tangier and out, before our pariah status turned to that of victim. I wanted to sleep, to relax, to consider the next stage and Alexis was too tired to face another long, sweaty bus ride that night. Tomorrow, then, on to Erfoud, the famed silence of the Tafalilet, home to the Alaouite dynasty.

We never reached Erfoud. Sitting on my bed, watching the alarm clock's hands moving round, drained and yet alert, I began to worry about the door. No amount of self-mockery, no pep talks or arguments with my inner voice could remove this sense of waiting and it was with a start of relief that I rose to the sharp double knock which came at ten past midnight. A man in a brown djellabah with white specks shoved his ID at me as I struggled out into the dark corridor, leafing through my bag for my passport. He knew my name already and I listened in disbelief as he addressed me by my surname, quoted arrival times and destinations.

'You will leave town in the morning. You cannot go to Erfoud. It is forbidden.'

This caught my attention. 'What is forbidden?' I asked, suddenly livid, hours of tension exploding in a terse snap.

'It is forbidden,' he repeated and walked off. I watched other doors being knocked upon further down the corridor, saw the receptionist's face in the murk, heard whispered conversations, a yelp of protest.

My neighbour emerged, took in the scene and said, '*Enchanté.*'

Brown djellabah pulled him close by the collar, then released his fist with a flick, pushing the middle-aged man into an armchair.

'Go back in your room and don't leave it before morning,' the policeman ordered me.

I obeyed, first glancing worriedly from one man to another. 'It's nothing,' my neighbour added. 'Good night, madame.'

Wide awake on the bed, I tried to make out what was being said outside. I heard low voices, a slap and then what sounded like the crumpling of paper notes. Yet another round of 'Would you like to buy me a coffee?' being played out by the purported forces of the law. Suddenly the tears came and I huddled on the floor, wondering why I was being so feeble, why I was not fighting back, demanding explanations, shouting 'foul' or 'attitude problem'. Every WC door which slammed had me trembling; every scuffle increased the shaking of my hands, the rigidity of my posture. Alexis slept on as I packed our bags in the dark, holding onto objects for support whenever another bout of dry retching threatened to choke me. I sensed a kernel of hate form.

We left Er-Rachida at noon, four hours after first presenting ourselves at the bus station. The harassment had continued all morning, from the helicopters which circled our café and came low every twenty minutes, causing us to throw our arms up, automatically, across our faces against the wind and dust, to the toilet attendants who acted deaf when we asked for the doors to be unlocked, the waiter who affected blindness, and the bread and egg salesman who told me he was out of stock, brazenly leaning on a large heap of flat brown loaves. I left my bags with a young Moroccan boy and went for a walk. When I returned, the bags were standing in the dirt, the boy was gone and Dave was pacing, his temper about to strike out from behind its pragmatically fashioned restraints.

'Your friend has been arrested,' he told me, 'and ...' Before he could complete the sentence, a compelling swell of exhaustion and grief had sent me over to the grey-uniformed man in charge and I'd burst into an incoherent stream of sobs and accusations.

I cannot halt the words: 'You're everywhere. What have we done? I'm frightened of you. You make me feel like an animal. Where is my friend? What do you want? What's going on? It's not my fault.' The last phrase ripped through the air like a piteous wail, shocking me back into self-control. The officer surveyed me coldly, with distaste, and told me to get back to the group. He refused to look at me, gazing blankly over my left shoulder instead, and lit a cigarette. Drained and dismissed, I wandered back to a comforting hug from Heather and fulminated. Perhaps one should argue, or would this be seen as a challenge? Perhaps demeaning myself completely would bring out the best in the man, make him lose interest, defuse the situation. A slight noise behind me and the Moroccan was stumbling onto the bus, to bury his head in his arms.

Sporting a purple weal on his left cheek, his eye a slit, he ignored us. Guilt washed over me. In spite of everything, I hadn't actually taken the lesson to heart, hadn't been able to accept how much we were loathed in this town. And it was this Western self-confidence, my wilful rejection of an unpalatable, new, reality, which had led to another person's humiliation and punishment. I felt ashamed, screamed inwardly for the bus to leave, to get us out of there, north and away.

Three hours and seven document checks later, I had accepted leper status completely and was standing on the road by another Sûreté Nationale van, answering questions on the Gulf war. The Iraqi ground forces had broken into Saudi Arabia and my interrogator wanted to crow at our expense. Heather and Dave had glazed looks as they leaned against the van, having once again tried to explain Enterprise Allowances and landscape gardening to a hostile audience. Alexis was worrying that the bus had been sent away to Midelt with our luggage still aboard. Pale and suffering from diarrhoea, he was not responding to talk of Maradona and John Barnes, but was poking a stick in the dirt and flicking pebbles at the tyre-bursting, spiked metal strip which had been laid to criss-cross the road. I was recklessly frivolous, totally burnt out, and cracked jokes with a laugh bordering on the hysterical cackle, as the grey-uniformed officer pounded through: Palestine, the Balfour Declaration, the Zionist conspiracy worldwide and the need for internal security. Three plain-clothes men stood nearby, while a soldier brewed tea behind the van and two uniformed men halted all approaching traffic. For once, I noted almost automatically, the question and answer session seemed to have an object, since the officer kept returning to his opening query: were there any military personnel in our families?

'No,' I answered for the fifth time. 'All our parents are dead.'

There seemed no point in talking about my laboratory technician mother, Dave's retired mother or Heather's parents since my French vocabulary wasn't up to coping with Bunsen burners, crofts and poll tax inspectors that morning.

'All dead,' he marvelled. 'Now, isn't that sad for you?'

'Yes, very sad,' I agreed.

'And what of Bush?' he continued, circling back yet again. I felt like screaming, repeated that I didn't know him personally, that my heart was with my Palestinian brothers and sisters, that as a housewife I had no opinions. I was too busy bringing up children. Our conversation ground to a standstill while he sipped tea and then tried a new tack. 'And what of Morocco?'

'Beautiful countryside, excellent political system, wonderful people, marvellous king,' I pattered on. 'England is poor in comparison. Our weather is terrible, our unemployment high, our government unpopular. And meat is very expensive,' I added, inspired, gathering speed and talking in a dislocated rush about jewellery and gardening, homelessness in London.

I think that this garrulousness, coupled with the hunted look in my eye, finally persuaded him that we, not to mention our society, were harmless and quite mad, for suddenly cigarettes were passed round and the bus was radioed to come back and collect us. I felt free to move around, for the Middle Atlas is chilly, and I reached into my bag for a sandwich. Heather and Dave relaxed and sat down, and the police turned their attention to the traffic, away from us. An hour passed and I no longer believed the bus was ever coming back. The officer took a tea break, chose to sit with us. We were so near to leaving and yet one false step, one careless word, and the bonhomie, and bus, would disappear forever. Frozen smiles and splitting headaches replaced relief. Eventually, we sighted the lumbering green car which was our transport and gathered up our bags, careful not to appear over-eager or abrupt. I risked a question; impulsively, asked him 'Why?'

To my surprise, the man leaned over and touched my cheeks with gentle fingers, stroked my hair. 'It's for your protection, pretty eyes. We don't want any deaths in the south.'

This gesture, coming out of the blue, and from an unexpected source, flabbergasted me into immobility and I stood on the rear stairs, tearfully waving at the officer, for all the world as if he were a lover I was doomed never to see again. My co-passengers peered at me curiously as I staggered into the back row and wiped my eyes, inclined to believe the worst, or relieved.

Predictably enough, a minority was very obviously disappointed that we hadn't been clapped in irons or beheaded and glares were exchanged.

The trip continued through a much under-appreciated part of Morocco – the Middle Atlas – that visually subtle expanse of contrasts which links the fertile Sais plain surrounding the imperial cities of Meknès and Fez with the barrenness of the south through a series of passes, flattish, grazed plateaux and volcanic outcrops. I was grateful to be able to immerse myself in something impersonal and, as the miles finally rolled by, my tension drained away. At first, yellow rock walls resembling pleated curtains stacked with cigarettes loomed over valleys where goats tugged at loosely rooted scrub. Volcanic peaks shone, reddish-brown and purple, symmetrically eroded. Gradually the palmeries, with their neat terraced patches, low fortified buildings and stubby minarets, faded down the slopes and gravel mountains, while the cliffs reflected back heat and light. As our boneshaker twisted round cliff-face after cliff-face, shadows were plucked from the jagged sides and thrown on the gold incline below, darkening the riverbeds with their deep pools. The lower slopes all around appeared to have been swept clean with a giant broom, which had heaped the extra soil into soft, large, tawny cylinders. The housing evolved from the ksour to the newly built as we spiralled upwards, the snow-capped peaks of the distant mountains filling in gaps in the line of pink hills nearby. As we rolled past Midelt, a Berber market town, to Azrou, pine forests darkened the horizon and the number of herds glimpsed increased. The first pitched-roof, low, yellow houses appeared in the cedar belt south of Azrou. This cedar forest is the home of Barbary apes, including those living on the Rock of Gibraltar, incidentally, and snow was slipping onto the road, hanging in heavy drifts on the roots which stuck out of the cliff-face, bowing the newly planted trees. The orange soil of the sun-sparkled valleys, the rich sap of the evergreens, jarred my senses into life. The palmeries and the ksour had little to offer in comparison with this feast of vibrant shapes and tones. Almond trees stood sentinel over the icy road which became a tunnel of cedars, the odd break in the thick wave of branches torn by pink shafts of light thrown by a dying red sun.

I got out to restore my circulation at Azrou, seven hours into the ride, and gazed around at the attractive Swiss-style chalets, the expensive prettiness of it all. Elaborate private lighting systems embellished three-storey verandahed houses, huge cars glided by, women in furs strolled past. Was this Morocco? I remembered that the king favoured this part of the Middle Atlas and owned a ski-lodge-cum-summerhouse in Ifrane; that it was impossible to find lodgings here during the summer when the rich escaped the baking, suffocating lowlands in favour of the cool mountain air, pampered rest cures and up-market hotels. Security was tight as a result and I was resigned to the next document check when it came, at the Ifrane turn-off.

The bus passengers must have loathed the four of us by now, simply because we had added nearly two hours to everyone's already arduous trip. A pompous policeman entered and, as usual, everyone fell silent, the radio was switched off, the lights came on. We waved our passports from the back row as he scanned faces, picking up the odd Moroccan ID card, asking a question here, a question there. The bus boy lost his packet of Marvel cigarettes, a fairly expensive brand at eleven dirhams, as it was slipped into the policeman's pocket. The youngster pleaded for one or two for the rest of the journey, said that it was a long time since he had bought a whole packet, that he couldn't afford to replace them. To no avail. This character seemed vicious. A man in new jeans and a tan leather jacket was forced to his knees to pick up orange peel and eggshells in the aisle.

Why did everyone look face-forward and pretend that nothing concerned them; why this automatic subservience, this fear of authority, this inability to challenge? The severity of reprisals immediately sprang to mind as an answer, but I thought it must originate elsewhere: in the fact that no one can trust his neighbour not to be an agent provocateur and that collective action is therefore doomed. Popular myth has it that taxi drivers, bus ticket sellers and waiters are all government spies. Obviously, if betrayal is a real possibility, then keeping one's own counsel and not rocking the boat or drawing attention to oneself is crucial. Originally, each time the bus was stopped Dave, Heather and I made an effort to talk animatedly, break the silence and encourage the others not to slump into self-effacing defeatism. This strategy failed dismally, probably because we were in the south, where hierarchical structures and habits of obedience run deep and political consciousness is underdeveloped. I doubted whether it would be so simple to cow a bus-load of Riffians.

The Meknèssi, those phlegmatic, insular and laid-back gentlemen of the plains were not playing at war and waved us through in the pitch-black night as this ugly, taxing day finally drew to an end. It was 11:00 p.m. Ironically enough, I thought back on how lucky we'd been: it would have been so easy to lock us up, to confiscate our money and papers, to blackmail us into handing over everything voluntarily in exchange for our freedom. In the last two days, we'd collectively spent two hundred and twenty dirhams on compulsory 'cups of coffee': seventeen pounds worth of bribes seemed cheap at the price.

What I had underestimated in putting together the final reckoning was a subtle but radical change in my ability to relax. It took me days to return to my normal self, not to start at knocks at the door, not to jump when the bus doors opened or someone walked into a café or a room. At first, these reflexes amused me, but then came the shame. I found myself being grateful when people answered my questions, grateful for every smile, surprised at everyday courtesies and the fact that no one recoiled from my blonde hair and Western face. How little it takes to diminish us, to undo years of expectations, to instil an acceptance of the victim's mentality. And if I felt like this, powerless, resigned and terrified into compliance, after three days of persecution, how much worse it must be for poorer Moroccans, who know no other system, cannot fly out of Casablanca airport, and draw the short straw every time they run into authority on the rampage in its many guises, its many uniforms.

I licked my psychic wounds in beloved Meknès. The physical ones, a suppurating mess of bites of unknown origin, responded to cortisone and antiseptic cream and healed quickly. For two days, I tentatively walked round the town, spending dirhams in order to feel some power over objects, since I was unclear where I stood with people. I ate strawberry tarts and bought pink socks; struggled, unseeing, in my headscarf through streets whipped by hailstorms; waded, soaked, through roads awash in water. The nameless fear which spurred me on gradually abated, and when the army trucks parked in the shadows of Bab Mansour, no longer froze my steps and I found myself considering whether or not to snatch a quick snapshot. I knew my confusion was clearing and I was ready to re-enter the world of the war and its partisans, untainted. Alexis had been working out a spit count. According to him, I'd come off lightly since I'd only been spat at six times and he'd chalked up ten spits, two punches and Er-Rachida's one-fingered salute. I laughed dutifully and reminded him that since I'd volunteered more 'Vive Saddam Hussein's than he had, and more loudly, it was not surprising that my dry-cleaning bill would be lower. What a bizarre conversation.

Dave and Heather were gone, back to the West, and RAM finally volunteered a flight home – 9 February via Tangier. I had to return to Rabat to change my tickets and argued the toss over supplements and cancellation insurance, but the uncertainty appeared to be over. I resolved to keep the FO's low profile, buy the plastic camels I promised Blaise, and wash the dust of the south out of my hair somewhere in town, even have a manicure. This hedonistic dream collapsed the moment I walked up the steps at Rabat Ville and onto Avenue Mohammed V.

The usually elegant, lively boulevard which, on a Sunday, should have been thronged with families carrying flat cardboard cake boxes and bunches of flowers, casually dressed students and courting couples sipping orange juice, was deserted. Instead of cars I saw crowd control barriers and troop carriers. Instead of Rabatis, I took in the sight of hundreds of police and army personnel, fast navy blue saloon cars with their plain-clothes drivers, flat-bottomed trucks choked with rifle-toting soldiers. Up in the balconies which overlooked the well-protected post office and parliament, women held children high in their arms. Everyone was waiting on this sunny morning of 3 February, still and motionless, but what for? A dull roar which gradually attracted smatterings of applause and the odd whistle built way down at the opposite end of the street. I gripped Alexis and my bags and looked for a side road (all were blocked), an open café (none) or a deep doorway. We trotted smartly towards Boulevard Hassan II, moving against the trickle of people who had suddenly appeared on the pavements and were seemingly intent on getting a better view of whatever was coming up the street, a murmuring swell of many, many voices. Some broke into a run; others flattened themselves against the crowd control barriers; odd looks were cast in our direction. I still cannot comprehend what I had inadvertently become part of when the appearance of *L'Opinion* vendors cleared the fog. Oh, my God, it was the demonstration which Istiqlal, the major opposition party, had organised to protest Allied aggression and to show solidarity with the Iraqi people.

PART THREE

Over the next, endless four hours, I stood, wedged in a shoe-shop doorway, as seven hundred thousand anti-Western demonstrators moved past. The noise was insupportable as, twenty to forty abreast, they poured into the road, umbrellas covered in Palestinian shawls against the heat: Iraqi, Moroccan and Palestinian flags waving, banners flying from thin long poles. An effigy of George Bush turned the corner. He had an ass's head, a 'Jewish' nose and was being pursued by grey representations of Scud missiles rattled aloft, the better to be mocked and admired respectively. An old policeman came to stand next to me and told me that the Union Jack, Stars and Stripes and the Tricolour had all just been burnt ceremoniously at Bab el Had. I gulped back a knot of nausea. There is something almost blasphemous about flag-burning, the symbolic reduction to ash of the symbol of an entire people. 'What are the banners saying?' I asked him quietly.

'"Our beloved Saddam will destroy Tel Aviv", "Bush is an assassin and Mitterrand is his dog," "Allah is our desert storm",' he rattled off, impassively, eyes moving from left to right, hand on his holster. Suddenly, he turned and looked at me. 'I know what I'm doing here, madame, but what the hell do you think you're doing here?' he asked.

I had no answer and shrank back against him as another fist-waving, singing, screaming section of the crowd burst past, wailing 'Mohammed,' children bouncing on shoulders in time to the incantation. A young teenager spotted us, alerted his friends, and, as if in slow motion, dozens of marchers their arms upraised, turned, calling 'Saddam,' over and over again, simultaneously assertive and threatening.

I bowed my head and looked at my feet until they had moved by, the FO words of advice – avoid large crowds – dancing in my skull. It was impossible to escape. All we could do was avoid eye contact and brazen it out. Once again, I longed for the anonymity of dark hair, as people stared openly at me, someone shouting 'Look at that one there,' with a tongue dipped in loathing. A large group rolled by, singing the Istiqlal anthem, men held aloft on others' shoulders, encouraging everyone to join in. It was a bouncy little number, reminiscent of the best of British football terraces, and I found myself humming it spontaneously until the inappropriateness of the gesture struck home. I wondered how many of the demonstrators were members of the Deuxième Bureau, how many cameras were trained on the pulsing mass of people a matter of six feet away from me? Who would end up rueing this day, incriminated by indiscretions born of mass hysteria and the euphoria of the crowd?

Eventually, quietly, my head automatically bent, Alexis's hand in mine, I slunk out of the doorway and moved from one Sûreté Nationale van to the next in short dashes. 'We are here for your protection' ringing in my ears. Today, I was happy to forgive the Sûreté Nationale everything, to praise them to the skies, to see their point of view, to push for an increase in their numbers and better pay and conditions – anything, just to move from one haven to another. The erstwhile enemy was my only hope of breaking out of central Rabat before the crowd dispersed and swallowed me up in its dangerous embrace.

Bab el Had was a sea of bobbing heads and I was temporarily stymied. Where now? Suddenly, a grey-uniformed arm opened a crowd control barrier, pulled me through and signalled to his companions to guide me out. Passed from arm to arm, I could feel the difference in each guide's grip: one squeezed tight in anger; another barely wanted to touch me; a third was concerned for my safety; a fourth comforting. Whatever their motives and emotions, the men of the Sûreté Nationale are efficient, and a matter of minutes later I was through, free, dusting myself down and hailing a petit taxi.

The driver laughed at the expression chiselled on my face, jovially threw my bag onto the roof rack and summed it all up.

PART THREE

'You Westerners,' he said with a note of incredulity, 'are completely mad!' The car pulled away and I joined in the laughter. In the end, what else was there to do?